Thucydides
The Artful Reporter

Thucydides
The Artful Reporter

Virginia J. Hunter

Hakkert   Toronto   1973

Cover design by R. Mitchell Design
Book design by Anya Humphrey

This book has been published with the help of a grant from the Humanities
Research Council of Canada, using funds provided by the Canada Council.

International Standard Book Number 0-88866-523-7
Library of Congress Catalogue Card Number 73-83514

Printed and bound in Canada
by The Hunter Rose Company

A. M. Hakkert Ltd., 554 Spadina Crescent, Toronto, Canada M5S 2J9

To Mabel Lang

Contents

ꙮꙮꙮ

Preface

In the spring of 1970 this study, in a somewhat different form, was submitted as a dissertation for the Degree of Doctor of Philosophy at Bryn Mawr College. At that time it was entitled *Paradeigma and Pattern in Thucydides' History: A Study in Motivation and Structure.* Since then it has undergone a number of minor changes and additions.

The writer wishes to express her gratitude to the following people: to William P. Wallace, her original teacher at the University of Toronto, and Malcolm F. McGregor, director of a graduate seminar in Thucydides at the University of British Columbia, for a thorough introduction to the problems of Thucydides and her abiding curiosity about that enigmatic author; to C. W. J. Eliot of the University of British Columbia for her interest in historiography; to Agnes Michels and Richmond Lattimore of Bryn Mawr College for reading and criticizing her dissertation in its original form; and finally and especially to Mabel Lang for her provocative seminar on Thucydidean historiography, for her advice and criticism in directing this study, and more particularly, for her tolerance in what must have seemed an unwieldy undertaking and her insistence on the question why as a key to the understanding of Thucydides.

I also thank Mary White of the University of Toronto for reading the original work and making many helpful suggestions; Alan Samuel for his care in preparing the manuscript for publication; and my sister, Helen Buzovetsky, for typing the original manuscript.

Toronto   Virginia J. Hunter
August, 1973

Abbreviations

Books and articles cited by the name of the author only are listed below. Elsewhere the customary abbreviations have been used.

Collingwood   R. G. Collingwood, *The Idea of History*, Oxford, 1961.

Cornford   F. M. Cornford, *Thucydides Mythistoricus*, London, 1907.

DK   H. Diels, and W. Kranz, *Die Fragmente der Vorsokratiker* (sixth edition), Vol. 2, Berlin, 1952.

Finley   J. H. Finley, Jr., *Thucydides*, Ann Arbor, 1963.

Gomme   A. W. Gomme, *A Historical Commentary on Thucydides*, Vols. 1-4, Oxford, 1945-1970.

Gommel   J. Gommel, *Rhetorisches Argumentieren bei Thukydides*, Spudasmata 10, 1966.

Kennedy   G. Kennedy, *The Art of Persuasion in Greece*, Princeton, New Jersey, 1963.

de Romilly   J. de Romilly, *Histoire et Raison chez Thucydide*, Paris, 1956.

Stahl   H. Stahl, *Thukydides: Die Stellung des Menschen im geschichlichen Prozess*, Zetemata 40, 1966.

Wallace   W. P. Wallace, "Thucydides," *Phoenix* 18, 1964, pp. 251-61.

Westlake   H. D. Westlake, *Individuals in Thucydides*, Cambridge, 1968.

Thucydides
The Artful Reporter

Introduction

F. E. Adcock concludes his recent work, *Thucydides and his History*, with the following statement:

> it becomes highly probable that Thucydides would not turn his eyes from what was happening or wait to see how it all turned out. He has been called a "retrospective prophet" and if that means that he was looking backwards while pretending to be looking forwards, it would not be in tune with what seems to be his purpose and his method. As has appeared from the study of his work, if the study matches the evidence, he proceeded, not by intuition or by having a preconceived philosophy and using events to justify it but by observation and deductions which rest on observation and human experience.[1]

The late W. P. Wallace, writing about the same time, has a different view of Thucydides' method:

> No totalitarian meeting of voters assembled to elect a single slate of candidates has ever been more unanimous than the readers of Thucydides in assessing the issues of the Peloponnesian War. The effect depends to a considerable extent upon what one may almost call subliminal persuasion, upon careful repetitions and echoes of words and phrases. It is probable that most of this does not reach the level of any reader's consciousness, but analysis of the text reveals the method, and its effectiveness is proved by the unanimity it has produced. Such a method of predigesting facts, such careful

1. *Thucydides and his History*, Cambridge, 1963, p. 109.

3

presentation of only the most palatable and nourishing provender, produces happy readers. Not for them the knitted brow, the puzzled mind. The drama hurries them along; they are in the grip of fear and pity; it would seem irrelevant to ask if that is really exactly how it happened.[2]

The viewpoints of Adcock and Wallace represent two quite contrary evaluations of Thucydides. Was he primarily an objective observer and recorder of "what was happening," setting down events as they occurred? Or were his observations and accumulated facts secondary to a larger meaning which he thought inhered in them, a meaning so vital that he employed his formidable talents to ensure that the reader would draw no conclusions but those to which he was directed, in short "see the facts as he saw them?"[3] For "predigestion" surely implies not only a vantage point outside events, but the *use* of events to justify one's own convictions.

Let us return briefly to Adcock, whose work typifies the kind of assumptions about historiography and the purpose of the historian which have dominated Thucydidean scholarship for almost a century. In the first place, like so many earlier studies of Thucydides' purpose and method, it ends up concerned not with the question of how and why but when. As surely as rivers find their way to the sea, so Thucydidean scholars inevitably end by subordinating their researches to the "composition question."[4] It is hardly surprising then that Adcock, having asked no new questions, arrives at no new answers. One might even go so far as to say that in his general approach he has not moved a single step beyond late nineteenth-century historiography. He states, for instance, that the history was written *"ad narrandum non ad probandum,"* its main purpose being "the clear record of what happened."[5] In neglecting part — and a very significant part — of Thucydides' statement of purpose,[6] Adcock leaves no doubt as to his nineteenth-century mentor, who also spoke of history in these

2. "Thucydides," *Phoenix* 18, 1964, p. 258.
3. Ibid., p. 257.
4. I think especially of Jacqueline de Romilly's well-conceived and excellent work, *Thucydides and Athenian Imperialism*, Oxford, 1963.
5. Op. cit., pp. 11-13.
6. Τ ῶν τε γενομένων τὸ σαφὲς σκοπεῖν cannot be separated from καὶ τῶν μελλόντων ποτὲ αὖθις κατὰ τὸ ἀνθρώπινον τοιούτων καὶ παραπλησίων ἔσεσθαι (1.22.4). The latter are, in fact, the very words which differentiate Thucydides' approach to history from that of Adcock.

terms. Leopold von Ranke, called the father of "modern historical scholarship,"[7] aspired "only to show what actually happened (wie es eigentlich gewesen)." Out of his and his contemporaries' reaction to the apriorism and teleological approach to history of Hegel arose "scientific history." For Ranke and his followers historiography became a strictly empirical science, history the knowledge of individual facts, and the historian "an impartial spectator and objective recorder of what really happened."[8] How familiar this is to any student of Thucydides.

I see no need to dwell at length on the genesis, nature, and history of "positivism" and its influence on Thucydidean scholarship, as it is reflected, for example, in the works of men like J. B. Bury, G. F. Abbott, C. N. Cochrane, and A. W. Gomme. Instead I refer the reader to the second chapter of Hans-Peter Stahl's *Thukydides: Die Stellung des Menschen im geschichtlichen Prozess*.[9] I welcome his attempt to break from this tradition and would only add the following. Whatever the value of positivism in the evolution of historiography, (e.g., systematic and detailed study based on definite critical principles), its methods, pursued too enthusiastically and too long, have led to sterility in two ways:

a) The preoccupation with individual facts has utterly fragmented and particularized knowledge. In turn attempts to abstract from or synthesize these facts are usually viewed with scorn as "overgeneralizing." Only research aimed at the accumulation of more facts is deemed worthy of pursuit. As a result, Greek History, that rich blend of social and political life, religion, philosophy, and art has been reduced to a series of repetitious and unrelated "problems." History is not history but chronology, military science, epigraphy, etc., seemingly without unifying principle. And Thucydides, far from being studied and valued as a human being and thinker eminently representative of his age, is wrenched from that age and made to spew up minor discrepancies, "problems" deemed worthy of inclusion in an endless proliferation of articles and monographs.

7. The description of Ranke is that of Fritz Stern. Both it and Ranke's own statement were taken from his anthology, *The Varieties of History*, Cleveland, 1956, pp. 54 and 57.

8. Taken from Hans Meyerhoff's Introduction to his invaluable anthology of contemporary historical thought, *The Philosophy of History in Our Time*, New York, 1959, p. 16. The Introduction presents a useful summary of earlier views.

9. *Zetemata* 40, 1966, pp. 12 ff. For a very precise account of positivism in general see R. G. Collingwood, *The Idea of History*, Oxford, 1961, pp. 126-133.

b) Worse still, engaged as they are in this "objective" pursuit of particulars, scholars have created a Thucydides in their own image, an empirical, sensible man who has no superstitions, no religion to speak of, and no philosophy of any kind. Since *they* find history meaningless, so does he. He merely observes and records; he never judges.

Consider the work of the foremost Thucydidean scholar of our time, A. W. Gomme. Whatever the merit of the particulars of his commentary — and surely there is much excellent scholarship there — it remains nonetheless just that, an assemblage of particulars, the result of viewing each passage, if not each line in isolation and thus in its totality not a coherent picture of the historian at all.[10] Perhaps there is no more apt description of Gomme's method than the remark of R. G. Collingwood made in reference to Mommsen's *History of Rome*: "The legacy of positivism to modern historiography on this side of its work, therefore, is a combination of unprecedented mastery over small-scale problems with unprecedented weakness in dealing with large-scale problems."[11]

I hope the publication of Stahl's book represents a permanent revulsion against this outlook and the reemergence of attitudes which have existed as a kind of undercurrent since the publication of F. M. Cornford's *Thucydides Mythistoricus*.[12] What Cornford had the temerity to emphasize were the irrational aspects of Thucydides' outlook and his manipulation of events and characters in order to make them conform to his own preconceptions about the Tragedy of Athens. Though Cornford's work met with almost universal indignation, some scholars still could not conceal their doubts and questions: the accepted evaluation of Thucydides was all too neat. Perhaps W. P. Wallace has asked the most important question, "What is he really doing?"[13] Wallace, of course, acknowledges his debt to R. G. Collingwood, who accused Thucydides of having a "bad conscience," and who considered

10. I refer particularly to Gomme's four-volume work, *A Historical Commentary on Thucydides*, Oxford, 1945-1970. Gomme's lectures on Thucydides in *The Greek Attitude to Poetry and History*, Berkeley, 1954, pp. 116-164, though admittedly more synoptic, are largely concerned with demonstrating Thucydides' "method of narrating successive events (p. 127)." His own view of Thucydides as "primarily a recorder of events (p. 151)" he defends against men like Cornford, Finley, Jaeger, and Collingwood.

11. Loc. cit., pp. 131-2.

12. London, 1907.

13. Op. cit., p. 253.

him no worthy successor to Herodotus because he smothered historical thought "beneath antihistorical motives."[14] Important as these questions were, it is, in my opinion, two eminent Thucydidean scholars who have contributed the most towards reversing the trend of Thucydidean historiography, John H. Finley, Jr. and Jacqueline de Romilly.[15]

Finley's major contribution was to place Thucydides firmly in the 5th century B.C. where he belongs, by establishing his relationship to his predecessors and contemporaries, especially Euripides and the Sophists. Once such connections were made the next question was obvious. How much and in what way did the intellectual currents of his time influence Thucydides? In a word, what preconceptions did he bring with him to his work? Finley also makes the following observation: "The marvel of Thucydides' achievement in the Sicilian books is to have fused the sense of pattern and the sense of accident into a terrible and lifelike unity."[16] In attempting to explain this combination of pattern and accident he probes beneath the factual surface of the *History* for the historian's basic assumptions. Far from being the work of an empirical mind, he discovers, Thucydides' account of the historical process assumes a strong degree of inevitability or historical compulsion and even the existence of "forces working themselves out in the period which were beyond the control of any human agent."[17]

De Romilly is also concerned with inevitability, though more in terms of the techniques used by the historian to make events seem inevitable. She has analyzed numerous passages to show the close relationship between *logoi* and *erga* and the repetitions and

14. Collingwood, pp. 29-30.
15. Unless otherwise indicated I refer to Finley's general work, *Thucydides*, Ann Arbor, 1963, which is based on the researches of three earlier articles now collected as *Three Essays on Thucydides*, Cambridge, Mass., 1967. Where de Romilly is concerned, I refer to *Histoire et Raison chez Thucydide*, Paris, 1956. In all fairness, some mention should be made of two German scholars, Werner Jaeger and Wilhelm Nestle, writing not so much in the field of history as the history of ideas. Jaeger's brilliant chapter "Thucydides: Political Philosopher" in *Paideia: the Ideals of Greek Culture*, Vol. 1 (second English edition), Oxford, 1947, pp. 382-411, has found general acceptance. It seems to me, however, that the English-speaking world has not made Nestle's insights a part of its heritage. His chapters on Thucydides in *Vom Mythos zum Logos*, Stuttgart, 1940, pp. 514-528, and *Griechische Studien*, Stuttgart, 1948, pp. 321-373, the latter entitled "Thukydides und die Sophistik," establish Thucydides' place in the history of Greek thought in a thorough fashion.
16. P. 204.
17. P. 307.

verbal echoes which influence, even brainwash the reader into thinking as he should think, i.e., as Thucydides would have him think. She thus demonstrates how Thucydides both motivates and anticipates events with the result that, in Wallace's words:

> Thucydides himself makes hardly any comments, and yet the reader feels deeply convinced at every stage that he understands exactly what is happening, that, like the spectator of a great drama, he sees events rushing to their only possible conclusion; he feels that he knows, where those who took part in the events could only guess.[18]

No attempt has been made throughout the present work to refer to Finley and de Romilly in every particular. Indeed, this would be impossible, since their influence has been a total one, a way of looking at Thucydides, not to be measured in isolated citations and references. At this point the writer would like to acknowledge her debt to these two scholars, before attempting to pose and answer the following questions raised by their works:

a) Granted de Romilly's close analysis, we are still uneasy. Again we ask, what *was* Thucydides doing? Why this tremendous concentration and intensity to make events turn out as they should? Surely it is insufficient to return, as de Romilly does, to the explanation, "En effet, l'histoire de Thucydide tend à laisser le plus possible les faits parler d'eux-mêmes."[19] Why must "facts speak for themselves?" Nor is it sufficient to refer to the conventions of tragedy. Thucydides is dramatic, yes, and undoubtedly tragic, but surely in a way that transcends mere style. Perhaps he *saw* life as tragic, and perhaps this outlook was so intense and all-engrossing as to demand the methods of tragedy to express it. In the end de Romilly's explanation leaves Thucydides' work discrete and aimless. Thus the first task of the present study will be to reconsider the historian's technique of anticipation to see if it has some larger significance.

b) If there are patterns in the *History*, how prevalent are they? Are they merely patterns of behaviour as Finley seems to imply?[20] Here we would ask the question, Why are Thucydides' characters so one-sided? They are not real people at all but mere personifications of one quality or another. They are types;

18. P. 252.
19. P. 84 and especially pp. 105-6 for a summary.
20. Pp. 57 ff., 98, 110, and 307.

Perikles, for example, is the statesman, Kleon, the demagogue, and Brasidas, the military man. Do characters in the *History* also conform to some pattern in the mind of the historian? Are they in fact idealized and schematized in order to fit into some larger pattern of history like Herodotus' characters?

c) If events *seem* inevitable, does this mean Thucydides thought they *were* inevitable? If there is an element of historical compulsion and forces "beyond the control of any human agent," how is it manifested and how far are men responsible for their own actions?

With these questions as a starting-point, the present study aims at a new synthesis based on a new unifying principle. Its method will be similar to that of de Romilly and Stahl, a careful analysis of the text of the *History*. For only the historian himself can ever yield an answer to the question of what he is doing and why. I do not intend to restrict myself to or avoid the problematic, nor deal exclusively with either speeches or narrative portions. In the case of the latter, de Romilly has demonstrated the integral connection of *logoi* and *erga*: they can only be considered in their interrelationship.

Each chapter will begin *in medias res*, so to speak, with an analysis of selected passages and the conclusions to be drawn therefrom. Beginning with a group of isolated passages, examining Thucydides' technique of motivation and anticipation, in a sense retracing de Romilly's steps, I then move onto a broader plane in an attempt to delineate the overall structure of which these isolated passages are a part, the architecture of the work and the historiographic methods Thucydides used to achieve it.

Chapter 1
Motive and Anticipation:
Archidamos' Invasion of Attika (Thuc. 2.10-22)
ꙅꙅꙅ

Immediately after the Theban attack on Plataia the Lakedaimonians and their allies assemble at the Isthmus, ready to invade
Attika. There King Archidamos, leader of the expedition, addresses the generals and officers briefly in an exhortation with
three main parts, warning, advice, and prognostication, each of
which has a statement of the course of action necessary (χρή)
under the circumstances, and a generalization or *gnome* explaining
why this is so (γάρ). The first two arguments (11.3-5) – a stricture
against negligence and advice about the correct balance between
confidence and apprehension – are based on the general rules of
war and meant to instil a realistic appreciation of the enemy in
advance. Of greater significance are Archidamos' predictions
(11.6-8), since they apply to this expedition alone and to the
Athenians in particular. In this case, the explanation which follows
the statement of what is necessary is twofold, the state of
Athenian preparations and a *gnome* about human behaviour. And
there is a third step to the argument introduced by εἰκός,
explaining why the preceding *gnome* is especially applicable to the
Athenians. It is an assumption based on probability.

Leaving aside the form of argumentation for the present, let us
consider Archidamos' prognostications and the language in which
they are written. A translation follows:

> In the present instance, the city against which we are going,
> far from being so impotent for defence, is on the contrary
> most excellently equipped at all points; so that we have every
> reason to expect that they will take the field against us, and

that if they have not set out already before we are there, they will certainly do so when they see us in their territory wasting and destroying their property. For men are always exasperated at suffering injuries to which they are not accustomed, and on seeing them inflicted before their very eyes; and where least inclined for reflection, rush with the greatest heat to action. The Athenians are the very people of all others to do this, as they aspire to rule the rest of the world, and are more in the habit of invading and ravaging their neighbours' territory, than of seeing their own treated in the like fashion.[1]

So much for the *logoi*, the previsions of Archidamos and his reasons for expecting the Athenians to take the field. How far do the *erga* conform to his predictions? For an answer let us anticipate events and look ahead to chapters 21 and 22. The Spartans are now in Attika encamped at Acharnai. "The territory of Athens was being ravaged before the very eyes of the Athenians, a sight which the young men had never seen before and the old only in the Median wars; and it was naturally thought a grievous insult. . . ." The essential situation and the vocabulary correspond exactly to the words of Archidamos in chapter 11.

11.7: πᾶσι γὰρ ἐν τοῖς ὄμμασι καὶ ἐν τῷ παραυτίκα ὁρᾶν πάσχοντάς τι ἄηθες ὀργὴ προσπίπτει·

21.2-3: . . . ἀλλ᾽ αὐτοῖς, ὡς εἰκός, γῆς τεμνομένης ἐν τῷ ἐμφανεῖ, ὃ οὔπω ἑοράκεσαν . . . δεινὸν ἐφαίνετο . . . . παντί τε τρόπῳ ἀνηρέθιστο ἡ πόλις, καὶ τὸν Περικλέα ἐν ὀργῇ εἶχον . . . .

11.7: καὶ οἱ λογισμῷ ἐλάχιστα χρώμενοι θυμῷ πλεῖστα ἐς ἔργον καθίστανται.

22.1: ἐκκλησίαν τε οὐκ ἐποίει αὐτῶν οὐδὲ ξύλλογον οὐδένα, τοῦ μὴ ὀργῇ τι μᾶλλον ἢ γνώμῃ ξυνελθόντας ἐξαμαρτεῖν. . . .

a) The sight was one to which they were not accustomed. In fact, based on past experience, they had hoped the army would not advance any nearer than Eleusis (21.1-2; cf. 11.7, the unaccustomed).

b) It was happening before their very eyes (21.2; cf. 11.7, injuries inflicted before one's very eyes).

c) It was considered "a grievous insult" (21.2; cf. 11.7, anger under the circumstances). This is repeated in 21.3 and 22.1. The

1. Unless otherwise indicated the translation used throughout this work is that of Richard Crawley.

whole city was "in a most excited state" and Perikles "the object of general indignation." "Anger and infatuation" were "in the ascendant."

d) Perikles thought their response was dictated by "passion and not by prudence" (22.1, cf. 11.7, where Archidamos contrasted reflection and emotion).

e) Such a reaction was what one might expect (21.2; cf. 11.8).

Thus do the *erga* conform to Archidamos' predictions, with one significant exception. Though he correctly anticipated the emotional response of the Athenians, he left no place in his calculations for the resolution of their leader Perikles. The latter, confident of his own course, refused to call an assembly or meeting of the people, knowing that only error could be the result of a debate based on anger rather than rational judgment. In thwarting Archidamos' plans, he evinced the same understanding and made the same assumptions about the Athenian masses as his Spartan counterpart.

It is clear from this that *logoi* and *erga* form a closely-knit unity. The point, of course, is not especially new. In the past it has been observed that a Thucydidean speech often anticipates the events which follow, thus revealing the essence of the situation before it actually occurs.[2] This raises a number of questions which have not been posed. Were these the only arguments open to Archidamos? Plan and effect do not usually correspond so neatly; events are not so inevitable. Was Archidamos' foresight really so infallible? Why, for that matter, must events happen twice, first foreshadowed in word, as it were, and then effected in deed, with the result that the reader knows what will happen and why before it actually takes place? Having been forewarned by the *logoi*, he can draw no other conclusion than that to which they have directed him, so that he sees events as Thucydides would have him see them. The technique is too effective to be accidental, yet to admit that it is conscious or purposive is to reduce Archidamos to a mere creature of the historian.

If   this   arouses   some   suspicions   about   Thucydides'

---

2. This is the major conclusion of Jacqueline de Romilly's *Histoire et Raison chez Thucydide* (e.g., pp. 123-128 and 159 ff.). (See also Wallace, pp. 257-258, for an excellent summary of her work.) In light of this thesis de Romilly later analyzes Thuc. 2.10-22 in "Les Intentions d'Archidamos," *REA* 64, 1962, pp. 287-299. Since our analyses are very similar, at the end of Chapter 1 I shall indicate how mine differs from hers and where I intend to go beyond her.

historiographic methods – and such suspicions are not unusual where the *logoi* are concerned – consider next the *erga* themselves, the "facts" of the first Spartan invasion. Perhaps no other passage in the *History* does more to undermine Thucydides' reputation as a mere recorder of "what was happening," for its composition is such that it offers an excellent opportunity to distinguish fact from interpretation. What actually did happen -- what were the facts – that gave rise to Thucydides' narrative? Reconsider briefly his account of the invasion. It provides only five major details:

a) Before the Peloponnesians reached Attika Perikles gave up his houses and lands to be public property (13.1).

b) The Spartans began by attacking Oinoe and spent considerable time there (18.1).

c) The Athenians moved into the city (18.4).

d) When the Spartans finally entered Attika, they encamped at Acharnai and used this as a base for their ravages (19).

e) Pandemonium broke loose in Athens, as the citizens pressed for a sally. Foremost among them were the Acharnians (21.2-3).

Thucydides' description of these events is, of course, much fuller. What has he added and why? How has he explained these facts and thus motivated the *erga*? It would be well to study these details and consider their value as "history."

Where Athens herself is concerned two of the above points are of major significance, c) the move into Athens and e) the reaction of the Acharnians.

The move itself obviously affected Thucydides very deeply, and he has underscored its difficulties by a digression on the rural life of the Athenians. In chapter 14 the Athenians began moving to the city in response to Perikles' advice. Thucydides stresses it was no easy matter, "as most of them had been always used to live in the country." Chapter 15 explains the difficulty: from the time of Theseus and even Kekrops most of them had lived in the countryside. Using a kind of ring-composition Thucydides completes his digression in chapter 16 with διὰ τὸ ἔθος, proving that the Athenians were used to life in the country, not the city. The result was that they were deeply troubled and discontented at leaving their homes. And yet, in spite of discontent and difficulties they did effect the move. Why? Because the invasion was not prompt. Instead of hastening to catch them still in the fields, Archidamos delayed at Oinoe. (The causal connection is clear; fact b leads to fact c.) But in order to put these facts in context the next question Thucydides had to answer was why Archidamos delayed at Oinoe. Chapter 18 attempts to offer an explanation. First Thucydides mentions some rumours about Archidamos. It seems he had acquired the reputation of being weak and pro-Athenian, for at every stage of the preparation and march his actions had been slow and half-hearted. At least this is the charge against him. But an alternate explanation is offered. Archidamos, it is said (18.5: ὡς λέγεται), waited because he expected the Athenians to shrink from letting their land be wasted and to give in while it was still untouched.

There can be no doubt that Archidamos delayed at Oinoe. This would be common knowledge. But Thucydides' explanations of it are contradictory. Either he was soft and pro-Athenian, as alleged, or he purposely delayed because he hoped the Athenians would submit. Which was it? Not only do the two explanations contradict each other, but the latter contradicts the *logoi* which Thucydides put in Archidamos' mouth at the Isthmus. There his strategy was to provoke a land-battle with the Athenians. He was, moreover, quite confident (and correctly so, as the *erga* later demonstrate) that the masses would rush into action on seeing their property wasted. Consider the two explanations and their possible sources. The first must be Spartan, a fairly normal *aitia* when a general was unsuccessful.[3] Perhaps the delay was merely a case of notorious Spartan slowness. Indeed, there would have been little incentive for Archidamos to display speed and initiative, for he had strenuously opposed the war from the start and all the evidence indicates that he led the expedition with great reluctance.[4] What better scapegoat for Spartan policy that failed? The alternative explanation, delay as a tactic, stands in sharp contrast to the above. The tell-tale phrase, ὡς λέγεται, rarely used by Thucydides, indicates a kind of variant version, perhaps not his

3. Thucydides himself mentions the example of Pleistoanax (21.1), who was exiled from Sparta because allegedly he had been bribed to retreat from Attika in 445. See too the brief account in 1.114.2.

4. If one accepts Thucydides' word that he adhered "as closely as possible to the general sense of what they (the speakers) really said (1.22.1)," then Archidamos' first *logos* (1.80-85) must be considered at least in its essence indicative of what was "really said": the old king opposed the war. (Why Thucydides represented him as using the particular arguments he did will be the subject of later chapters.)

own but someone else's viewpoint.[5] Possibly he felt obliged to record it as a rejoinder to what must have seemed malicious Spartan slander. Perhaps it represents the climate of opinion in Athens.

By suggesting two possible and contradictory explanations Thucydides reveals his ignorance of Archidamos' real motives. He himself did *not* know why Archidamos delayed at Oinoe. He knew only what anyone in Athens might know. What is significant is that as an historian he felt at liberty to supply motives — to convert what were clearly results or effects into purposes on the part of Archidamos.

Fact e, the reaction of the Acharnians, can be viewed in the same way. Why were they foremost in pressing for a sally? Obviously because Archidamos was ravaging their land. Again there is a direct causal connection between fact d and fact e. And again the narrative connections are much fuller, as Thucydides attempts to answer the further question why Archidamos chose Acharnai. In the beginning, it is said (λέγεται), Archidamos had expected the Athenians to be tempted into attacking him at Eleusis or Thria to stop their land from being devastated. When no army met him, he next thought that a camp at Acharnai would serve as a sure provocation. For, once the Acharnians, a significant portion of the population, were exasperated, they would incite the rest of the citizens to action. (Also it was a very good place for a camp.) If this plan failed, he would still have the plain to ravage in future invasions. Then the Acharnians, having lost their property, would lack enthusiasm and cause a division among the Athenians.

That Archidamos encamped in and ravaged Acharnai is historical truth. And so is the reaction of the demesmen. Aristophanes' play *The Acharnians* confirms Thucydides' account.[6] But what evidence does Thucydides present to prove that Archidamos planned this beforehand or that he knew the relative size, mood, or even the location of Acharnai. His motives, embraced between the two nouns γνώμη τοιᾶδε (20.1) and

5. E.g., H. D. Westlake, *Individuals in Thucydides*, Cambridge, 1968, p. 128, believes the phrase refers to statements made at Sparta by Archidamos or his friends "in repudiation of the charges against him."

6. Admittedly the play was not produced until 425, but in singling out the Acharnians as the most bellicose opponents of peace because of the destruction of their lands, it at least corroborates the kind of popular divisions caused by the invasions. Though Thucydides does not indicate the factional divisions after the second invasion (2.59), there is no reason to believe those begun in 431 did not last a number of years.

τοιαύτῃ διανοίᾳ (20.5), take the form of an expectation, "He hoped that the Athenians. . . ." Actually this is nothing more than a repetition of his predictions in 11.6. Here, however, they are particularized and spelled out step by step. The chapter is not unlike a speech in indirect discourse. Indeed, one may go so far as to assert that there is not a single fact presented in chapter 20, for it consists entirely of thoughts in the mind of Archidamos or what his thoughts would have had to be in order to make this move a purposeful one in view of the results. There are three main points:

a) Considering the number of their young men and the efficiency of their armament — both at their height — the Athenians might be provoked into battle rather than let their land be ravaged.

b) The Acharnians, being a significant portion of the population, might refuse to submit to the ruin of their property and force a battle on the rest of the citizens.

c) In future invasions it would be possible to ravage the plain without fear since, once the Acharnians were deprived of their property, they would no longer be so willing to risk themselves for that of their neighbours. There would be a division in Athenian policy.

Now compare chapter 21:

a) When the Athenians saw their land being ravaged, the determination was universal, especially among the young men, to sally forth and stop it.

b) Foremost in pressing for the sally were the Acharnians, since they considered themselves no small part of the state. The following will make even more clear just how closely 20 and 21 approach each other:

20.2: τοὺς γὰρ Ἀθηναίους ἤλπιζεν, ἀκμάζοντάς τε νεότητι πολλῇ . . . ἴσως ἂν ἐπεξελθεῖν καὶ τὴν γῆν οὐκ ἂν περιιδεῖν τμηθῆναι.

21.2: - - - καὶ ἐδόκει τοῖς τε ἄλλοις καὶ μάλιστα τῇ νεότητι ἐπεξιέναι καὶ μὴ περιορᾶν.

20.4: ἅμα δὲ καὶ οἱ Ἀχαρνῆς μέγα μέρος ὄντες τῆς πόλεως . . . οὐ περιόψεσθαι ἐδόκουν τὰ σφέτερα διαφθαρέντα, ἀλλ᾿ ὁρμήσειν καὶ τοὺς πάντας ἐς μάχην.

21.3: οἵ τε Ἀχαρνῆς οἰόμενοι παρὰ σφίσιν αὐτοῖς οὐκ ἐλαχίστην μοῖραν εἶναι Ἀθηναίων, ὡς αὐτῶν ἡ γῆ ἐτέμνετο, ἐνῆγον τὴν ἔξοδον μάλιστα

c) Naturally the final point cannot be demonstrated in this chapter, since it anticipates later expeditions and the Athenian mood then. Suffice it to point out that in 2.55, a detailed account

of the second invasion of Attika, the Spartans did ravage the plain
and even advanced into the Paralia as far as Laureion. The invasion
was followed by despair, a desire to come to terms with the
Lakedaimonians, and such discontent with Perikles' leadership
that in the end he was fined. In chapter 21 this division is already
evident. Factions were forming in the city, foremost among them
the Acharnians.

Like his speech earlier the thoughts of Archidamos — or those
attributed to him by Thucydides — anticipate events. Once again
the *logoi*, indirect in this case, force the reader to see events as
Thucydides would have him see them. Once again we ask, was
Archidamos' foresight really so infallible? Obviously not. There is
no reason to believe that Archidamos chose Acharnai for any
other purpose than that suggested by Thucydides in 20.4. It was a
good location for a camp. (Also it left the plain for future
devastation.) Everything else followed — despair, agitation, sur-
misals. According to Thucydides the whole city was "in a most
excited state." Even oracles were recited. Rumours must have
spread quickly. Amid the confusion and clamour of the Acharnians it is easy enough to understand how a vast and sinister
scheme would be attributed to Archidamos. Thucydides calls it a
dianoia. The whole episode, moreover, is introduced by λέγεται,
suggesting an informant, or better still, a climate of opinion. This
is reasoning after the fact, heard in Athens and recorded by
Thucydides because he himself could offer no more plausible
motives and more important, because it suited his own concept of
the writing of history. In other words, Thucydides has events and
their probable (or possible) motives turned on their head. He knew
what resulted at Athens when Archidamos camped at Acharnai;
these results he converted to purposes on the part of Archidamos.

In discussing Archidamos' delay at Oinoe we pointed out the
contradictory nature of the two explanations offered by Thucydides. The second explanation, delay in hope of capitulation,
also contradicted the earlier *logoi* (2.11) which Thucydides put in
Archidamos' mouth. This confusion of purposes is sustained by
the present passage which serves to particularize Archidamos'
strategy and prognostications at the Isthmus. Once again Archidamos is represented as confident in his expectations of provoking
the Athenians into battle. The awkwardness of this reversal has led
some commentators to invoke the "composition question."[7] Such

7. Gomme 2, p. 73 feels that "c. 18 sits ill with 19 and 20, though the beginning

a *deus ex machina* is hardly necessary, however. *When* Thucydides composed the passage is not so important as *why*. The answer to the latter lies in the way he attributed motive — by deriving purposes from results. Since two distinct results, the successful move of the Athenians and the anger of the Acharnians, required motivation, he was forced to assume cross-purposes. Archidamos, he decided, must have delayed in the hope of peace. On the other hand, in choosing Acharnai as his camp, he must have been trying to bring on a battle.[8]

With the exception of the rather problematic delay, the account of the invasion is otherwise consistent, *logoi*, both direct and indirect, and *erga* all combining to anticipate even to the smallest detail what actually did occur in Athens.[9]

of 19 fits well enough." He suggests (p. 77) that 18.3-5 as well as 20-22 were part of an earlier draft. Westlake, p. 130 (n. 1), accepts de Romilly's arguments in "Les Intentions d'Archidamos," that "the sequence of thought in the sections dealing with the intentions of Archidamus is perfectly logical and there is no real basis for the criticisms of scholars ... who have suggested that they belong to drafts composed at different times." Nevertheless he believes, "It may well be that this portion of his work was among the first to be written, when he had not yet fully mastered the technique, which he later perfected, of combining narrative with commentary, information with evaluation (p. 130)."

8. I have not dealt at length with fact a, Perikles' sacrifice of his estate, since it is not essential to the main thread of the narrative. Note, however, that it has been elaborated in the same manner as the other facts. An event which happened in Athens is converted to suspicions on Perikles' part (13.1: ὑποτοπήσας). Did Perikles voice such suspicions or even harbour them? Or did Thucydides again know only the *fact* of his giving up his lands and explain it with what seemed likely reasons? It is logical for Thucydides to have thought in these terms, for he must have believed that had anything undermined Perikles' authority at this point, the Spartans might well have succeeded in provoking the Athenians into battle. As it was, seen through Thucydides' eyes, Perikles demonstrated his characteristic foresight. (Perikles' handing over of his property seems more like an immensely clever political move; he made the first sacrifice, where sacrifice was required, and thus brought credit to himself, while setting an example for others.)

9. Thus nothing could be further from the truth than Westlake's evaluation of Archidamos' speech at the Isthmus (p. 126): "It is thoroughly conventional and uninspired and probably reflects the real character of Archidamus more accurately than the speech assigned to him in the first book.... It is not altogether clear why Thucydides includes a summary of this speech, which does not appear to provide any very significant elucidation of his narrative." Westlake's treatment of 2.10-22 does little more than summarize Thucydides, thus pointing up the obvious problems. On the whole he accepts Thucydides' portrait of Archidamos at face value and offers no real solution to the discrepancies in motivation. Since he insists on viewing Archidamos as "a typical Spartan" he ends by making the following statement (p. 131): "... all his reported predictions proved to be incorrect; he is thus seen to have been unable to understand fully the psychology of other Greeks. . . ." Our analysis has shown the very opposite. Cf. also for Archidamos H. Gundert, "Athener und Spartaner in den Reden des Thukydides," *Antike* 16, 1940, pp. 98-114; F. M. Wassermann, "The Speeches of King Archidamos in Thucydides," *CJ* 48, 1953, pp. 193-200 and "The Voice of Sparta in

The analysis of 2.10-22 has led to the following conclusions:

a) Far from being a mere narration of facts, Archidamos' invasion of Attika is a masterpiece of selection, a tightly-knit unity held together by a veritable tissue of motives and anticipations.

b) Thucydides achieves this unity by converting results to purposes. The reader thus knows what will happen and why before it actually takes place.

c) So purposive is the historian in the use of this technique of anticipation that the facts themselves pale before several larger points which seem to be the purpose of the whole episode or at least dictate the way in which the historian viewed the facts:

i) As narrated by Thucydides, Archidamos' first invasion is primarily a study in mass psychology and as such a living proof of the king's own prognostications in 11.6. A prediction about human behaviour is made in the *logoi* and then confirmed by the events themselves. Expectation and result reinforce each other. The reader confronts both and is overwhelmed by the truth of the generalization, indeed, seems to reason it out for himself. He has a kind of surrogate experience whereby he learns and so knows because he has been the observer of a model situation.

ii) It must be remembered that the Spartans never did succeed in provoking the Athenians into battle. For this failure they were themselves, as Thucydides represents them, partially responsible. Their (or Archidamos') delay at Oinoe, whatever its reasons, gave the Athenians time to complete their move to Athens. In losing this opportunity they allowed a second factor to come into play — Perikles. He was the one incalculable factor in Archidamos' scheme. Like the latter he too understood mass psychology. Moreover, his defensive strategy was no whim of the moment but the result of rational calculation and foresight. And his resolve was firm. Where Archidamos lost the debate in Sparta and so was leading an expedition perforce, Perikles had the upper hand in Athens. Thus was Archidamos frustrated by a leader more decisive than himself. What emerges is not merely Perikles' knowledge of human behaviour, which serves to confirm Archidamos' generalizations, but his effectiveness as a leader

Thucydides," *CJ* 59, 1964, pp. 289-297; P. A. Brunt, "Spartan Policy and Strategy in the Archidamian War," *Phoenix* 19, 1965, pp. 255-280.

in the face of mass hysteria. In a sense he reversed the inevitable.[10]

10. De Romilly's analysis of Thuc. 2.10-22 (op. cit.) demonstrates in clearest fashion the relationship between *logoi* and *erga* and the way in which the former anticipate the latter. Implicit in the above, though nowhere *stated*, is the manner in which Thucydides attributed motives, by deriving purposes from results. Had de Romilly been more explicit about this point of methodology she would have found it less difficult to explain Archidamos' cross-purposes. As it is, her distinction between general as opposed to particular motives (Archidamos' *logos* and the indirect *logoi* respectively) provides only a partial answer. Furthermore, when she concludes that Thucydides wished to put into relief truths about human behaviour and the limits of prevision as well as Perikles' role as leader, she shrinks from taking her argument a step further by asking if the historian did not have some broader purpose in his interpretation of these events. Having accused Thucydides of creating a model situation (and the *History* abounds in such episodes, as de Romilly herself has shown in *Histoire et Raison*) I would hope to go beyond de Romilly in asking whether the historian did have some purpose in employing this method. I.e., unlike de Romilly we will study the episodes not in isolation but in relation to one another.

Chapter 2
Εἰκός and Εἰκάζειν:
Brasidas' Successes (Thuc. 4.125-127 and 5.6-10)
🕉🕉🕉

Chapter 1, by analyzing what seemed a typical episode in the *History*, revealed certain features of Thucydides' method of composition. But was this just an isolated example? At the risk of some repetition, I will attempt to confirm the findings of Chapter 1 by a similar analysis of Book 4.125-127 before going on to elucidate how Thucydides reasoned about events.

The circumstances which precipitated Brasidas' retreat from Lynkos are briefly as follows (4.124-125). In 423, not long after the revolt of Mende, Brasidas joined forces with Perdikkas of Macedon for an expedition against Arrhabaios, king of the Lynkestians. Before any decisive attack was possible, however, news arrived that their Illyrian allies had betrayed and joined Arrhabaios. Even as retreat was being meditated, the Macedonians deserted in panic, leaving Brasidas and his men alone and greatly outnumbered by an army of warlike barbarians.[1] In the face of imminent enemy attack Brasidas prepared to retreat. There are two parts to his preparations: a) tactics meant to provide the best defence possible and b) a speech of encouragement.

a) Brasidas disposes his troops in the following manner (125.2-3): forming his hoplites into a square with the light-armed in the centre, he orders his youngest soldiers to dash out wherever the enemy should attack, while he himself with 300 picked men holds the rear.

1. Here I am merely summarizing Thucydides' account in order to provide background for the passage I intend to analyze. I shall follow the same method at the beginning of most chapters.

b) In the brief time that remains he steps forward to encourage his men. He first asserts that his speech is no mere exhortation (παρακέλευσις), and to counter their obvious dismay he offers διδαχή, of two kinds, ὑπόμνημα and παραίνεσις. The main problem would seem to be the desertion of their allies and the numbers of the enemy (125.1-2). And Brasidas does indeed refer to this dilemma at the outset of his remarks (126.1), but surprisingly, only to dismiss it with a curt statement, a reminder to the Spartans that in war they usually depend not on allies but on their native *arete*. As for numbers what terror can they hold for citizens of a state where the few rule the many by virtue of their superior martial skill?[2] This said, he addresses himself to what he considers the main issue, their inexperience (ἀπειρία) which has produced a vain fear of the barbarians. His advice — a good part of it prognostication — follows the formal pattern laid down in Archidamos' speech: statement, explanation, then application to the particular problem.

Obviously experience is not the acquisition of a moment. But knowledge, it seems, can replace it. Thus what the Peloponnesians must do is realize that the enemy will *not* prove formidable. A *gnome* explains this statement. "Where an enemy seems strong but is really weak, a true knowledge (διδαχή ἀληθής) of the facts makes his adversary the bolder. . . ." This "true knowledge" Brasidas then proceeds to supply. From his own understanding of the barbarian mode of fighting and its inherent weakness, lack of discipline, he predicts that the enemy will scatter in fright in the face of men who hold their ground. Terrifying as they seem to the eyes and ears of the inexperienced, they are really all bluff. The peroration recapitulates neatly:

> Stand your ground therefore when they advance, and again wait your opportunity to retire in good order, and you will reach a place of safety all the sooner, and will know for ever afterwards that rabble such as these, to those who sustain their first attack, do but show off their courage by threats of the terrible things that they are going to do, at a distance, but with those who give way to them are quick enough to display

2. For οὐ πολλοί (126.2) I would read οἱ πολλοί (Stephanus). The logic of Brasidas' speech seems to demand it. Just as he counters their fears about the desertion of the Macedonians with the argument that they normally depend not on allies but their own *arete*, so he counters their fear of superior numbers with the fact that they are used to being outnumbered.

their heroism in pursuit when they can do so without danger.

In the encounter which follows there are three essential points to watch for: a) a spectacular display on the part of the barbarians, especially if they believe the enemy is in retreat; b) the collapse of this bravado in the face of determined and disciplined resistance to their first attack; c) flight and pursuit of a safer target, those who have already given way to them. In chapter 127 the following occurs:

a) Thinking that Brasidas and his men are in flight, the barbarians attack "with much shouting and hubbub."

b) When the Peloponnesians resist in a disciplined manner using the tactics outlined in 125.2-3, and thus withstand the first attack, the barbarians are unable to cope with the resultant close combat.

c) Instead they go off in pursuit of the fleeing Macedonians.

125.3: ἐκδρόμους δέ, ἔι πῃ προσβάλλοιεν αὐτοῖς, ἔταξε τοὺς νεωτάτους, καὶ αὐτὸς λογάδας ἔχων ... γνώμην εἶχεν ὑποχωρῶν τοῖς τῶν ἐναντίων πρώτοις προσκεισομένοις ἀνθιστάμενος ἀμύνεσθαι.

127.2: καὶ ὡς αὐτοῖς αἵ τε ἐκδρομαὶ ὅπῃ προσπίπτοιεν ἀπήντων καὶ αὐτὸς ἔχων τοὺς λογάδας ἐπικειμένους ὑφίστατο. ...

126.5: καὶ γὰρ πλήθει ὄψεως δεινοὶ καὶ βοῆς μεγέθει ἀφόρητοι. ...

127.1: οἱ δὲ βάρβαροι ... πολλῇ βοῇ καὶ θορύβῳ προσέκειντο. ...

126.6: ... τοῖς μὲν τὴν πρώτην ἔφοδον δεξαμένοις. ...

127.2: ... τῇ τε πρώτῃ ὁρμῇ παρὰ γνώμην ἀντέστησαν. ...

Once again *logoi* and *erga* form a closely-knit unity and, forewarned by the former, the reader is well aware how events will happen and why. In fact, so well have the *erga* been anticipated that Thucydides is able to sum up the actual encounter in 9 lines. The Spartan tactics need little or no explanation, since Brasidas' intentions were spelled out in detail in 125.2-3. But the description of the barbarian reversal is almost too sparse. Just why were they forced to give up their offensive? Lack of discipline? Thucydides does not explain. The reader must assume that it happened as Brasidas predicted. The battle itself, the *erga*, seems to serve merely to confirm the prognostications of the *logoi*.

Chapter 1 concluded that Thucydides converted results or effects to purposes. This is surely the case here as well. What did he know? What actually did happen? A small force of Spartans held off — even put to flight — a veritable horde of barbarians.

How? Being Spartans they were naturally disciplined and followed orders. (Hence Brasidas' orders in 125.2-3 and his peroration.) Quite simply, the undisciplined barbarians could not withstand a disciplined resistance. But that hardly sems enough. The barbarians must have been a terrifying sight. Why, Thucydides might have asked, were the Spartans not paralyzed with fear? Where did they get the *tolma* even to make their stand? They had been forewarned. Brasidas' *logos* and especially his prognostications had made them realize they could withstand the barbarians.

How neatly plan and effect correspond. The key, of course, is correct prevision. Of what does this correctness consist? How does Brasidas — like Archidamos before him — arrive at the conclusions upon which he acts so successfully? Or, since Brasidas' arguments are only those with which the historian has supplied him, how does Thucydides himself reason about events? A more detailed study of Brasidas' *logos* may hold the answer.

There are three steps to his argument, each one a statement followed by an explanation introduced by γάρ.

a) The barbarians are terrifying to men who lack experience. Why? Their appearance is frightful and the noise they make dreadful.

b) But when it comes to fighting men who stand their ground, these terrible barbarians are not what they seem. Why? It is a question of discipline. Since they have no set order, it is all the same to them whether they attack or fly; their independent mode of fighting leaves them every excuse to run away if they so desire.

c) The barbarians are more sure of themselves when frightening their opponents from a distance. Why? Otherwise they would be attacking, not just making threats.

On what does Brasidas base these assumptions? Fortunately in the same chapter (126.3) he is very specific about how one reasons in an emergency like the present. In fact he supplies a kind of recipe. That knowledge which he asserts his men must have, which he calls διδαχὴ ἀληθής in 126.4 and which he proceeds to supply in 126.5 has three sources. The men themselves have already fought the Macedonians αὐτῶν, i.e., among the barbarians. (Presumably Macedonians and Lynkestians are lumped together as the same people, or at least close kinsmen.)[3] The point is that they

---

3. He means, of course, the recent encounter with the Lynkestians (124.3). For evidence that Thucydides considered the Lynkestians a Macedonian people see 2.99.2 and 4.83.1.

have personal experience of the enemy upon which to draw. Combined with this is Brasidas' own "judgment" (ἐγὼ εἰκάζω) and "knowledge" (ἐπίσταμαι). The first, εἰκάζειν, is connected with εἰκός. It is the ability to relate past and present experience, find their essential similarities, and then conjecture or predict what is most likely to occur under the given circumstances. It is reasoning based on probability.[4] About his "knowledge" Brasidas is fairly specific; it is ἄλλων ἀκοῇ, which may mean merely what one hears "from others," perhaps by questioning them about the enemy. It goes without saying that Brasidas would do this. On the other hand, ἀκοή often has the connotation "history," i.e., knowledge which goes beyond one's own personal experience and perhaps more important, confirms one's own experience. If this is its meaning, it adds another dimension to Brasidas' formula.[5] The result is a potent combination of experience, knowledge, and reason brought together to determine how the enemy will most likely act (126.5) and what tactics will best rout them.

Let us return to arguments b and c above, both assumptions about how the barbarians act or will act. It must be obvious that there can be no certainty about these assumptions: they are merely probabilities. What was described above as a statement followed by an explanation can be defined more precisely in Aristotelian terms as an enthymeme or rhetorical syllogism – a syllogism starting from probabilities or signs.[6] In simplest terms it

4. For the various connotations of εἰκός see Jürgen Gommel, *Rhetorisches Argumentieren bei Thukydides. Spudasmata* 10, 1966, pp. 18-19.

5. Gomme 3, p. 616, also suggests "history" as a possible translation. It goes without saying that most 5th century history was a kind of "hearsay," since it was based primarily on oral tradition or the oral reports of informants. Thucydides himself uses ἀκοή a number of times in the sense of "oral tradition" (e.g., 1.4.1, of Minos; 1.20.1, 6.53.3, 55.1 and 60.1, of the Peisistratidai). One of Thucydides' major concerns, however, is the uncritical way in which men deal with ἀκοαί (1.20.1: ἀβασανίστως). Ἀκοή is contrasted with ὄψις (1.73.2: autopsy) and elsewhere with πεῖρα (4.81.2: personal experience). It would seem that both Alkibiades' and Nikias' information about Sicily (6.17.6 and 20.2) was based on this kind of untested ἀκοή. Where the more distant past is concerned, Thucydides asserts that he corroborated ἀκοή with other kinds of proof (6.55.1: in reference to Hippias). An instance of ἀκοή which comes very close to that used in the present passage is found in 4.81.2: "Later on in the war, after the events in Sicily, the present valour and conduct of Brasidas, known by experience (πείρᾳ) to some, by hearsay (ἀκοῇ) to others, was what. . . ." "Hearsay" or "oral reports" is here tantamount to a kind of history. This same kind of history Brasidas might have known of the barbarians and their methods of warfare.

6. See Aristotle, *The Art of Rhetoric* 1356b1 ff. for the two modes of argument, induction and deduction, and his definition of the enthymeme as a rhetorical syllogism. See also 1357a29 ff. for the materials of enthymemes and the further discussion at

is a proposition with a reason, the premises of which "are only true for the most part, or usually true."[7] In other words, the logical tool Brasidas uses to arrive at his conclusions is the argument from εἰκός. The process itself is εἰκάζειν, implying as it does previous similar experiences and knowledge against which to compare the present. Brasidas would have had ample opportunity in his Thracian campaigns to observe the shortcomings of Macedonian discipline; this was the notorious failing of all barbarian armies. He had, moreover, just recently fought and routed the Lynkestians themselves (124.3). On the basis of his combined personal experience and all the knowledge gleaned from other sources it was reasonably safe to assume that the present enemy, Lynkestians and Illyrians, would act accordingly. Thus tactics were devised to meet this probability.

While Brasidas himself assumes the task of εἰκάζειν, it is important to notice that his men are themselves led to reason from εἰκός. Furthermore, they have a definite basis for accepting his arguments, since they too can refer to their own personal experiences, specifically the recent encounter with the Lynkestians. Realizing the truth of Brasidas' evaluation they are encouraged to face a strange and formidable enemy, for they know his weaknesses. "True knowledge" dispels *atolmia*, making them bold (126.4).

At this point it is tempting to consider another passage where the concept of εἰκάζειν also appears. In Book 1.138.3 Thucydides is elaborate in his praise of Themistokles, whose genius he seems to consider second to none, not even Perikles'. What emerge as his two major qualities are significant: ". . . he was at once the best judge (κράτιστος γνώμων) in those sudden crises which admit of little or no deliberation, and the best prophet of the future

1394a24 ff. The clearest and most well-reasoned discussion of the enthymeme is J. H. McBurney's "The Place of the Enthymeme in Rhetorical Theory," *Speech Monographs* 3, 1936, pp. 49-74. The work provides full references to Aristotle, showing the relationship of rhetoric to logic and also distinguishes nicely between "probabilities" and "signs" (56 ff., εἰκότα =-ratio essendi and σημεῖα =-ratio cognoscendi).

7. G. Kennedy, *The Art of Persuasion in Greece*, Princeton, New Jersey, 1963, p. 98. Kennedy's exposition of the two processes of logic (pp. 96 ff.) and his summary of Aristotle are excellent. Cf. also the following works for the enthymeme: E. M. Cope, *The Rhetoric of Aristotle with a Commentary* (revised and edited by J. E. Sandys), Vols. 1 and 2, Cambridge, 1877; R. C. Seaton, "The Aristotelian Enthymeme," *CR* 28, 1914, pp. 113-119; E. H. Madden, "The Enthymeme: Crossroads of Logic, Rhetoric, and Metaphysics," *Phil. Rev.* 61, 1952, pp. 368-376. (For further bibliography see Kennedy, loc. cit.)

(ἄριστος εἰκαστής), even to its most distant possibilities." Above all Themistokles is praised for his foresight (ποεώρα). Obviously, the latter derived from his powers of εἰκάζειν, indicating that the basis of *pronoia* or *prognosis* — the statesman's primary virtue — is the ability to reason from εἰκός. This alone, however, is not sufficient. He must also formulate a policy to fit the circumstances. This is γιγνώσκειν, the ability to arrive at a correct *gnome*. The function of both together allows one to αὐτοσχεδιάζειν τὰ δέοντα, "meet an emergency" or "extemporize what must be done."[8] The latter is just what Brasidas does, evincing Themistoklean virtues. He is an excellent εἰκαστής: this is the basis of his *prognosis*. And once he discerns "the better or worse in the unseen future"[9] he extemporizes τὰ δέοντα in two ways. First, recognizing that the essential problem is to dispel fear with knowledge, he provides it for his men in an exhortation. Thus τὰ δέοντα of his speech becomes synonymous with τὰ δέοντα of real life. Then, using military science, *episteme*, he counsels the correct tactics — "what is required" on the most practical level.

But if, as we have demonstrated, Brasidas' arguments are only those with which the historian has supplied him in order to make his success purposeful, it follows that the logical tool Thucydides himself used to convert results to purposes was the argument from εἰκός. Thus in depicting Themistokles as an εἰκαστής, he was not just highlighting the qualities he thought necessary to the statesman but also those he himself required as an historian. Unlike the statesman, however, whom he portrayed as clairvoyant, he had at least the advantage of reasoning after the fact, of knowing what actually did occur before supplying reasons and motives. This process is nonetheless εἰκάζειν, for given the facts he must use his own experience and knowledge to compare and conjecture. In order to provide arguments from εἰκός, he must himself reason from εἰκός.

Much has been written on the argument from εἰκός, its importance to fifth-century rhetorical theory and practice and its prevalence in Thucydides' *History*. It was one of the earliest innovations of Sicilian rhetoric, elaborated by Korax and Tisias and introduced to Athens sometime before 430, since it is found in plays of both Sophokles and Euripides as well as in Antiphon's

8. My translation.
9. My translation.

Tetralogies.[10] Hence it is not unusual that it should appear as a rhetorical device in Thucydides' speeches. What has not been sufficiently appreciated, however, is just how all-pervasive this kind of reasoning is in the *History*, *erga* as well as *logoi*. The main reason is that critics like Danninger and Gommel have restricted themselves to those passages where the word or one of its compounds actually appears.[11] But arguments from probability such as those used by Brasidas need not contain the word εἰκός. Εἰκάζειν is a way of reasoning. Indeed, what often passes for fact is really after-the-fact reasoning based on εἰκάζειν. Consequently, the next step in this work will be to analyze another passage in the *History*, Book 5.6-10, in order to study further how Thucydides used the argument from εἰκός to convert results to purposes.

Book 5.6-10, Kleon and Brasidas at Amphipolis, is not unlike Archidamos' invasion of Attika in its basic characteristics, offering once again a neat combination of *logoi*, both direct and indirect, and *erga*. In this case the latter are such an inextricable combination of fact and motive as to baffle commentators. A. W. Gomme, for example, finally throws up his hands in despair and admits: ". . . I am not by any means sure that Thucydides was, on

10. On the origin of the argument from εἰκός see Bromley Smith, "Corax and Probability," *QJS* 7, 1921, pp. 13-42; D. A. G. Hinks, "Tisias and Corax and the Invention of Rhetoric," *CQ* 34, 1940, pp. 61-69; S. Wilcox, "Corax and the *Prolegomena*," *AJP* 64, 1943, pp. 1-23. While there is no conclusive evidence as to how the argument reached Athens, Finley, pp. 46 ff. has shown that it was certainly in use there before 427 (the date of Gorgias' visit). His work, which refers to Sophokles, Euripides, the Old Oligarch, and Antiphon, is based on two earlier studies which now appear in *Three Essays on Thucydides* as chapters one and two, "Euripides and Thucydides" and "The Origins of Thucydides' Style." In the latter, pp. 63-65, he argues for dating Antiphon's *Tetralogies* before 430. (See especially p. 65, n. 28 and cf. Gommel, pp. 81-84.) For Thucydides' use of rhetoric see also F. Blass *Die attische Beredsamkeit*, Vol. 1 (second edition, Leipzig, 1887), pp. 203-244 and on the history of rhetoric O. Navarre, *Essai sur la Rhétorique Grecque avant Aristote*, Paris, 1900, pp. 3-77 and Kennedy, pp. 52 ff.

11. O. Danninger, "Ueber das εἰκός in den Reden bei Thukydides," *WS* 49-50, 1931-32, pp. 12-31. Danninger's thesis is that the argument from εἰκός is a later development in Thucydides. Examples of it found in the first four books he considers awkward and in many cases *vaticinia post eventum*. Thus he believes they are later insertions, part of a revision. Concerned as he is with the "composition question" he not only neglects a number of important passages where εἰκός appears but never recognizes that arguments from probability do not require the word εἰκός. Gommel's work is far more serious. Its main aim is to show how Thucydides himself used contemporary rhetorical techniques to make his history more credible (p. 80). However he also does not consider arguments from probability unless the word εἰκός appears. Apart from this limitation his work is an excellent, if somewhat formal, study of 5th century rhetorical techniques — arguments, proofs, typology — found in the *History*.

this occasion, sufficiently awake to his own principles explained in 1.22.3. . . ."[12] Because of Thucydides' failure to cite his informants or sources or for that matter to draw a distinction between the "facts" observed by himself or garnered from others and the suggested motives which lay behind them, it is clearly impossible to disentangle the various elements of his history with *absolute* certainty. On the other hand, by noting some of the contradictions in his reasoning, one can be made to realize that a genuine problem does exist and one of such proportions as to demand some explanation.

First the problem itself, best demonstrated by chapters 6-8. Chapter 6 is in the main a straightforward account of Kleon's activity at Eion and Brasidas' response to it. After some success in the area, notably at Torone and Galepsos, Kleon remains inactive at Eion awaiting reinforcements from Macedon and Thrace. Informed of this, Brasidas takes up a position on Kerdylion, calling together all the forces he can muster. Some he leaves in Amphipolis, the rest he takes to Kerdylion. Strategically, this is a good move, since the place is on high ground not far from Amphipolis commanding a view on all sides and thus making it impossible for Kleon's army to attack without being seen. In other words, Brasidas is taking no chances on a surprise attack such as he himself so successfully made two years earlier. It is, then, with some surprise that one reads that Brasidas expected (6.3: προσεδέχετο) Kleon to advance on Amphipolis with the forces he had on hand. Why should Kleon make such a bold move even as he is awaiting reinforcements? Brasidas supplies a motive: he might do so out of disdain for the enemy's forces (ὑπεριδόντα σφῶν τὸ πλῆθος). Now this question of numbers is a problem in itself, since Thucydides nowhere specifies the exact number on either side. Kleon has 1200 infantry, 300 horse, and an unspecified number of allies (2.1). The *known* forces of Brasidas are greater, 2000 infantry, 300 horse, 1500 Thracians, over 1000 targeteers, and "all the Edonians, horse and targeteers (6.4-5)." The insufficiency would seem to be on Kleon's part. At least he is taking the precaution to send for reinforcements before attacking. The matter is clarified somewhat in chapter 8.2, where reasons are

---

12. "Thucydides and Kleon," *More Essays in Greek History and Literature,* Oxford, 1962, pp. 118-119. The work is written specifically on the second battle of Amphipolis — reconstruction, comments, etc. — but also deals with the general question of Thucydides' bias against Kleon.

presented to explain why Brasidas distrusts his forces enough to employ a stratagem. He believes them inferior not in number (for they are *about equal*) but in quality. Why then should Kleon disdain his forces? Amphipolis being no easy place to take either by storm or siege, it would be a move of the utmost stupidity on Kleon's part to attack before his reinforcements arrive. In fact, a premature attack would clearly be in Brasidas' favour, since it would be the one chance of catching the Athenians alone before more forces arrived. (See 8.4.) Consequently, while Brasidas may wish to provoke an encounter, he has no reason to assume that Kleon will comply. In any case, whatever Kleon does, Kerdylion will have the same strategic advantages as an advance outlook. Thus the motive which Thucydides attributes to Brasidas and indirectly to Kleon does not follow from the circumstances and must be one which he supplied himself after the fact *for his own reasons*. It is contradicted in the next chapter.

Chapter 7 opens dramatically. Kleon does just what Brasidas expected (ὅπερ ὁ Βρασίδας προσεδέχετο). But note: the reason has changed. Kleon himself does not initiate the move. Rather he is compelled (ἠναγκάσθη) by an incident which neither Brasidas nor anyone else could have anticipated. His soldiers begin muttering about their inactivity and the quality of Kleon's leadership. Rather than allow their discontent to get out of hand Kleon moves nearer Amphipolis. Two questions arise. Why should the soldiers be so bored? Just how long have they been there — a day, a week? Thucydides is vague — just τέως. Surely the soldiers would be able to appreciate the difficulties of capturing Amphipolis and be content to await reinforcements? Secondly, it does come as rather a shock to discover the contempt in which they hold their leader. No one can quarrel with their evaluation of Brasidas. All that Thucydides has written about this brilliant general points to the qualities *empeiria* and *tolma*. But where has Kleon ever shown himself either incompetent or weak? His famous success at Pylos has recently been enhanced by the capture of Torone and Galepsos. Thus is it not suspicious that his soldiers now criticize him for the very faults he will reveal in the *succeeding chapters*? Granted the existence of some discontent, might it not be tempting *after the fact* to assume that the soldiers recognized and despised Kleon's failings all along?

Still, it seems that Thucydides realized that there is something wrong with this explanation which places the onus not on Kleon but his soldiers. He therefore adds a second reason somewhat in line with Brasidas' original prediction about "disdain." Kleon is in the same mood as he was at Pylos. Because he had been successful, (or although he had only been lucky – εὐτυχήσας), he is quite sure of himself.[13] Then Thucydides finds himself in difficulties. Kleon, it now seems, has no intention of marching on Amphipolis. "Disdainful" or "confident" as he is, he is admittedly only going out to look around and does not expect anyone to come out to meet him. This is repeated in 7.5: "He thought to retire at pleasure without fighting. . . ." Obviously Kleon's mission is a reconnaissance which will allow him to examine the city and terrain while still awaiting reinforcements and then on their arrival to put into effect his real strategy, surround and storm the city (7.3). He does not want a premature encounter. But he makes a mistake, not so much in disdaining Brasidas' forces, as in underestimating his daring, and once he realizes he has made an error and attack seems imminent, he sounds the retreat at once (10.3). This hardly indicates overconfidence. Here one must cite A. W. Gomme again: "I am doubtful whether Thucydides had made clear to himself what was wrong with Kleon's strategy."[14]

What strikes the reader of chapter 7 immediately is the number of verbs of thinking or feeling in contrast to which the facts of the matter are few indeed. Of 19 lines in the Oxford text only five indicate what actually did occur. Kleon moved to a position on a strong hill in front of Amphipolis and proceeded to examine the terrain round about. Apart from these few details the chapter consists of a variety of thoughts in the mind of Kleon's soldiers and Kleon himself (for the latter, αἰσθόμενος, βουλόμενος, ἐπίστευσε, ἤλπισεν, ἐνόμιζεν, ἐδόκει). Just how Thucydides had such insight into Kleon's moods and feelings one might wonder.[15] Presumably these motives and reasons are to be accepted as on a par with the facts themselves. (Indeed, they have all but taken on the status of "fact.") Yet, as has been shown, many of them do not stand up under criticism. Something is clearly wrong. And it becomes even more glaring when one finds that Thucydides has

13. Chapter 4 will deal at length with Pylos-Sphakteria.
14. *Commentary* 3, p. 639.
15. Cf. A. G. Woodhead, "Thucydides' Portrait of Cleon," *Mnem.* 13, 1960, p. 308: "By contrast with the obscurity of the battle narrative, the historian seems remarkably well acquainted with what was *in the minds* of both commanders." Later (p. 313) he calls Thucydides "a remarkable thought-reader where Cleon is concerned."

the same insight into Brasidas' mind.

Chapter 8 is devoted to Brasidas' strategy. The upshot of it is that Brasidas does *not* go out to meet the Athenians in regular order but prepares a surprise attack in two stages. This is of course what actually does take place and is described, if somewhat confusedly, in chapter 10. Once again Thucydides' task is to present a convincing explanation of this stratagem. Why is there no regular battle? Again participles. Brasidas "fears his preparation (δεδιώς)" and "thinks (νομίζων) his men inferior."[16] This must mean the men themselves, for he compares them to the Athenians, described as καθαρόν, and the flower of the Lemnians and Imbrians. One could question this. What about the experience of Brasidas' men? Does this go for nothing against "green" Athenians? What about Dorian courage and discipline which sustained them against tremendous odds in the retreat from Lynkos? Brasidas himself takes this for granted in the speech which follows. But perhaps it is not the men themselves after all. In 8.3 Brasidas' concern alters again. Now it is numbers and the poor quality of their arms which gives him pause. He thinks to himself that if Kleon should see his deficiencies, he (Brasidas) "should have less chance of beating him than by not letting him have a sight of them, and thus learn how good a right he had to despise them." Observe that it is the lesson of 4.126.4 all over again: "Where an enemy seems strong but is really weak, a true knowledge of the facts makes his adversary the bolder. . . ." If Brasidas thought in this neat way, it would be most surprising. To reconstruct his plight: He must have known that Kleon's move was one of reconnaissance preparatory to a major assault on Amphipolis as soon as help arrived. Kleon was not going to be tempted into a premature confrontation. To offer battle in the conventional manner would merely allow him all the time he needed to move back to Eion. (This was what Kleon was counting on.) *But* a quick sortie might catch him unawares and force him to a confrontation while isolated or, better still, while in retreat. This was the only course open to Brasidas and it succeeded. Based on this success, the result of the encounter, Thucydides supplies Brasidas with a strategy which makes his moves purposeful. In so doing, however, he supplies motives which do not meet the circumstances.

Before proceeding further along these lines some consideration

16. My translation.

must be given to the speech which Thucydides has put in Brasidas' mouth, the purpose of which is to explain his *epinoia* (strategy). It is in fact an expansion of his general intentions in 8.4. In studying the speech what strikes one immediately is its similarity in structure and reasoning to his earlier exhortation (4.126). It falls into the same five sections: a) introduction explaining why such a speech is necessary; b) reasoning from εἰκός; c) a *gnome* which fits the circumstances; d) an *epinoia*; e) a παρακέλευσις. To expand briefly:

a) (9.1-2) Once again Brasidas and his men are about to face tremendous odds, a select body of only 150 against all Kleon's forces. Nevertheless, their leader sees no need to speak at length about courage; he takes it for granted, especially as they are Dorians against Ionians. What he does want to ensure is that his troops understand all the possibilities inherent in what looks like a dangerous situation. This he proposes to "teach" them in order to dispel *atolmia* based on ignorance. Recalling 4.126.4 one might conclude that διδαχὴ ἀληθής is an essential part of effective leadership.

b) (9.3) Pointing to what he himself can observe and what must be obvious to his men, that the enemy has marched out and is now on a neighbouring hill looking about in a rather careless manner, he uses his powers of εἰκάζειν to deduce their probable motives. Why are they there? They must have a low opinion of Brasidas' forces and not expect anyone to come out to meet them. Note the similarity of the reasoning to that of 4.126.5: an enthymeme is implied in Brasidas' argument. Note too how carefully the reader has been prepared in advance for this assumption. Not only does he know Kleon is on a reconnaissance mission, but in the *erga* which precede (7.3) he has also been told Kleon's motives, which correspond exactly to what Brasidas merely reasons out as a probability.

c) (9.4-5) Brasidas grasps the situation at once and sums it up in a *gnome*:

> But the most successful soldier will always be the man who most happily detects a blunder like this, and who carefully consulting his own means makes his attack not so much by open and regular approaches, as by seizing the opportunity of the moment; and these stratagems, which do the greatest service to our friends by most completely deceiving our

enemies, have the most brilliant name in war.

In other words, because Brasidas does not have (or Thucydides thinks he does not have) the forces to make a conventional attack, he resorts to *techne*. What was explained in 8.2 as due to the inequality of their respective forces, is now reduced to a *gnome*, or general rule of war, in order to underscore the essence of the situation.

d) (9.6-8) The problem made clear, Brasidas next unfolds tactics based on his specialized knowledge and experience as a military man. First he repeats his earlier evaluation of the enemy. They are overconfident (θαρσοῦσι; cf. 9.3, καταφρονήσει) and intent on retreat rather than battle and thus unprepared (ἀπαράσκευοι; cf. 9.3, ἀτάκτως). Though the words ἐξ ὧν ἐμοὶ φαίνονται indicate these are still only assumptions, Brasidas infers further that such an enemy must be lacking in resolution and caution. The obvious tactic is a sudden attack which will in all probability (κατὰ τὸ εἰκός) fill them with terror. So confident is Brasidas of this *prognosis* that he even maps out a second stage to his strategy. Once he himself has attacked with the desired results, Klearidas must dash out suddenly and engage the enemy with all speed. Why two attacks? Brasidas expects (*elpis*) that such a tactic will cause the most terror. Again why? A *gnome* explains that "a fresh assailant has always more terrors for an enemy than the one he is immediately engaged with." (Note that the second step of the argument is actually the application of the *gnome* to the present situation. *Elpis*, moreover, is all but synonymous with εἰκός. Thus the construction — imperative followed by *elpis* and γάρ — is tantamount to the χρή, γάρ, εἰκός of earlier speeches.)

Needless to say the encounter transpires *exactly* as Brasidas predicts. Since the close relationship of *logoi* and *erga* has been our major subject up to this point, it will be sufficient here merely to indicate a few of the more obvious repetitions.

Kleon does just what Brasidas wants him to do. Still looking about he is surprised by the news that an attack may be imminent. Wishing to avoid this and thinking he can get away, he sounds the retreat without taking the precaution to organize or instruct his men or even protect himself against attack. In his haste he leaves his unarmed side exposed to the enemy (10.2-4). Brasidas recognizes his opportunity at once (10.5: *kairos*) and attacks, instructing his men to the very end. Listed below are some of the correspondences in vocabulary.

logoi	*erga*

Brasidas' attack

9.6: ... προσπεσοῦμαι δρόμῳ κατὰ μέσον τὸ στράτευμα·

10.6: ... ἔθει δρόμῳ ... καὶ προσβαλὼν τοῖς Ἀθηναίοις ... κατὰ μέσον τὸ στράτευμα τρέπει

The Athenians' reaction

9.7: ... ὅταν ἐμὲ ὁρᾷς ... φοβοῦντα αὐτούς. ...

10.6: ... τοῖς Ἀθηναίοις πεφοβημένοις τε ... καὶ τὴν τόλμαν αὐτοῦ ἐκπεπληγμένοις. ...

Effect of a second attack

9.8: ἐλπὶς γὰρ μάλιστα αὐτοὺς οὕτω φοβηθῆναι·

10.7: ξυνέβη ... τοὺς Ἀθηναίους θορυβηθῆναι.

The close relationship of *logoi* and *erga* is not surprising, since it was characteristic of the two previous episodes discussed above. It is also clear that the reasoning used to explain and anticipate the enemy's behaviour as well as to evolve a successful strategy and tactics for the Peloponnesians is once again εἰκάζειν. The present example is somewhat more complex, however, in that there are now two stages of anticipation, as it were, *erga* – *logoi* – *erga*. In Brasidas' earlier speech the recent encounter with the Lynkestians (the *erga* of 124.3), though specifically referred to, was hardly more than implicit in the *logoi*. Here, on the other hand, not only does Brasidas' speech anticipate the action which follows but his speech itself depends on the *erga* which precede it. For example, when Brasidas suggests in 9.3 that the Athenians' carelessness is due to their contempt for his own forces, the reader is already aware of this. Kleon's overconfidence permeates chapter 7, which was itself anticipated even earlier in 6.3, Brasidas' original prediction. Again, when Brasidas sums up the general situation in a *gnome* about using an enemy's mistakes to one's own advantage (9.4), he takes it for granted not only that Kleon is making a serious error, but that he is justified in disdaining his forces because they *are* inferior. This looks back in turn to Brasidas' own ponderings in 8.2 which resulted in his decision to employ *techne* so that the enemy might not see his forces and realize just how inferior they were. The *erga* which precede, however, are no mere set of verifiable facts but a complex mesh of fact and motive. When studied above many of the latter were found inconsistent, if not illogical. Furthermore, our reconstruction indicated no reason to believe Brasidas' forces were much, if at all, inferior to Kleon's — quite the contrary. As for Kleon's decision to reconnoitre, in itself it was not disastrous or even bad. In actual fact then Brasidas' stratagem was not based on his inferiority but his hope of forcing Kleon to meet him before reinforcements arrived. Conventional warfare would just not do. Kleon would have no part of it. A surprise attack was the only way. Thus the essence of Brasidas' evaluation, disdain and the use of stratagem against a superior force, collapses. Since this was *not* the situation, he would never have spoken this way. But if the speech is inconsistent with *our* reconstruction, it is not inconsistent with that of Thucydides. It fits the circumstances very well, (τὰ δέοντα), since it best responds both logically and practically to the *erga* which precede. In other words, it reflects a situation *set up* by the historian and consisting of both fact and motive.

As we have demonstrated above, Thucydides' reconstruction of the events which preceded the battle (the *erga* of chapters 6-8) is full of inconsistencies. What might have given rise to such a reconstruction? I.e., what were the facts upon which he based his interpretation? They are surprisingly few. 1) Kleon arrived at Eion and sent for reinforcements. 2) Brasidas took up a position on Kerdylion with part of his men; the rest he left with Klearidas in Amphipolis. 3) Kleon moved to a strong hill in front of Amphipolis. (The move was preceded by some unrest among his men.) 4) Brasidas returned to Amphipolis and prepared a surprise attack, which he carried out successfully in chapter 10.

In simplest terms Brasidas took Kleon by surprise and Kleon was defeated trying to retreat. Why? He was careless and left his unarmed side exposed. Again why? It was a question of leadership, Thucydides might have answered: on the one side was a skilled general with a masterful strategy and the daring to execute it (the *empeiria* and *tolma* of 7.2) and on the other a totally incompetent man (7.2: ἀνεπιστημοσύνης). Having thus judged the respective leaders in the battle, Thucydides next assumed that this was the character of their leadership right from the beginning and reasoning backwards supplied appropriate motives for the events which preceded. Since Brasidas was successful he once again provided him with a *logos* which makes his success purposeful. He not only evolves a correct strategy and tactics for his men but forewarns them how the enemy will probably act. It is mainly reasoning from εἰκός. But what reason did Brasidas have for making a surprise attack? In the first place it is the kind of move one might expect from such a man. From his first appearance in the *History* his main characteristic is *tolma* (2.25.2). Another is speed. Very often words like δρόμῳ or τρέχω describe his movements, (e.g., 2.25.2: διαδραμών; 5.10.6: ἔθει δρόμῳ). Most of all he is a man of surprises, either sudden attacks or stratagems, such as at Megara (4.70 ff.) or Amphipolis (4.103 ff.). On other occasions he used such stratagems because his forces were insufficient for a conventional battle. This was probably the case here as well, Thucydides must have believed. Without knowing Brasidas' real reasons then, he assumed those most probable in light of the man's past history and reputation. Hence the series of participles in chapter 8 explaining Brasidas' motives for using *techne*.

In the same way the behaviour of Kleon in the encounter — or what Thucydides assumed was his behaviour (for note that participles motivate him even in 10.3) — carelessness is made his major characteristic right from the beginning. Since he was defeated he could present no *logos* outlining a strategy. Where Brasidas anticipated, he merely responded. He did not act so much as react to his men. While we judged his move a reconnaissance — perfectly reasonable under the circumstances — Thucydides has not given him the benefit of the doubt. How might he have reasoned about why Kleon moved? Perhaps somewhat as follows. "He will imagine he can achieve another Pylos, especially if he is convinced Brasidas' forces are inferior to his own. He will probably boast about it too and end up being challenged by his own men to act, if he really is so clever. Then he will be forced to move or lose face. Still he is sure to accept the challenge since he is impetuous and has plenty of confidence."[17] Even Kleon's response to the soldiers fits neatly into a picture of a man too irrationally

---

17. I have taken the liberty to refer to Pylos because Thucydides himself mentions it (7.3), even though on the whole I am restricting myself to this particular passage. The problem is, of course, much larger. In particular the question of whether Thucydides was prejudiced against Kleon has stimulated a great deal of scholarship. The two best works on the subject are those of Gomme and Woodhead, both cited above (notes 12 and 15 respectively). Woodhead believes Thucydides was prejudiced against Kleon and conditioned the reader "by his choice of words and interpolation of comment" to share his dislike (p. 297). As to the passage under study, he expresses "a very considerable doubt as to the validity of Thucydides' account of the battle of Amphipolis. . . (p. 310)." See also Westlake's chapter on Kleon, especially pp. 75-81.

sure of himself to refuse any challenge. Thus he did not look ahead and anticipate possible dangers but acted from purely personal motives, concern for his reputation, on the one hand, and on the other, overconfidence verging on disdain for the enemy and in the end, carelessness.

Note finally that Brasidas is allowed to anticipate Kleon's every move right from the beginning, even predicting his original disdain in conformity with Thucydides' own evaluation of Kleon. Thus the whole passage is an elaborate combination of *logoi-erga-logoi-erga* with Brasidas masterminding each step. Where the historian himself is concerned it is an intricate process of working back from known results to purposes, from facts to probable motives. In this process he made use of his own powers of εἰκάζειν in two ways. First he interpreted and explained the facts by supplying what seemed to him the most probable motives under the circumstances; to achieve this he used direct *logoi*, actual speeches, indirect *logoi*, lengthy passages of "thoughts," and in the *erga* participles. Secondly in the direct *logoi* he provided the successful protagonist with rhetorically sound arguments from probability forecasting what was to happen and why. It is surely no wonder then that a work so elaborately constructed, in which *logoi* and *erga* parallel and reinforce one another, should make the reader feel "that he knows, where those who took part in the events could only guess."[18]

These first two chapters have not merely suggested but illustrated certain methods Thucydides employed in the composition of his *History*. In turn this discussion raises the following questions:

1) If Thucydides has manipulated events in such a way as to make them seem inevitable, to happen as they should happen, does this mean that he thought they *were* inevitable? If not, what larger purpose did he believe he was serving in making plan and effect correspond so neatly?

2) Correct prediction, of course, is a large part of it. And so far it seems that men reason and so predict correctly when they use the logical tools of εἰκός and εἰκάζειν. On the other hand, that is hardly sufficient, since it is possible to argue from εἰκός on both sides of a question.[19] Obviously, both sides cannot be at one and

18. Wallace, p. 252.

the same time correct. Thus εἰκάζειν is in itself no infallible guide to the truth. Is there then some other, less obvious, ingredient of *prognosis*, the knowledge of which, in addition to εἰκός and εἰκάζειν, may be an all but infallible guide to the future?

19. For instance in Antiphon's *Tetralogies* speakers for both the defence and the prosecution use arguments from εἰκός.

Chapter 3
Κρείττων Λόγος:
Phormion's Exploits (Thuc. 2.83-92)

In 429 the first major naval confrontation of the Archidamian War takes place. Under the *strategos* Phormion, a mere 20 Athenian ships defeat the Peloponnesian navy not once, but twice in succession, an exploit unparalleled for daring in the whole history of the war. In the first engagement Phormion prevents the Peloponnesians from transporting troops across the Gulf of Patrai to Akarnania by forcing them to fight in mid passage, where he causes their 47 ships such confusion that they end by fleeing. Then in a second battle off Naupaktos, though outnumbered almost four to one, having only the same 20 ships against a Peloponnesian fleet reinforced to 77, Phormion turns near defeat into a second victory.

Phormion's brilliant exploits captured the imagination of his contemporaries and he became a veritable legend.[1] Thus it is not surprising that Thucydides should share this admiration and not only devote a considerable portion of the *History* to describing the two victories, but underscore their significance with a verbal duel, an *antilogia*, between Phormion and his opponents. It is the antilogy and the battle which follows it which will be the primary concern of this chapter. Since, however, the *logoi* are very much dependent on the *erga* which precede, i.e., the initial victory in the Gulf of Patrai, some consideration must first be given to this event.

1. See especially Aristophanes, *Knights* 562, *Peace* 347, and *Lysistrata* 804. There is, however, another tradition critical of Phormion reflected in Diodoros 12.48.3 and discussed by Gomme 2, p. 235. One should perhaps keep it in mind while reading Thucydides' account.

Even a cursory reading of chapters 83-84 reveals the same relationship between purpose and result described in the preceding chapters. Phormion's motives — for the most part assumptions based on probability — are set in indirect discourse introduced by verbs of thinking and wishing. Subsequent events then conform perfectly with his "plan." Consider chapter 83. Right from the beginning Phormion takes the initiative by keeping close watch on the Corinthians and their allies on their way to Akarnania. A participle explains his motives; he wishes to attack in the open sea. The Peloponnesians, secure in their numbers and believing the Athenians would not dare to engage them, are not prepared for a battle; in fact they do all they can to avoid it until they are at length compelled to fight in mid passage. (Twice the verb ἀναγκάζω appears, in 83.1, ἠναγκάσθησαν, and in 83.3, ἀναγκάζονται.) Forfeiting the initiative to Phormion, the Peloponnesians adopt a defensive strategy: they form a circle, prows out and sterns in, all the smaller boats inside and five of their best sailers ready to emerge quickly wherever the enemy attack. So far then all is in accordance with Phormion's original wish.

The Athenians respond by forming a single line and forcing the enemy to contract their circle. Though they feign attack, they do not strike immediately. Phormion has told them in advance *not* to attack until he signals. His motives for waiting are as follows (84.2):

> His hope was that the Peloponnesians would not retain their order like a force on shore, but that the ships would fall foul of one another and the small craft cause confusion; and if the wind should blow from the gulf (in expectation of which he kept sailing around them, and which usually rose towards morning), they would not, he felt sure, remain steady an instant. He also thought that it rested with him to attack when he pleased, as his ships were better sailers, and that an attack timed by the coming of the wind would tell best.

In other words he is waiting for the wind to blow.

Events unfold just as Phormion predicted. Almost as if on signal the wind begins to blow; whereupon the enemy ships, already hemmed into a narrow space and with the small craft now dashing against them, are thrown into confusion. Thucydides describes the scene in some detail: as the ships fall foul of one another and the crew tries to push them off with poles, amid the yelling and swearing orders become inaudible. Worse still, through lack of experience (ἄπειροι) they are unable to lift their oars clear of the rough water and so fail to obey the helmsmen. This is the very moment Phormion had anticipated and he signals at once. In the confusion (ὑπὸ τῆς ταραχῆς) no one thinks to act with valour (alke). They flee.

The relationship of the erga to the thoughts and intentions which precede them is clearly the same as that observed in the exploits of Archidamos and Brasidas. How much might Phormion have anticipated? It is impossible to determine; the details are sparse and the tactical assumptions plausible.[2] But since we have already demonstrated elsewhere Thucydides' habit of reasoning after the fact and given lengthy examples of purposes derived from results, we are surely justified in expecting the same kind of reasoning here. I.e., what were in reality Phormion's responses to the Peloponnesian defensive strategy and to their confusion, especially after the wind began to blow, the historian converted to purposes which correctly anticipate what were in fact only probabilities, thus revealing a consistent preoccupation with intention and prediction in every sense as great as his concern for "fact."

In this case, however, what will be most important for the analysis which follows is a correct understanking of the erga themselves (84.3). What actually did occur and to what did Thucydides attribute the Peloponnesian defeat?

Obviously Athenian daring and skill and Phormion's leadership play a major role. And the Peloponnesians show their usual lack of initiative. But this is only a partial answer. The latter might have compensated for their initial slowness in the action itself except that they lacked one thing, practical skill based on experience.[3]

---

2. Phormion, one must observe, was not able to choose his time of attack but responded to a Peloponnesian movement. How lucky that this was the very hour at which the wind usually blew. The story sounds apocryphal. According to one tradition Themistokles did the same thing at Salamis (Plutarch, Them. 14.2). Gomme 2, p. 219, n. 1, comments that "we may have an interesting instance of a common error among the learned, the duplication of an action for another occasion — 'for Themistokles would have acted as Phormion did' — without due observation of all the facts. . . ." If such a tradition was current in Thucydides' day — C. Hignett, Xerxes' Invasion of Greece, Oxford, 1963, p. 233 rejects it, while A. R. Burn, Persia and the Greeks, London, 1962, p. 461 accepts it — then I would be inclined to say just the opposite: Phormion would have acted as Themistokles did.

3. Gomme 2, p. 218, says of the Peloponnesian formation, "The device was a sensible one, and would have worked if the Peloponnesian seamen had been more skilled and more confident and their ships not overloaded. . . ."

Faced with an unexpected difficulty – choppy waters, the result
of a sudden wind – circumstances which they did not anticipate
or perhaps had never experienced before (or at least manoeuvred
while under attack), the Peloponnesians are thrown into confusion. Experienced sailors might have extricated themselves. Being
green, they shout, cannot control their oars, and end up in total
disorder. Phormion's prediction proves true: the *taxis* required on
the sea is very different from that on land. And when confusion
replaces *taxis*, *alke* (prowess or courage) also disappears with the
result that "no one thought of resistance for the confusion. . . ."
Alke then depends on *taxis*, which in turn depends on *empeiria*. It
was the lack of *empeiria* which caused the defeat.[4]

The defeated Peloponnesians next sail to Kyllene in Elis,
where they are joined by the *nauarchos* Knemos and ships from
Leukas. At this point the Lakedaimonians themselves intervene,
sending out three commissioners with orders to prepare for a
second, more successful battle and not let a few ships drive them
from the sea. Thucydides explains their motives (85.2). Their main
feeling is one of surprise; what happened was beyond their
calculations, especially

> as it was their first attempt at sea; and they fancied that it
> was not that their marine was so inferior, but that there had
> been misconduct somewhere, not considering the long
> experience of the Athenians as compared with the little
> practice which they had had themselves. The commissioners
> were accordingly sent in anger.

As soon as they arrive the commissioners begin to repair and
augment their fleet for a second battle. (Phormion, meanwhile, is
not so fortunate; though he sends for and is voted reinforcements
from Athens, they delay their arrival by first sailing to Crete.)

The Peloponnesian fleet, now 77 strong, takes up its position
at Achaian Rhion near Panormos opposite Phormion's ships at
Molykrian Rhion. There they wait six or seven days, resolved, one
side not to sail into the open sea, the other not to sail into the
narrows. The motive of the Peloponnesians is fear, fear inspired by

---

4. Cf. de Romilly, pp. 125-128, who also discusses Phormion's previsions and the
probabilities on which they were based. She ends with the observation, ". . . la narration
proprement dite est nise en relation avec le plan dégagé en tête, les quelques lignes
consacrées à l'évocation du désordre sont le seul élément descriptif qui vienne s'ajouter à
cette épure."

the previous disaster. In the end the generals (Knemos and Brasidas named specifically) decide to take the initiative and bring on a battle before Athenian reinforcements arrive. First, however, they address their men.

The speech is an exhortation (παρακέλευσις), its purpose like those of Brasidas to dispel fear and replace it with *tolma*. (The men are described as φοβουμένους καὶ οὐ προθύμους ὄντας.) It is also similar to earlier speeches in structure and reasoning and falls into three main sections: explanation, advice, and exhortation.

a) 87.1-3 looks back to the *erga* which precede and attempts to offer an explanation for the defeat, or better still, justify it.

b) 87.4-7 offers encouraging advice for the encounter which is to follow and ends with a kind of prognostication.

c) 87.8-9 is the exhortation proper.

Our primary concern will be the first two sections, the formal reasoning of which is at once familiar from our analyses of earlier speeches: statement, followed by explanation, usually a generalization, often a *gnome*, then the application of the latter to the particular situation, or, where there is prediction, some form of εἰκός. The following is a summary of a and b:

a) 87.1-3. The Peloponnesians have no reason to fear just because they have been defeated. The evidence does not justify it (οὐχὶ δικαίαν ἔχει τέκμαρσιν: note the implicit χρή). What is the evidence? Four explanations are offered for defeat: their preparation had been insufficient; their object had been a *strateia*, *not* a sea-battle; they had had plain bad luck (τὰ ἀπὸ τῆς τύχης); their inexperience — it was their first sea-battle — also must share *some* blame (πού τι καὶ ἡ ἀπειρία). Thus cowardice had nothing to do with it and their resolution remains, or should remain, undefeated. At this point the speaker reveals which of the four above explanations he believes takes precedence. For a second time he refers to accident or chance as a cause of defeat (τῆς γε ξυμφορᾶς τῷ ἀποβάντι and ταῖς μὲν τύχαις). But this should have no effect on resolution or bravery. As far as experience goes, this seems to worry him least. In any case, he does not consider them justified (εἰκότως) in using inexperience as an excuse for cowardice. (I.e., the main concern both as to the past and in the coming encounter is courage, *andreia*. As long as they have not shown *malakia*, which the Lakedaimonians suspected in 85.2, they have no reason to fear.)

b) 87.4-7. Inexperience can not be set aside that easily,

however; therefore they next proceed to show how it is outweighed by other advantages. These are twofold: inherent bravery and numbers. The first is rather complex and must be quoted verbatim (87.4):

> Nor are you so behind the enemy in experience as you are ahead of him in courage (ἀπειρία and τόλμη); and although the science of your opponents would, if valour accompanied it (ἐπιστήμη vs. ἀνδρεία), have also the presence of mind to carry out at an emergency the lesson it has learnt, yet a faint heart will make all art powerless in the face of danger (τέχνη vs. εὐψυχία).

To substantiate their preference for natural qualities rather than acquired ability they offer a *gnome*. "For fear takes away presence of mind (μνήμην), and without valour art is useless (τέχνη vs. ἀλκή)." Thus they should counter experience with daring. Secondly they have the advantage of numbers and of engaging off their own coast. Again a *gnome*: In most cases numbers and preparations mean victory. On the basis of the above reasoning a prediction follows. At no point is defeat probable (εἰκότως). The whole section then is an argument from εἰκός. (There is one further point: they will learn from their previous errors.)

Is this the διδαχὴ ἀληθής of former speeches? To be sure, formally the same elements are present, viz., *gnomai* or generalizations, arguments from probability and a kind of prognostication. But one is uneasy with the speech; there seem to be misinterpretations, errors in reasoning. In fact, if the reader recalls the details of the *erga* which preceded, he can carry on a dialectic with the Peloponnesians even before he knows Phormion's reply. In light of the known "facts" then let us attempt a refutation of their arguments.

a) Basically there is nothing wrong with the four reasons offered in 87.2 for their defeat; it is the emphasis which is misleading. Yes, they were unprepared for a sea-battle and only transporting troops to Akarnania. And it is true that the wind and consequent rough sea might be considered bad luck, even though Phormion had taken them into account. Yet the fact remains that it was their inexperience which made them ignore possible weather conditions and their lack of practice which made them respond as they did and lose control. The *erga* demonstrated this clearly. Therefore, the Peloponnesians are incorrect in underestimating "experience" or "skill" and looking only to personal courage.

b) First, the assumption that the enemy does not have courage is a rather risky one to make in light of past events. It is easily refuted. But what the previous encounter contradicts specifically is the *gnome* about the relationship between *alke* and *techne*. No one can deny that fear takes away presence of mind, but 84.3 proved that *alke* disappears if *techne* is lacking. Indeed, one might make the very opposite assertion, ἀλκὴ ἄνευ τέχνης οὐδὲν ὠφελεῖ. Or perhaps there is some more subtle relationship between the two which evades the Peloponnesians. Certainly, they have not learned from experience. As for numbers, it may be true that numbers and preparations (*dynamis* elsewhere) are *generally* decisive, but there can be exceptions, the incident in the Gulf of Patrai being one. It is then not an absolute truth but only a probability that *dynamis* brings victory.

Finally, have they really learned from their errors, as they stated? The above suggests they have not. The key to this is 85.2, the motives given for sending the commissioners. Not having experienced the battle themselves, the Lakedaimonians can only assume what went wrong from a distance or from the accounts of informants. Hindered by a static view of the demands of war, a view based on land-battles rather than naval encounters, their first and only assumption is cowardice or misconduct. They therefore act out of passion, anger, and *not* from careful reflection. In Thucydidean terms they have not considered every aspect (*log-ismos*). Their reasoning is bound to be faulty. And this is the very reasoning reflected in the speech. In fact, the speech itself is in substance nothing more than an elaboration of 85.2. The Peloponnesians cling to one lesson and one alone and this not the result of careful calculation but of fear: they refuse to fight in open waters.

Thus the first *logos* stands revealed as full of inconsistencies. It offers no concrete *dianoia* — overall strategy or tactics. And in a most striking manner it brings into question the argument from εἰκός. For it can lead to *incorrect* assumptions.

Phormion's address to his men follows, a speech which parallels that of the Peloponnesians in every respect. For example, its general purport is the same. When Phormion notices that his men are frightened at the sight of so many ships arrayed against them and becoming demoralized, he offers them advice and encouragement. His aim is to dispel fear with confidence (88.1 and

3: θαρσῦναι and θαρσεῖν). But the speech is more than a mere isolated παρακέλευσις; it is closely related to the one that preceded. In fact, it is a refutation and counter *logos*.

There are four main sections: a) 89.1-5 answers the Peloponnesians' main arguments; b) 89.5-7 sets up a counter *logos* based on different generalizations; c) 89.8 is a kind of *dianoia*, though negative in character, outlining the strategy they should avoid and why; d) 89.9-11 is the exhortation proper. The following, while summarizing these arguments briefly, will also show their relationship to the earlier speech and the reasoning upon which they are based.

a) 89.1-5. The Athenians have no reason for fear (οὐκ ἀξιῶν = χρή). Why? Phormion attacks the enemy on three counts, numbers, courage, and allies. First, if the Peloponnesians do not meet them on equal terms — and it is apparent that their forces are many times greater — it is due to their previous defeat. They do not think themselves a match for the Athenians. Thus, like Brasidas facing the Lynkestians Phormion uses the numerical superiority of the enemy against them by assuming fear as their motive and putting them at a psychological disadvantage in the eyes of his own men. (Incidentally he answers 87.6.) Secondly, what is the basis of Peloponnesian confidence? Their courage, of course. But from what does it derive? Past success based on their experience in land service. This, they imagine, will bring them like success at sea. But their reasoning is faulty. And this Phormion nicely points up in a generalization. Both have courage, but the Athenians are more likely to have the advantage of confidence *in this situation*, since "we are each of us more confident, according to our experience in our particular department." In other words, where confidence is concerned, native courage is of less importance than experience. Thus Phormion refutes the long argument of the Peloponnesians about the relative merits of natural qualities and acquired "ability" (87.4). Phormion's third point is an assumption based on εἰκός. The enemy is bringing sailors into battle against their will, otherwise they would not venture into the sea, having already been decisively defeated once. (Implicit in this argument is his *gnome* of 89.11 that defeated men do not twice face the same danger with equal resolution.) Phormion's conclusion is that they need *not* fear the *tolma* of the Peloponnesians.

b) 89.5-7. A counter *logos* follows setting out reasons why they are themselves the more formidable. First, they have already been victorious. Secondly, just *because* they are so few, Phormion sketches what he assumes to be the *probable* feeling of the enemy, disbelief that the Athenians would oppose them unless about to do something noteworthy. This statement is reinforced by a *gnome*. "An adversary numerically superior, like the one before us, comes into action trusting more to strength than to resolution (τῇ δυνάμει as opposed to τῇ γνώμῃ); while he who voluntarily confronts tremendous odds must have very great internal resources to draw upon (μέγα τι τῆς διανοίας)." This the Peloponnesians know and so "fear our irrational audacity more than . . . a more commensurate preparation." (Literally, they fear the "improbable" τῷ οὐκ εἰκότι, i.e., what the Athenians may do that the enemy cannot foresee on the basis of their experience. This is contrasted with "preparation κατὰ λόγον," what they could reasonably assume or calculate, not a *paralogos*. Indeed, τῷ οὐκ εἰκότι is here all but synonymous with *paralogos*.) And as for trust in numbers (87.6), very often armaments succumb to their inferiors from inexperience (ἀπειρίᾳ) or sometimes lack of daring (ἀτολμίᾳ). The Athenians have neither. The implication is that *these* qualities will be decisive. Thus the counter *logos* goes beyond a mere refutation of the Peloponnesians by propounding contrary generalizations which subtly foreshadow the coming battle.

c) 89.8. The *dianoia* is nothing more than an expansion of 86.5, the resolution of the Athenians not to sail into the narrows. Why Phormion refuses to fight in the strait he explains. It is a matter of making the best of one's advantages, here experience and skill. When many unskilled ships face a few experienced good sailers, for the latter the στενοχωρία is of no advantage, because they cannot use their characteristic skills (and he names several, such as διέκπλοι and ἀναστροφαί). Instead, what must result is a land-battle fought on board ship. And there numbers are decisive. In other words, though Phormion offers no concrete tactics to his men, (and clearly this would be impossible because they do not have the initiative), he is emphatic about what they must avoid — a fight in narrow waters. *How* they are to do this, they must leave to him. "For all this I will provide as far as can be." Presumably, he will watch for the *kairos* and then give his orders.

d) 89.9-11. The exhortation is interesting for three points. First, it describes what is essential to *taxis* in naval encounters, order and silence. Secondly, it underscores the importance of the coming encounter. Athens may have only 20 ships involved, but on their success or failure hinges the future of Peloponnesian aspirations by sea. (See 80.1. The latter hoped to interfere with Athens' *periplous* of the Peloponnese and even take Naupaktos. The loss of the latter would be a blow to all westward activities.) Finally, a last encouragement to the sailors, "... beaten men do not face a danger twice with the same determination."

The *antilogia* is a kind of *dissoi logoi*, two opposing arguments on the same subject. Which of the two is the more valid? Is there such a thing as "truth" in the abstract? Put in Thucydidean terms, what constitutes διδαχὴ ἀληθής? A comparison with the earlier *erga* did reveal certain flaws in the Peloponnesian argument. But this was quite provisional. No matter what their reasoning, the second defeat was still not inevitable. As for Phormion, granted he seemed to have drawn the lesson of the previous victory and was determined not to lose the advantage of experience and skill, yet his chances for success were very slim indeed. Our analysis showed that his speech, no less than that of the Peloponnesians, was a tissue of assumptions based on his own set of *gnomai* or generalizations. Both present a series of arguments from εἰκός. And probability is never absolute truth. Thus, however critical one may be of particulars, especially when they contradict past *erga* or "facts," it is still difficult to deny both *logoi* an equal validity in so far as they refer to the future.

How then does one determine which argument is the "stronger" (κρείττων λόγος)? (And presumably Thucydides would not have wasted his labours on an antilogy unless he recognized a meaningful antithesis in which one *logos* is κρείττων, the other ἥττων.)[5] Superficially, the answer appears simple. Phormion was successful; therefore, his must have been the stronger argument. But for this to be so, Phormion's victory must somehow be the result of his speech. Does such an integral

5. The *antilogia* as a kind of *dissoi logoi* is not a reference to the late 5th century work of that name (DK 90), although this would be another example of opposing arguments. Rather we refer to the general concept of antilogy as attributed to Protagoras (DK 80A 1.51: καὶ πρῶτος ἔφη δύο λόγους εἶναι περὶ παντὸς πράγματος ἀντικειμένους ἀλλήλοις; 1.52: the originator of λόγων ἀγῶνας). It was he who distinguished a "weaker" and "stronger" argument (DK 80B 6). Thucydides' early rhetorical training would necessarily have included practice in this kind of antithetic debate. Cf. Finley, p. 46, "... it is not too much to say that political questions, phrased by the method of searching antithesis introduced by Protagoras, must have formed the essence of Thucydides' early training." De Romilly, p. 181 also comments, "... il n'est pas improbable que Protagoras lui ait fourni ses bases et son essor."

connection exist between Phormion's *logos* and the *erga* which follow?

First what did happen? In chapter 90 the Peloponnesians finally take the initiative and force Phormion to follow them into the gulf. There they attack him as he coasts along shore and succeed in defeating nine ships. The other 11 head for more open water and then hasten towards Naupaktos, the enemy's 20 best sailers in pursuit. Only one fails to outsail the Peloponnesians and this is chased by a Leukadian somewhat in advance of the rest. The latter are already singing the paean for victory, when the following incident occurs (91.3): "But there happened to be a merchantman lying at anchor in the roadstead, which the Athenian ship found time to sail round, and struck the Leucadian in chase amidships and sank her." Faced with the unexpected, a *paralogos*, the Peloponnesians react exactly as they did in the previous encounter. They panic and lose their presence of mind. Already out of order from overconfidence, some of them now drop their oars and come to a standstill, looking to the main group for support. Others meanwhile run aground in the shallows.

The Athenians also give a second example of their skill. They are filled with confidence and at one command rush forward to take advantage of the enemy's mistakes and disorder. Needless to say, the latter flee at once.

Could such an outcome ever have been predicted? Thucydides himself describes it as "unexpected"; it was quite fortuitous (ἔτυχε). Obviously, he knew that the particulars could not be foreseen. Thus Phormion cannot and does not spell out a *dianoia*. Yet the event *was foreshadowed*, in that Phormion's *logos* sets forth a number of arguments which *must* depend on the outcome. In a general way he *does* predict the unpredictable.

Consider his strictures against the στενοχωρία (89.8). Is this not the point of 90.5? The ships which meet the enemy head-on are disabled at once with no opportunity to use their skill. Numbers decide. It is the 11 who escape the enemy and head for more open water (ἐς τὴν εὐρυχωρίαν, repeated in 91.1) that are able to display their skill.[6] First, speed; they outsail the enemy to

---

6. Gomme 2, p. 231, calls this "very awkward, a careless piece of writing" and takes ἐς τὴν εὐρυχωρίαν with τὴν ἐπιστροφήν rather than ὑπεκφεύγουσι. This, of course, cuts across what Thucydides is demonstrating, especially through Phormion's stictures in 89.8. Perhaps the Peloponnesians did "turn and enter the open waters" but only *because the Athenians were already there*. This passage serves to point up the close

Naupaktos (91.1: φθάνουσιν ... προκαταφυγοῦσαι). And then that feat which turns the tide. Speed again (φθάσασα) and one of those tactics which Phormion called the *erga* of good sailers (91.3; cf. 89.8, διέκπλοι and ἀναστροφαί). Meanwhile, to what do the Peloponnesians trust? Their superior numbers (89.6, δυνάμει rather than γνώμῃ). So confident are they in their superiority that they lose their order (ἀτάκτως). What finally causes panic is a *paralogos* (91.4). Is this not that very "improbable" (89.6: τῷ οὐκ εἰκότι) which Phormion said they fear? Thus the debate about courage versus experience is resolved in action and Phormion's *logos* proves the stronger. The Peloponnesian courage is of no avail once they lose their presence of mind, for they then forget even the most basic nautical skills and drop their oars. Their inexperience leads to mistakes and disorder and in the end defeats them (cf. 89.7, τῇ ἀπειρίᾳ). For this is the signal for Athenian θάρσος (92.1). It was just this Phormion tried to instil in them (88.1 and 3). It was just this he believed was the gift of experience (89.3; where men are ἐμπειρότεροι, they are θρασύτεροι). The Peloponnesians flee. One almost expects a repetition of the words of 84.3, ". . . no one thought of resistance for the confusion. . . ." There is no word of *alke*.

Never has there been a more revealing example of Thucydides' use of after-the-fact reasoning than when he makes Phormion predict the unpredictable.[7] But we have already discussed at length the derivation of purposes from results. Now we are led to a fresh observation. Is it not strange that Thucydides devotes so little space to the actual encounter that followed the Athenian surprise attack? Apparently there was no battle; none is described. And Phormion's name is not even mentioned as the source of the "one

relationship which exists in Thucydides' work between *erga* and *logoi*. Not a single word is chosen haphazardly. In any case, as we shall show in later chapters, the concept of the στενοχωρία with its disadvantages for Athenian nautical skill and tactics is one which never leaves Thucydides. It is what lies behind the final defeat at Syracuse.

7. The whole *erga-logoi-erga* combination is elaborated with formidable skill, being full of verbal and conceptual echoes and interconnections. Thus it is somewhat surprising to read Gomme's evaluation, 2, p. 228: "The two speeches here introduced do not seem to have any special aim other than to lend weight to the description of the most notable battle at sea of the Archidamian war, and to remind readers of the principal features of naval tactics." For an excellent analysis see de Romilly, pp. 140-148, especially her comments on the central issue, "la force d'âme" versus "l'intelligence" (p. 143). In her work she attempts to elucidate "prevision" in Thucydides and here in particular discusses how and why he turned the fortuitous into an event forewarned.

word" (92.1). One might reply, of course, that Thucydides was more concerned with the *paralogos* and its effect on the Peloponnesians. This is true; it is surely what would have stood out in his own or his informants' memory. But note something else. The missing details can be supplied from chapter 84.2-3. What Phormion anticipated there and could not reasonably predict here, (since it was to depend on the "unexpected"), happens again – ταραχή. Furthermore, the description of the confusion and disorder in 84.3 might well describe the mêlée in 91.4. And surely the command here corresponds to Phormion's earlier signal given the instant he recognized the *kairos*. Here too is a *kairos* and immediate response. But the reader knows all this, for the second encounter is nothing more than a repetition of the first. History repeats itself, with this difference: Phormion has learned from life what he merely assumed in 84.2 and thus can present a *logos* based on this knowledge.[8] How unlike the Peloponnesians who did *not* learn from the *erga*, as their speech revealed, and so were doomed to repeat their previous errors.

Our first conclusion, a tentative one at this point, concerns the relationship between past, present, and future. Past *erga*, what happened, can serve as a model for the future. What mediates in the present is the *logos* or διδαχή, in human terms, the man who has learned from experience and so can make predictions about the future. Phormion spoke of *pronoia* (89.9). Like Brasidas and Themistokles he too is κράτιστος γνώμων and ἄριστος εἰκαστής (1.138.3). In an emergency he is able to arrive at a correct *gnome* or generalization and then use it as a premise to make assumptions and predictions, i.e., reason from εἰκός. In Chapter 2 (p. 29) we wrote:

> the basis of *pronoia* or *prognosis* – the statesman's primary virtue – is the ability to reason from εἰκός. This alone, however, is not sufficient. He must also formulate a policy to fit the circumstances. This is γιγνώσκειν, the ability to arrive at a correct *gnome*. The function of both together allows one to αὐτοσχεδιάζειν τὰ δέοντα, "meet an emergency" or "extemporize what must be done."

It now becomes evident that the reasoning process just described

---

8. Or such is the role of the *logos* in this incident. Actually, what Phormion predicted in chapter 84 one can assume he learned from his own previous experience, for he had a great deal (Thuc. 1.64-65 and 117, 2.29, 58 and 68-69).

depends in turn on one's ability to understand past *erga*, experience, which alone contain "truth."

To return to our previous discussion of the "stronger argument," we have now shown that what makes one *logos* κρείττων is not its reasoning *per se*, but the fact that life, the *erga*, demonstrate its superiority. Phormion's *logos* was only tentatively the stronger until events conformed to it. Then it *was* the stronger. Then truth was established, truth *for that particular situation*, and *perhaps* truth of value for the future.

Let us now revert to the year 432 and the second congress at Lakedaimon. The Corinthians are speaking, as ever demanding that the war should begin. Full of confidence they give a number of reasons why they expect success (1.121.2: εἰκὸς ἐπικρατῆσαι). The following is but one of their predictions (121.4):

> A single defeat at sea is in all likelihood their ruin (κατὰ τὸ εἰκός): should they hold out, in that case there will be the more time for us to exercise ourselves in naval matters; and as soon as we have arrived at an equality in science, we need scarcely ask whether we shall be their superiors in courage (ἐπιστήμη vs. εὐψυχία). For the advantages that we have by nature they cannot acquire by education (φύσις vs. διδαχή); while their superiority in science must be removed by our practice (μελέτη).

A familiar issue? Surely the very point of the Phormion episode, the relationship between natural qualities and acquired "skill." And in this case also there is a counter *logos*. In his first speech Perikles answers the Corinthians by pointing out the difficulties the Peloponnesians will face in trying to acquire naval experience (142.6-9):

> Familiarity with the sea they will not find an easy acquisition. If you who have been practising at it ever since the Median invasion have not yet brought it to perfection, is there any chance of anything considerable being effected by an agricultural, unseafaring population, who will besides be prevented from practising by the constant presence of strong squadrons of observation from Athens? With a small squadron they might hazard an engagement, encouraging their ignorance by numbers; but the restraint of a strong force will prevent their moving, and through want of practice they will

grow more clumsy, and consequently more timid. It must be kept in mind that seamanship, just like anything else, is a matter of art, and will not admit of being taken up occasionally as an occupation for times of leisure; on the contrary, it is so exacting as to leave leisure for nothing else.

Three points emerge from the above. First, note once again that the argument from εἰκός is *not* confined to the side which proves correct. As in the law-courts *both* parties to a debate resort to this kind of reasoning in order to make assumptions about both present and future. Here the Corinthian *logos* is demonstrably wrong, since later events do not correspond to their predictions. *In itself* then εἰκός is not infallible or even dependable as a guide to the future.

Secondly, which argument in *this* debate is κρείττων? Obviously Perikles'. There never was a "first defeat" to finish off the Athenians. Even when the Peloponnesians did confront a small squadron "encouraging their ignorance by numbers," they were defeated not once, but twice (Phormion's victories). And the reason? They did not appreciate the relationship between courage and "science" nor the importance of experience and practice. But it is only, finally, in the light of the *erga*, Phormion's exploits, that Perikles' *logos* proves the "stronger." In other words, the empirical truth we described as established "for that particular situation" (i.e., 2.83-92) has a more general relevance. It looks back to one of the larger questions raised in the pre-war debates of Book 1: what kind of military power, based on what qualities of character will most likely lead to success in the coming war.

Thirdly, we can come to a conclusion from the above. Just as individual *logoi* such as exhortations foreshadow the *erga* which follow close upon them, so some *logoi*, major debates, foreshadow whole periods. In providing the Corinthians with the "weaker" argument and Perikles with the "stronger," Thucydides follows the very same method he employed in the debate between the Peloponnesians and Phormion before Naupaktos. In both cases events themselves decide between the *logoi*.[9] If then, as we have

9. Stahl, pp. 86 ff. also notes this technique, referring in particular to Perikles' first speech (1.140-144) and the second speech of the Corinthians (1.120-124). He suggests (p. 96) that Book 1 was composed in light of the concrete reality of Book 2 and that the latter seems to correct the predictions of the former, thus highlighting the relationship, or better the discrepancy, between plan and execution. Since he lays

demonstrated in all the individual episodes up to this point, such "anticipations" are based on after-the-fact reasoning, does the same hold true for *logoi* which foreshadow whole periods? For example, was the debate between the Corinthians and Perikles written *with Phormion's exploits in mind*? I suspect it was, for the latter *do* resolve concretely the question of naval power and abstractly the argument about φύσις vs. ἐπιστήμη.

The very nature of the central issue, φύσις vs. ἐπιστήμη, raises another point. Again and again words or synonyms recur, εὐψυχία, ἀνδρεία, ἀλκή on the one side, διδαχή, ἐπιστήμη, τέχνη on the other and most especially practice (μελέτη) and experience (ἐμπειρία).[10] Evidently Thucydides saw in the Phormion episode a demonstration of the importance of practice and experience in the acquisition of "science" or "skill" (cf. Perikles' remarks above). The latter, in turn, proves to be one of the major ingredients of *tolma*, daring and initiative. Or perhaps we can turn this statement on its head and say that Thucydides was convinced of the importance of διδαχή and ἐμπειρία, (whether because of this incident or some experience of his own), and so set down Phormion's exploits in such a way that their meaning might be clear to all. He so selected his details — *erga-logoi-erga* — that the reader is inexorably led to reason as Phormion reasoned and discover for himself the truth contained in the events themselves. Furthermore, the central question involved here is hardly accidental, since it was *one of the major debates of the 5th century*. The Sophists argued at length about this question of φύσις vs. ἐπιστήμη, part of the larger problem of φύσις vs. νόμος.[11] There is

particular stress upon *discrepancy*, in his discussion of Phormion's exploits (pp. 84 ff.), Stahl overemphasizes the element of chance. Certainly the two battles did hinge on a number of purely accidental factors. But if the present chapter has shown anything, it is that Thucydides was so intent on motivating both victories that he *underplayed* the role of chance and at Naupaktos in particular made Phormion predict the unpredictable. In other words the possibilities of the rational process (*gnome* or *pronoia*) concerned him no less, perhaps more, than the irrational (*tyche*). Later chapters of this work will attempt to relate the rational and irrational and describe man's place in the historical process.

10. Forms of ἐμπειρία are especially numerous: 84.3, ἄπειροι; 85.2, ἐμπειρίαν; 87.2, ἀπειρία; 87.4, ἀπειρία; 87.5, ἐμπειρότερον; 89.2, ἐμπειρίαν; 89.3, ἐμπειρότεροι; 89.7, ἀπειρία; 89.8, ἐμπείροις. Thucydides overdoes it a little. Supposedly it was the first attempt of the Lakedaimonians at sea (85.2). But what about Corinthian experience? They were just as much a naval and trading people as the Athenians.

11. Protagoras, DK 80B 3; Demokritos, DK 68B 33 and 242; Antiphon the Sophist, DK 87B 60; and Kritias, DK 88B 9 are just a few examples. See too P. Shorey, "Φύσις, Μελέτη, Ἐπιστήμη," *TAPA* 40, 1909, pp. 185-201; Jaeger, *Paideia* 1, pp.

no reason that Thucydides, a keen observer and a student of his own times, should not express his own opinion on this matter. By demonstrating it in life, in the *erga*, he was groping for a level of "truth" which goes far beyond "that particular situation" and becomes almost universal.

In relation to the major problem of the *History*, the decline of Athens, the Phormion episode is as much a model situation or *paradeigma* as the Funeral Oration. The latter describes and eulogizes all the best in Athenian life and character before sickness, both literal and figurative, sets in. In the same way Phormion and his men demonstrate *in action*, on their native element, the sea, those qualities the Athenians possessed both by nature and training which brought them to the height described by Perikles.[12] What these qualities were, Perikles himself indicated in his first speech (1.144.4):

> Did not our fathers resist the Medes . . . and more by wisdom than by fortune, more by daring than by strength (γνώμη τε πλέονι ἢ τύχῃ καὶ τόλμῃ μείζονι ἢ δυνάμει), did not they beat off the barbarian and advance their affairs to their present height?[13]

Wisdom and daring together appear again and again as the very essence of the Athenian character. For example, in the Funeral Oration Perikles characterizes them thus (2.40.2-3):

> instead of looking on discussion as a stumbling-block in the way of action, we think it an indispensable preliminary to

305 ff.; Nestle, *Vom Mythos zum Logos passim*; W. C. Greene, *Moira*, New York, 1963, *passim* and especially Appendix 31, which provides a bibliography of works on φύσις and νόμος.

12. Cf. Gomme 2, p. 233.

13. Cf. Phormion's *gnome* (89.6), which the *erga* confirmed: "An adversary numerically superior, like the one before us, comes into action trusting more to strength (τῇ δυνάμει) than to resolution (τῇ γνώμῃ). . . ." A. G. Woodhead sums up his argument in Chapter 2 of *Thucydides on the Nature of Power*, Cambridge, Mass., 1970, with a list of five "characteristics or factors or qualities which had made the Athenian democracy great and had brought it success (p. 46)." They are *kratos, dynamis, tharsos, gnome*, and *perousia. Tharsos* (or θαρσεῖν) he rightly emphasizes, delineating it (my *tolma*) and *gnome* as specifically Athenian qualities. I would reverse the order of these five characteristics, however, and establish a different relationship among them, since I do not believe that *tharsos* and *gnome* are so much concomitants of power and "its successful use" as the source of Athenian greatness, the qualities which enabled her to acquire and exercise power (*dynamis*), both men and resources. In Perikles' time this included *arche* and resulted in *perousia*. On the whole I agree with Woodhead's very interesting discussion of the virtues and defects of democracy.

any wise action at all. Again, in our enterprises we present the singular spectacle of daring and deliberation, each carried to its highest point, and both united in the same persons. . . .

Finally in his last speech Perikles makes his most significant statement about the relationship between *tolma* and *gnome* (2.62.5):

And where the chances are the same, knowledge fortifies courage by the contempt which is its consequence, its trust being placed, not in hope, which is the prop of the desperate, but in a judgment grounded upon existing resources, whose anticipations are more to be depended upon.

These are the very qualities evinced by Phormion and his men.

But if the *History* is a record of Athens' decline from the peak of the Funeral Oration, it also records her loss of these two important and interrelated qualities. Moreover, the Phormion incident not only serves as a *paradeigma* of these qualities, but also establishes truths based on experience which will be significant for the future. Thus the technique we have called "anticipation," the deriving of purposes from results, is not one found only in isolated incidents but suffuses the whole work.

Chapter 4
Ὁ Χρόνος καὶ ἡ Ἐμπειρία:
Demosthenes' Adventures (Thuc. 4.1-41)
ꙮꙮꙮ

Book 4.1-41, Pylos-Sphakteria, is in many respects comparable to the subject of the last chapter, Phormion's exploits. Its structure, *erga-logoi-erga*, is similar. What is more, it also describes a complete *paralogos* suffered by the Peloponnesians and an amazing display of virtuosity on the Athenian side. But there is a significant difference between the two passages: one is purposive, the other is not. Here, though one might expect Thucydides to employ his usual method of spelling out purposes to anticipate the *erga* so that his reader might better understand how they happened and why, he does no such thing. With this in mind, let us consider the first set of *erga* (4.2-16) under three headings: Demosthenes' "adventure," the Peloponnesian response, Demosthenes' speech.

Demosthenes' "adventure" (2-5).

The first thing to observe about this affair which becomes a major turning-point in the Archidamian War is that it begins as a very *minor* part of a larger expedition to Kerkyra and Sicily under the generals Eurymedon and Sophokles. "Demosthenes also, who had remained without employment since his return from Akarnania, applied and obtained permission to use the fleet, if he wished it, upon the coast of Peloponnese" (2.4). Where he obtained this permission and what was his status, indeed what exactly was the object of his trip and where in the Peloponnese, of all this nothing. It appears that no public decision was taken in which the two generals shared, for the latter never really seem to

61

know what Demosthenes is up to and balk at every suggestion. Off Lakonia, for example, hearing that the Peloponnesian ships are already at Kerkyra, they wish to sail there at once. This is as it should be, since it was their destination. But at this point Demosthenes orders them to put in at Pylos and do "what must be done" (3.1).[1] Thus his destination comes to light, even if his purpose is still rather vague. The reaction of the generals confirms that they do not hold joint orders with Demosthenes specifying "action" at Pylos, for they put up an argument which is only ended by a storm's carrying the fleet into Pylos.

Once there the reader and the generals too, it seems, find out "what must be done." Demosthenes urges them to fortify the place. This is what *he* has come for. Note that the last is in indirect discourse, part of his assertion, and *a revelation of his purpose for the first time*. He even makes use of the appearance of the place to convince them; it was strong and unoccupied. Thucydides then gives a geographical digression situating Pylos. There follows further confirmation that the generals knew nothing about Pylos until now: as far as they are concerned, one part of the Peloponnese is as good as another. They even imply that the whole thing is a waste of money. Finally Demosthenes shows that he does know what he is doing. The reasons which we might have expected earlier and which might have impressed his colleagues he now presents: Pylos has a harbour and its former inhabitants the Messenians could do the most harm by making incursions from there, and generally they would form a good garrison. The generals are still not convinced, nor anyone else for that matter.

Bad weather, meanwhile, keeps the fleet at Pylos, until the soldiers, bored with their inactivity, begin to fortify the place. Apparently, there was no prompting from Demosthenes. It was a whim (ὁρμή). But they do not have proper tools, rather surprising, since it had begun to look as if Demosthenes did after all know where he was going and why. Why would he not have brought equipment along? In any case, the soldiers set to work in order "to complete the most vulnerable points before the arrival of the Lacedaemonians. . ." (4.3). It is certainly odd that they should be worrying about the Lakedaimonians if they do not plan to stay. It is a game with a purpose. At this point the generals accept the inevitable, and without further ado leave Demosthenes a parting

---

1. My translation.

gift of five of their 40 ships.

What impression does this account convey? Not anticipation, but reaction. The reader is like the generals; he does not know what is going on. Purposes are not spelled out in advance but dragged in after the fact or as they seem to come to Demosthenes, and his decisions have the air of being made on the spot. All this is significant in light of Thucydides' usual keen interest in the relationship of plan and effect. Elsewhere, even if he contradicted himself, he assumed motives for his protagonists. Thus, even if he were not absolutely certain what Demosthenes' motives were, he would have been doing nothing new in assuming them after the fact. But he does not. He leaves Demosthenes without motivation, as it were. There is a total lack of *gnome* or prevision.[2] But, one might retort, this is just what we always expected from Thucydides, the *facts*, and proves he did not supply motives gratuitously. This would be a good argument except that the same *erga* are full of "motives," spelling out every thought the *Peloponnesians* have.

The Peloponnesian response (5-8).

News of what the Athenians are doing does not elicit any immediate response from the Peloponnesians for three reasons: 1) It coincides with a festival they are celebrating. 2) They make light of it in the belief that they can take it any time they choose. 3) Their army is away at Athens. How valid are these three explanations, any one of which would in itself have been sufficient?

1) This is the conventional explanation of Spartan delay and inactivity, but it is rather weak here. The festival had apparently not stood in the way of the invasion of Attika; so there seems no reason it should keep them from defending their own country.

2) There is a striking contradiction between the attitude of the Spartans at home and those in Attika. As soon as the latter learn that Pylos is occupied, they rush home "thinking that the matter touched them nearly" (6.1).

3. Thucydides implies that this is the least important reason (5.1: καί τι καί), but it is surely the true reason for their initial inactivity. In simplest terms, the Spartans had to wait for their army to return before taking action. They summoned it at once

---

2. Or as Cornford, p. 90 puts it, "What is left out is whatever would explain the motives and designs of the principal actors. . . ."

and it returned immediately. The festival was beside the point and no one "belittled" the occupation. A perfectly rational explanation outweighs coincidence or overconfidence. And here note a concomitant of Demosthenes' adventure. It brings the Spartans home, making this the shortest invasion ever, only fifteen days. One begins to suspect a masterful scheme. But no, Thucydides presents other circumstances that might have induced the Spartans to leave anyway. First, their invasion was so early that they were short of supplies, the corn being still unripe. Also, the unusually bad weather distressed the army. The last two reasons are mere assumptions and make little sense. What kind of army takes the field knowing full well the corn is still unripe and yet fails to take along sufficient supplies? And what a boon to Athens, if mere bad weather can stop the annual invasion. The Spartans are not such hardy folk after all. Again only one reason was necessary. But Thucydides seems intent on multiplying fortuitous circumstances which combined to bring the Spartans home.

In other words, where he might have brought the Spartans home *as a fact*, their motives being self-evident, he supplies *more* motives than he needs. How unlike his treatment of Demosthenes. But how like the Thucydides of earlier chapters.

Chapter 8 confirms our previous suspicions. With the Peloponnesians home from Attika the Spartans themselves rush to Pylos. The rest of the Lakedaimonians follow more slowly "as they had just come in from another campaign" (8.1). The Peloponnesians are ordered to get to Pylos with all speed, and what is more, the 60 ships at Kerkyra are brought home, managing to avoid the Athenians at Zakynthos. All this against a tiny force which, we are told, was previously disdained. The puzzles on the Athenian side are also increasing. Why anyway is the fleet, previously in such a great hurry, only 70 miles away at Zakynthos? They have been gone at least a week. We may shut our eyes to that one but not the next. Demosthenes manages to send them a message about his plight. It is actually an order and they obey at once. Gone is the mission to Kerkyra and Sicily and *no explanation* given of why Pylos, a seeming whim of Demosthenes and some of the soldiers, suddenly becomes so important. Once again the reader is led to suspect some brilliant strategy, part of which is the stay of the fleet at Zakynthos. For there is a second concomitant of Demosthenes' little adventure. The Peloponnesian fleet has been forced to leave Kerkyra and is now in the open.

Let us return to the Peloponnesians and their plans, for Thucydides has spelled them out in great detail. Of 16 lines in chapter 8 (4-8) only three lines are factual. All the rest — apart from a digression on Sphakteria itself, not included in the above — depends on a series of participles and verbs of thinking. With respect to Pylos itself they hoped (ἐλπίζοντες) to take it easily, since it was "constructed in haste, and held by a feeble garrison." Meanwhile, as they expected (προσδεχόμενοι) the fleet to arrive from Zakynthos, they intended (ἐν νῷ εἶχον), if they failed to take Pylos before, "to block up the entrances of the harbour to prevent their being able to anchor inside it." (The description of Sphakteria with its harbour and two inlets follows.) Thucydides continues, "The inlets the Lacedaemonians meant (ἔμελλον) to close with a line of ships placed close together. . . ." As for Sphakteria itself, fearing (φοβούμενοι) the enemy might make use of it against them, they stationed infantry both there and along the coast. An explanation of this strategy in indirect discourse follows. Confronted by a hostile continent and island the Athenians would have no place to land. (The shore of Pylos which faced the open sea had no harbour and so offered no base of operations.) On this basis the Lakedaimonians assume that "without sea-fight or risk (they) would in all probability (κατὰ τὸ εἰκός) become masters of the place, occupied as it had been on the spur of the moment, and unfurnished with provisions."

Where does all this come from? *With one exception* one might easily assume such a strategy after the fact; it is, after all, what happened, even if it did not succeed. And a major reason for its failure was that the Lakedaimonians did not carry through all the intentions Thucydides attributes to them (see below). For the moment what interests us is that Thucydides *does* assume these motives. He does allow the Lakedaimonians to offer a reasonable *dianoia* and a prediction based on εἰκός. This, of course, is his usual method and stands in stark contrast to his account of Demosthenes' adventures. Indeed, the Peloponnesians' "thoughts" emphasize Demosthenes' total absence of plan or foresight by pointing out indirectly that the defence-work was hasty, its defenders few, and food not available.

Demosthenes' speech (9-12).

The Peloponnesians seem to be right. Chapter 9 emphasizes the utter hopelessness of Demosthenes' plight. Now that they must defend themselves, they have nowhere to acquire arms. Actually they *do* have a few rather poor shields obtained from some passing Messenians. Fortunately there were also 40 hoplites on board ready and willing for employment. Of course, all this is perfectly ridiculous. Days before this the soldiers had hastened their work on the fortifications expecting the Peloponnesians to attack. How then did they ever expect to defend themselves without arms? Surely they would not have allowed the fleet to depart without leaving them *some* weapons. And the Messenians. Did the traditional enemies of Lakedaimon always float around off her shores this way? Rather risky in times of war, especially as they could hardly call it a pleasure-cruise dressed up as they were in hoplites' garb. Even if such a "destinationless" vessel could be imagined, why should they now be prepared to risk their lives in what must have appeared a fight against impossible odds?

Once again some master plan comes to mind. Once again no such plan is attributed to Demosthenes. The impression created is a total want of foresight culminating in a final oversight. Demosthenes, we are told, had a good idea where the enemy would try to land — at a weak part of the wall, "as the Athenians, confident in their naval superiority, had here paid little attention to their defences . . ." (9.3). Does this mean that Demosthenes felt confident in his three ships now in stockade, or in the whole fleet?[3] But it had gone to Kerkyra, presumably for good. Or was this some recent oversight? It is very mystifying. Thus are we prepared for the tenor of the remarks which follow.

The speech is a παρακέλευσις, very brief to be sure, but similar in reasoning and structure to others analyzed above. Its purpose is to replace fear with *tolma*. 10.1 presents the situation:

> Soldiers and comrades in this adventure, I hope that none of you in our present strait will think to show his wit by exactly calculating all the perils that encompass us, but that you will rather hasten to close with the enemy, without staying to count the odds, seeing in this your best chance of safety. In emergencies like ours calculation is out of place; the sooner the danger is faced the better.

3. In 4.3 they were hastening "to complete the most vulnerable points before the arrival of the Lacedaemonians. . . ." Why then in the intervening period with the fleet gone to Kerkyra would they leave *any* part of the wall vulnerable? Their confidence in naval superiority can only be a recent development, specifically since they summoned the fleet from Zakynthos.

Demosthenes then presents the following *dianoia* (2-5). The Athenians must stand fast and not give ground to the enemy, lest they lose the few advantages they have. The awkwardness of the landing, for example, is in their favour so long as they do not retreat, for it will be easier to repel the enemy while they are on board ship than "after he has landed and meets us on equal terms." As for numbers, these need not frighten them. Though numerous, the enemy can only engage in small groups, because they cannot land. In sum, they must display courage and tenacity to beat back the enemy at the water's edge.

The first thing to observe is that Demosthenes was perfectly correct in his assessment of what to expect from the enemy and thus what tactics they must employ. The Peloponnesians do land where he predicted, do row up in small groups trying to force a landing and, in spite of Brasidas' efforts, are unable to land "owing to the difficulty of the ground and the unflinching tenacity of the Athenians" (12.2). This close relationship between purpose and result is heightened by verbal correspondences:

9.2: ... ᾗ μάλιστα ἐκείνους προσεδέχετο πειράσειν ἀποβαίνειν. ...

11.2: προσέβαλλε δὲ ᾗπερ ὁ Δημοσθένης προσεδέχετο·

10.3: τοῦ τε γὰρ χωρίου τὸ δυσέμβατον ἡμέτερον νομίζω, ὃ μενόντων μὲν ἡμῶν ξύμμαχον γίγνεται, ὑποχωρήσασι δὲ καίπερ. ...

12.2: ... ἀδύνατοι δ᾽ ἦσαν ἀποβῆναι τῶν τε χωρίων χαλεπότητι καὶ τῶν Ἀθηναίων μενόντων καὶ οὐδὲν ὑποχωρούντων.

10.4: κατ᾽ ὀλίγον γὰρ μαχεῖται ... ἀπορίᾳ τῆς προσορμίσεως. ...

11.3: οἱ δὲ κατ᾽ ὀλίγας ναῦς διελόμενοι, διότι οὐκ ἦν πλέοσι προσσχεῖν. ...

In this situation then Thucydides does employ his usual method of supplying purposes in the *logoi* which anticipate the *erga*, just as he let the Peloponnesians' "thoughts" foreshadow their deeds. We are thus driven to the conclusion that in the earlier *erga* Thucydides consciously left Demosthenes without an overall plan. But, one might retort, perhaps he really was baffled and just could not think of a plan. This, of course, contradicts all we know of his method. Elsewhere — and here too where the Peloponnesians are concerned — he was so intent on relating purpose to result that he often supplied motives that were contradictory, making it obvious that he did not know why an event happened as it did but still thought it part of his task to assume motives after the fact. Given this propensity, it is a slight to his intelligence to suggest he threw up his hands in despair here. No, Thucydides deliberately chose not to supply motives. Whatever he thought significant about Demosthenes' adventure was *not* to be conveyed by relating purpose to result, but by leaving them unconnected, by presenting Demosthenes as devoid of *pronoia* or *gnome*.

Surely this is also the point of the first part of Demosthenes' *logos*. Reconsider the words he uses to describe the emergency. Is it not paradoxical that the most important Thucydidean virtues are now tossed to the wind? He cautions against "intelligence" and calculation (ξύνεσις and λογισμός). And what does he put in their place? Blind hope (ἀπερισκέπτως εὔελπις)[4] and native courage. This is the counsel of despair in circumstances which left nothing else to depend on but hope and *tolma*. As it happened, it was sufficient and the Athenians won the day by sheer tenacity. For this success Thucydides does give Demosthenes credit.[5] Like Brasidas, primarily a military man, he is a model of soldierly *tolma* and manages to inspire his men with the same dash. Normally such a quality would in itself be insufficient, especially coming at the end of a long series of oversights, or rather the oversights implied by Thucydides. For the beginning of the speech and all that preceded it indicate that if he had not lacked that prevision which is part of a far-sighted strategy, he would never have found himself in such a plight. Not once did he ever think ahead, until he finally had no choice but to stand or die. And though he evinces *tolma*, it is the *tolma* of a daredevil, *tolma alogistos*.[6] In its totality then Demosthenes' adventure at Pylos is an example in life, in the *erga*, of a statement of Perikles already well known to us. In the last analysis the reason Demosthenes found himself in such desperate straits that he had only hope to rely upon (ἐλπίδι . . . ἧς ἐν τῷ

---

4. Cf. 4.108.4 immediately after the fall of Amphipolis, where Thucydides comments not without bitterness on "blind wishing" as opposed to "sound prevision; for it is a habit of mankind to entrust to careless hope (ἐλπίδι ἀπερισκέπτῳ) what they long for, and to use sovereign reason (λογισμῷ αὐτοκράτορι) to thrust aside what they do not fancy." He chooses his words carefully.

5. Demosthenes and his men were after all successful and their feat as well known as Phormion's. Nor does it detract from the overall "planlessness" of the occupation to spell out their motives here. They had no choice but were responding to ἀνάγκη (10.1) much as the Peloponnesians did, though with less effect, in 2.83.1 and 3, "compelled to fight in mid passage."

6. Taken from 3.82.4. The epithet certainly characterizes his behaviour in Aitolia the previous year (3.97.2). "Led on by his advisers and trusting in his fortune (τῇ τύχῃ ἐλπίσας)," and without even waiting for needed reinforcements he led his men into a veritable massacre (98.3-4). Cf. 6.59.1, where the same words (*alogistos tolma*) describe the action of Harmodios and Aristogeiton.

ἀπόρῳ ἡ ἰσχύς) was that up to that point all his activities were characterized by a total lack of that "judgment (*gnome*) grounded upon existing resources, whose anticipations (*pronoia*) are more to be depended on" (2.62.5).

If ever there was a portion of the *History* completely at variance with the evidence, it is this one. If Thucydides could not or, as we suggest, *would* not supply an explanation of Demosthenes' adventure, modern historians can and do and find the whole affair carefully planned in the extreme. Even the most casual reader might well come to this conclusion, as we have hinted above in our discussion of the *erga*. The most appealing reconstruction is H. Awdry's suggestion[7] that the Athenians were on a mission to destroy the Spartan fleet wherever they found it, and left Demosthenes on Pylos as a decoy. Incidentally, this explains the presence of the Athenian fleet at Zakynthos about a week after their hasty departure for Kerkyra. As for the unexplained arrival of the Messenians, there is general agreement that some scheme existed between them and Demosthenes. They were, after all, to be left there as a garrison and general annoyance to the Lakedaimonians. It has even been suggested that Demosthenes hit upon this brilliant scheme in conversation with the Messenians the previous year in Akarnania and arranged the details with them, for they knew the country well and spoke its dialect.[8]

One puzzle does remain, the failure of the Spartans to close the inlets. We know that they intended to (8.5) and Thucydides repeats that intention in 13.4, "The Lacedaemonians . . . having omitted to close the inlets as they had intended, remained quiet on shore. . . ." Yet they had ample opportunity to carry out their intention. When the Athenian fleet arrived from Zakynthos, its immediate aim was to engage the Spartans in the open sea. When this failed and it was impossible to land on Sphakteria, the fleet retired for the night to Prote, a desert island nearby (13.3). In

7. "Pylos and Sphacteria," *JHS* 20, 1900, pp. 14-19. Also consulted were Gomme 3, pp. 482-488 and *passim*; B. W. Henderson, *The Great War between Athens and Sparta*, London, 1927, pp. 192-223; G. B. Grundy, *Thucydides and the History of his Age*, Vol. 2, Oxford, 1948, pp. 122-133; W. K. Pritchett, *Studies in Ancient Greek Topography*, Part 1, Berkeley and Los Angeles, 1965, pp. 6-29.

8. See, e.g., Gomme 3, p. 488, " . . . that the Messenians had arrived by arrangement with Demosthenes is obvious . . ." and Finley, pp. 190-191, "He had perhaps learned of it (Pylos) from the Messenians of Naupactus. . . ." The latter also believes that "an arrangement had no doubt been made the year before." Cf. Cornford, p. 93, and Henderson, op. cit., p. 197.

other words, for at least 12 hours the Spartans were aware of the Athenians' presence, and their men on Sphakteria must have seen the fleet. Yet they failed to close the inlets. There is, of course, nothing outside Thucydides' assertion to indicate that this *was* the Spartan intention. In a short but sound discussion of this problem Awdry has pointed out the impracticability of blocking the southern channel, which is wide, deep, and choppy. He states: "I do not think therefore that we are bound to lay any great stress on Thucydides' statement that the Spartans intended to block the channels. They thought of it, but dismissed it as impracticable. . . ."[9] Thucydides assumed this intention. And look how neatly it fits into the overall impression created about the Spartans! They display the same characteristics as they did in the Gulf of Patrai and at Naupaktos. They procrastinate, trust too much to numbers, and end by making mistakes.[10] Granted they were celebrating, but still they made an error in disdaining the occupation of Pylos and not attacking immediately. (These are the reasons Thucydides stresses, rather than the absence of the army.) It was too bad also that they did not intercept Demosthenes' messenger-ship somehow (8.3). And now this final inexplicable *error*.

Up to now we have made no reference to "chance." Instead we argue that even if Thucydides had never used the word *tyche* or its compounds, this episode would stand in contrast to passages analyzed earlier just *because* of the absence of motivation or anticipation. On the one side is error, (the Peloponnesians), on the other, a total lack of plan, (Demosthenes). What better place for *tyche* to play a role? If there is an element of chance even when men formulate a policy based on careful calculation and foresight,[11] how could it fail to be a most active force when both are lacking? Pylos is such an occasion. Quite simply, *tyche* has taken the place of *gnome*.[12] What is more, the second set of *erga*,

9. Op. cit., p. 18.

10. In a word they fail to recognize and act at the decisive moment, the *kairos*.

11. Such was the plague with respect to Perikles' policy. See his remarks at 2.61.2-3.

12. In the first set of *erga* there are the following references to "chance": 3.1, the storm κατὰ τύχην; 4.1, ὁρμὴ ἐνέπεσε resulting in defence-works; 5.1, ἔτυχον ἄγοντες a festival; 9.1, ἔτυχον παραγενόμενοι, arrival of the Messenians; 12.3, περιέστη ἡ τύχη, paradoxical manner of fighting; 13.4, οὔτε . . . ἔτυχον ποιήσαντες, failure to close inlets; and 14.3, τῇ παρούσῃ τύχῃ, good luck on Athens' side. All this has been admirably dealt with by Cornford, pp. 82 ff., and de Romilly, *Thucydides and Athenian Imperialism*, pp. 172 ff.

events at Sphakteria (29-41), sustains this impression.

It will not be necessary to analyze these events in the same detail as the earlier *erga*. Rather we shall devote our attention to chapters 29 and 30, where Demosthenes is at last making ready for a descent on the island. Thucydides offers the following explanation (29.2): " . . . the soldiers distressed by the difficulties of the position, and rather besieged than besiegers, being eager to fight it out, while the firing of the island had increased the confidence of the general." That Demosthenes' lack of $\dot{\rho}\dot{\omega}\mu\eta$ was the major cause of delay is evident from what follows. Thucydides presents Demosthenes' motives for not making a descent until now. The upshot of the long passage in indirect discourse is that "circumstances" prevented him. In the first place, the fact that the island was entirely wooded and pathless frightened him, for he thought it in the enemy's favour. If he landed, he could be attacked from an unseen position. On the other hand, if he attempted to attack them in the woods, he thought they had advantages which would allow them to use guerrilla tactics. Thus, though his hesitation caused the soldiers distress and made the people at home repent rejecting the Spartan offer (27.2), Thucydides makes it clear that Demosthenes' tactical considerations were sound. They were in fact based on a previous experience. "The Aetolian disaster, which had been mainly caused by the wood, had not a little to do with these reflections" (30.1).

Fortunately we can consult this *pathos* of the previous year which Demosthenes uses as a kind of *paradeigma*, for Thucydides has recorded it in 3.97-98. Specifically, he must be referring to 98.2: ". . . the greater number (of Athenians) however missed their road and rushed into the wood, which had no ways out, and which was soon fired and burnt round them by the enemy." A problem arises: who is who? Is Demosthenes trying to avoid a similar *pathos* for his own men by not allowing them to be caught in the woods on unfamiliar terrain? Ταῦτα ἐσῄει (30.1) would seem to refer back to his reflections. But what about the fire? Surely this implies a tactic to be used *against* men in a wooded area. It stands to reason then that given this experience and his present difficulties, Demosthenes would fire the island to bring the Spartans out in the open. But no. The fire was not deliberate at all but an accident. It seems that Demosthenes' men were so short of space that they were compelled (ἀναγκασθέντων) to use the extremities of Sphakteria as a kind of "picnic area." They took their dinners there, and on one of these outings (30.2) a certain soldier "set fire to a little of the wood without meaning to do so (ἄκοντος); and as it came on to blow soon afterwards, almost the whole was consumed before they were aware of it" (ἔλαθε). Of what is all this reminiscent? Chapter 4, of course, where the men's whimsical behaviour combined with their enforced stay in Pylos resulted in the fortuitous building of defence-works. Once again compulsion (ἀνάγκη) combines with unplanned human activity. Here too fortuitous weather conditions play a major role, and once again Demosthenes has failed to think ahead. The event upon which he builds his whole subsequent strategy, the burning of the island, he did not plan at all. Rather he *reacts* to the fire with a surge of confidence. This is the Demosthenes of Pylos, totally devoid of *gnome* or *pronoia*.

But if in the case of Pylos we showed there *was* a plan, why should we uncritically accept Thucydides' account here? Rather let us query the words ἀναγκασθέντων, ἄκοντος, and ἔλαθε.

Suppose Demosthenes really *did* learn something from the Aitolian *pathos*, has not Thucydides brought this *paradeigma* in at the wrong point? If one reads the entire account of Sphakteria, it is clear that Demosthenes put the Spartans in the *very* position in which the Athenians themselves had been when surrounded by light-armed Aitolians, (cf. 3.97.3 to 4.32.4 and 33.2). Having evolved this strategy, what Demosthenes required were light-armed troops, specifically targeteers and archers. As a matter of fact, *this is just what Kleon brings with him from Athens*, arriving soon after the fire (30.4). Does it not seem obvious that Demosthenes had to wait until he knew these troops were coming before he fired the woods? Hence the delay. He was playing for time. And how clever to accustom the Spartans to a harmless daily picnic. Little did they suspect that the Athenians, like poor campers, would one day fail to put out their fire. This also makes it clear that whatever other problems the debate between Kleon and Nikias raises (4.27-28), the former knew just what he was doing in choosing his troops, "archers" and "targeteers" (28.4). And yet Thucydides no more motivates *him* than Demosthenes. In fact, he makes it appear that he only chose Demosthenes because he later heard that he was intending a descent on the island. This failure to explain Kleon's reasoning *at this point* is in sharp contrast to his incredibly detailed description of Kleon's mental gymnastics in 27.3-28.2! No, we have provided a rational explanation of

Demosthenes' strategy and believe that Kleon too knew just what he was doing.

But, one might retort, surely the remaining account of the Athenian success at Sphakteria shows that Thucydides did not consider it fortuitous. We agree that Demosthenes' tactical skill (*techne*) is impressive. Just as at Pylos, in actual combat *where long-range plans are not required*, his behaviour is admirable.[13] But one must keep in mind that the odds were very much in the Athenians' favour, and that according to Thucydides' account, the victory depended on two *unplanned* circumstances, the firing of the woods and the Messenian advice (36.1). Who is this stranger that appears to Demosthenes much as Mnesiphilos appeared to Themistokles before Salamis (Her. 8.57.1)? We question Herodotus, but never Thucydides. In a sense it was he who was responsible for turning the final struggle into a little Thermopylai. Did Demosthenes not have equal powers of εἰκάζειν? (Note in 36.3, ὡς μικρὸν μεγάλῳ εἰκάσαι.) Although in action he displayed them in drawing the lessons of the Aitolian *pathos*, in Thucydides' account Demosthenes does not see ahead. In fine, it is not to *gnome* but to *tyche* he owes his success.

That Thucydides honestly believed that *tyche* was the determining force here is confirmed by his own later references to these events. He consistently uses some form of *tyche*. For example, in 4.55.3 he explains Spartan demoralization thus: "Besides this their late numerous reverses of fortune (τὰ τῆς τύχης), coming close one upon another without any reason, had thoroughly unnerved them, and they were always afraid of a second disaster (περιτύχῃ) like that on the island. . . ." Coming as it does only a few chapters after the events of Pylos-Sphakteria with no "reverses of fortune" in the interval, what else can it refer to? Again in 5.75.3 in commenting on the Spartan victory at Mantineia, Thucydides alludes to this disaster:

> The imputations cast upon them by the Hellenes at the time, whether of cowardice on account of the disaster in the island, or of mismanagement and slowness generally, were all wiped

---

13. Again the action was effective, very famous, and its details probably known to many. Thucydides himself seems particularly well-informed about the fighting on both sides. It just was a brilliant coup for the Athenians. Besides, he has made his point about the Athenian spirit in rejecting the Spartan offer (21.2), about the haphazard election of Kleon, and about Demosthenes and "chance."

out by this single action: fortune (τύχη), it was thought, might have humbled them, but the men themselves were the same as ever.

Tyche then is a force as far as Thucydides is concerned. Nor does it appear here for the first time; as we shall see, it permeates the work from the beginning to the end. But why should it not, when the concept was as much in the air in Thucydides' day as the debate about φύσις – νόμος? To ignore this or to try to explain it away is *not* to understand Thucydides but to wrench him out of time and place and force upon him that self-satisfied rationalism of 19th and 20th century man.[14] But, accepting *tyche* as a meaningful force in Thucydides' day, we may try to answer the following question: why did he see Demosthenes' successes as a result of *tyche* and fail to credit him with the *gnome* which is immanent in his actions? Can this "astigmatism" have some meaning for his work as a whole?

Consider next the *logoi* which connect the two sets of *erga* (4.17-20). With their men trapped on Sphakteria and an armistice declared, the Spartans send envoys to Athens to plead for peace. Their speech has three main parts: a) preamble, b) warning, c) proposals.

a) The preamble (17.1-3) serves as a kind of apology for the tone and length of what is to follow. It will be didactic to be sure (διδάσκοντας and διδασκόμενοι), but the Athenians should not be surprised by its length, since it is not unusual for Spartans to speak at length in a crisis (*kairos*). The length of the speech will not concern us: though longer than Sthenelaidas' harangue (1.86), the envoys' remarks are nothing out of the ordinary when compared to Archidamos' lengthy warning in Book 1.80-85. What *is* interesting and decidedly unSpartan is the terminology they employ. *Kairos*, for instance, has rhetorical connotations. "In rhetoric *kairos* is the principle which governs the choice of the organization, the means of proof, and particularly the style."[15] *Kairos* is, of course, not a new word to these pages; it appeared a number of times in the *erga*. Remember that both Phormion and Brasidas recognized the "crucial moment" and acted at once with

14. Cf. Stahl, pp. 140 ff. At this point — Pylos-Sphakteria — our analyses are surprisingly similar. In later chapters of this work, however, it will become clear that we differ in our emphasis on the irrational and its role in the "human tragedy." (Interestingly enough, both Stahl and I arrived at the latter concept independently.)

15. Kennedy, p. 67.

favourable results.[16] Both connotations, literal and rhetorical, are possible here. It is certainly a crisis, even a turning-point, which the envoys recognize and which demands διδαχή. At the same time to make such a speech is τὸ δέον πράσσειν (17.2). The latter is also rhetorical. In the pseudo-Plato ὁ καιρός and τὸ δέον are all but synonymous (ἐν . . . τῷ δέοντι καὶ τῷ καιρῷ).[17] The rhetorical kairos thus "has as its object τὸ δέον ἐν τῷ δέοντι, 'the right thing at the right moment.'"[18] Such an expression found in this context immediately calls to mind Themistokles' ability to αὐτοσχεδιάζειν τὰ δέοντα. Presumably, it is this the envoys will achieve by διδαχή. One wonders if it will be διδαχὴ ἀληθής, Thucydides' approximation of truth in that the erga which follow usually confirm its validity. All this, reflecting as it does Thucydides' rhetorical training and interests, is especially inappropriate in the mouths of Spartans. The question arises, is this Thucydides himself speaking? One suspects that such an accumulation of specifically Thucydidean concepts heralds an important message. Since the promised διδαχή takes the form of a "suggestion on the best course to be taken,"[19] it may be that the kairos will be one that the Athenians should also recognize as a "turning-point."

b) In the warning (17.4-18.5), the Spartans address themselves to the question of chance — life's vicissitudes — and human behaviour in the face of it. Pointing to themselves as an example they plead with the Athenians not to be carried away by their unexpected good fortune, lest catastrophe follow for them too.

c) The peace proposal (19 and 20) offers in return for the men trapped on Sphakteria "to make a treaty and to end the war, and offer peace and alliance and the most friendly and intimate relations in every way and on every occasion. . . ." What follows is a lecture on moderation reasoned out in a way already familiar to us from previous speeches. Moderation, the Spartans assert, is best in disputes. This statement they support by a series of gnomai.

16. Cf. 2.84.3; 4.126.6; 5.10.5.
17. Περὶ δικαίου 375A.
18. M. Untersteiner, The Sophists, Oxford, 1954, p. 177.
19. If Sthenelaidas was a typical Spartan, a plea for careful counsel might also be considered out of place in the mouths of Spartans, or at least ironical as addressed to Athenians. On the other hand, it may well be necessary to reassess our stereotype of a Spartan, so unhesitating has Thucydides been in making them his spokesmen or in any case endowing them with his highest qualities, (e.g., Archidamos, Brasidas, and later Gylippos). Cf. Cornford, p. 120, for a similar statement on this speech: "We suspect that the matters to be set forth are more to the point in explaining what Thucydides has in his mind than in influencing the Athenians to abandon the fruits of victory."

E.g., moderation, if displayed by the victor, inspires a debt of gratitude rather than provokes vengeance in the conquered. To apply this to the present situation, let the Athenians show such moderation and make peace before some irremediable catastrophe occur and eternal hatred be its consequence. Let them be reconciled before the Lakedaimonians suffer some indignity.

These proposals are simple enough and fairly concrete. The Peloponnesians, one must remember, began the war and thus legally, at any rate, are in the wrong. At the same time it was never particularly in Athens' interest to carry on hostilities. In fact, demoralization had been so great at the time of the plague that they had even sent ambassadors to Lakedaimon asking for peace, though to no avail (2.59.2). In short, it is the moment they have been hoping for: peace is now a real possibility. In spite of the long lecture on moderation then, chapters 19 and 20 are not inappropriate. Indeed, given the circumstances, they might well be the very proposals the Spartans made. For really they did not have much to offer except a return to the *status quo ante bellum* with assurances.

What will concern us primarily is the warning. In the context how is it τὰ δέοντα? If our evaluation of the events at Pylos is correct, the Athenian success did have a rational explanation, superior planning and strategy. The Peloponnesians fell right into a trap and "unexpected good fortune" had little or nothing to do with it. Surely the Lakedaimonians would not be blind to this fact and the Athenians might have some inkling of it too. Thus such a warning, so little in accord with reality, must have seemed absurd in the extreme. Yet it is seriously made and obviously τὰ δέοντα in Thucydides' eyes because it nowhere contradicts the *erga as he presents them*. Both Demosthenes' success at Pylos, the *erga* which precede, and the even greater success of Kleon and Demosthenes at Sphakteria, the *erga* which follow, he represents as due to *tyche*.

Let us then examine the warning more closely (17.4-18.5). In cautioning the Athenians, the Spartans do leave them some room for choice. It is possible for them to secure their present good fortune (εὐτυχίαν) and not share the experience of those who "meet with an extraordinary piece of good fortune." The latter, they explain, "are led on by hope to grasp continually at something further (τοῦ πλέονος ἐλπίδι ὀρέγονται), through having already succeeded without expecting it" (ἀδοκήτως εὐτυχῆσαι).

The alternative they express in a *gnome*: men who have most suffered life's vicissitudes put the least trust in good fortune (εὐπραγίαις). This they assume would in all probability be as well known to the Athenians as themselves on the basis of experience.

Some part of their own experience the Spartans next reveal by holding themselves up as an example. In rhetorical terms they use a *paradeigma* to prove their case.[20] The Athenians should look at their misfortunes, for they have suffered a complete reversal (one of the μεταβολή above). And it was due neither to a decline in power nor to the *hybris* attendant on growth, the two usual reasons for downfall. Quite simply, they made an "error of judgment" (γνώμῃ σφαλέντες). And anyone is subject to that. To apply this *paradeigma* to the Athenians, it is unreasonable (again εἰκός) for them to imagine that good fortune (τὸ τῆς τύχης) will always be with them because their city is in a flourishing state and has made recent gains.

How should the Athenians behave? Once again a *paradeigma*, the example of sensible men. The latter, they point out, consider that gains are precarious and that chance (αἱ τύχαι), not human decision dictates the course of war, "and thus, not being puffed up by confidence in military success, they are less likely to come to grief, and most ready to make peace, if they can, while their fortune lasts" (ἐν τῷ εὐτυχεῖν). This is a model of behaviour for the Athenians (*if* they are sensible men). Otherwise, let them stand warned and suffer the consequences – disaster.

(There is no need to expatiate at length on the incidence of words implying chance or good fortune. The Greek is clear and perfectly in accord with the *erga* as we have analyzed them.)

The envoys' speech marks the first great turning-point in the war. Chastened by experience and wise after the fact, the Spartans now admit to that error of judgment or wrong policy against which Archidamos warned. Just as he predicted (1.81.6), the Spartan policy of invading Attica proved obsolete and ineffective. His strictures against underestimating the power of Athens were ignored. Instead the Corinthian policy prevailed, a policy based more on land than naval power and one which underestimated Athenian resources, experience, and determination. (See especially

---

20. The *paradeigma* is as much a rhetorical concept as the argument from εἰκός, yet it has never been considered in relation to Thucydides' work. Gommel, p. 26, devotes only a paragraph to it. See the discussion in Aristotle's *Rhetoric* 1356b3 ff. and 1393a25 ff. and Kennedy's summary, pp. 98-99.

1.120-124.) Surely this is the *gnome* which the *erga* have shown was "an error." Phormion's victories were only one *paralogos* of many suffered as a result of it. Their entire strategy was wrong and they now admit it and are prepared to make peace.

Surely too this is that destruction and disgrace which Archidamos predicted would be the outcome of a war rashly begun (1.81.4 and 82.5). Now also the Spartans can point to their own experiences as an example of Archidamos' pronouncements on chance (1.84.3), ". . . the freaks of chance are not determinable by calculation" (λόγῳ). How ironic that these envoys must echo similar warnings made by the Athenian envoys at Lakedaimon in 432 (1.78.1-2):

> consider the vast influence of accident in war, before you are engaged in it (τὸν παράλογον . . . προδιάγνωτε). As it continues, it generally becomes an affair of chances (τύχας), chances from which neither of us is exempt, and whose event we must risk in the dark.

The above predictions and intimations are not accidental; they are as much after the fact as isolated anticipations we have studied. Thucydides consciously allowed the major debates of Book 1 to foreshadow the Archidamian (if not the entire) War.[21] He wrote with Pylos-Sphakteria in mind, knowing who was wrong and who right. But in the battle of *logoi* only events can decide, for *erga* alone establish truth. Only then, on the basis of this truth, the truth of experience, is a new *logos* possible. This is the envoys' speech. Earlier we expressed the same thing thus (p. 55): "Past *erga*, what happened, can serve as a model for the future. What mediates in the present is the *logos* or διδαχή, in human terms, the man who has learned from experience and so can make predictions about the future." Now we will add a remark of Antiphon the rhetor (5.14), "Time and experience show mankind what is imperfect" (my translation of ὁ γὰρ χρόνος καὶ ἡ ἐμπειρία τὰ μὴ καλῶς ἔχοντα ἐκδιδάσκει τοὺς ἀνθρώπους). Time has done just that and a cycle been completed.

But, if this speech looks backward, it also looks forward. A *paradeigma* implies futurity, in this case, an example to be avoided lest one suffer a similar fate. In particular the envoys issue

---

21. Cf. the suggestion in the last chapter (p. 58) that the debate between the Corinthians and Perikles was written with Phormion's exploits in mind.

warnings about "unexpected good fortune" in words which have a familiar ring. Their message is not new. Kleon spoke in a similar vein when he chastized the Mytileneans for not drawing the lesson of their neighbours' fate. (He uses the word παράδειγμα in 3.39.3.)

> The truth is that great good fortune (ἀπροσδόκητος εὐπραγία) coming suddenly and unexpectedly tends to make a people insolent; in most cases it is safer for mankind to have success in reason than out of reason (παρὰ δόξαν); and it is easier for them, one may say, to stave off adversity than to preserve prosperity (3.39.4).

In the context the remarks are totally inexplicable; the Mytileneans have experienced no sudden and unexpected good fortune.[22] But they *do* forecast the future in language identical with that used by the Spartans. (This is not the first instance of irony in Thucydides. For it is Kleon who will personify this *hybris*.[23]) Diodotos too has words on the same subject. Speaking of those passions which lure men to their ruin, he mentions "plenty" which "fills them with the ambition (πλεονεξίαν) which belongs to insolence and pride" (3.45.4). He then goes on to describe a psychological process, the relationship between hope and cupidity, and ends with a comment on *tyche*: "Fortune, too, powerfully helps the delusion, and by the unexpected aid that she sometimes lends, tempts men to venture with inferior means. . ." (45.6).

All this anticipates the Spartan warning and the mood which followed the "unexpected success" at Pylos and then Sphakteria. The mood is *pleonexia*. Thucydides later makes it clear that the envoys' warning was a forecast of how the Athenians actually would respond, by repeating their words twice in the *erga* which follow. The Athenians, he tells us, were so confident of their position that they did not accept the Spartans' peace offer but

22. Gomme 2, p. 307, observing the inappropriateness of 3.39.4, comments, "doubtless true, but not strictly relevant here; for the only thing unexpected about Mytilene's good fortune was the ill-fortune of Athens (the pestilence). It is another case of love of generalization making its way into a speech."

23. For example, the Athenian envoys' advice to the Lakedaimonians in 432 (1.78.1-3) would be equally appropriate if spoken in Athens in 415 before the Sicilian expedition. In 2.87.4 the Peloponnesians' *gnome* that "fear takes away presence of mind" describes exactly what they will themselves experience in 2.91.4. Such examples could be multiplied and might be an interesting study.

"grasped at something further" (4.21.2: τοῦ δὲ πλέονος ὠρέγοντο). The same mood prevails after their success at Sphakteria (4.41.4), when they "kept grasping at more ..." (οἱ δὲ μειζόνων τε ὠρέγοντο). Nor was this a transient mood. Thucydides apparently believed that a new and destructive spirit had been unleashed by the "unexpected" success, for in recording the events of the next year he harks back to this incident again. In 424 the Athenians banish Pythodoros and Sophokles and fine Eurymedon for "having taken bribes to depart when they might have subdued Sicily." (In actual fact they had no reason or excuse to remain there once the Sicilians united at Hermokrates' urging.) Thucydides passes a severe judgment on his countrymen at this point (4.65.4):

> So thoroughly had the present prosperity (εὐτυχία) persuaded the citizens that nothing could withstand them, and that they could achieve what was possible and impracticable alike, with means ample or inadequate it mattered not. The secret of this was their general extraordinary success (ἡ παρὰ λόγον τῶν πλέονων εὐπραγία), which made them confuse their strength with their hopes.

Once again the same language and once again nothing for it to refer to but Pylos-Sphakteria and the Spartan warning. We must conclude then that the envoys' remarks on unexpected good fortune represent Thucydides' own considered judgment.

Much of the above merely reaffirms the views of earlier writers.[24] In the conclusions which follow we shall try to relate these views to the rest of this work.

a) There are two ways human beings can learn. Either the *paradeigma*, the example of others, teaches them, or, if they refuse to draw that lesson, they must learn the hard way. Then "time and experience" will be their teachers. The *paradeigma* has come and gone and the Athenians totally ignored the Spartan warning. Thus the latter play the same role as Archidamos, tragic warners. And even as Archidamos predicted correctly, so it seems will the envoys.

b) The warnings about the destructive influence of unex-

24. Both Cornford and de Romilly have come to similar conclusions on the basis of the same passages. See also Finley, p. 195: "Thus from his (Perikles') point of view, and that of Thucydides, the Spartan offer should have been accepted. ... Kleon had roused the people to visions of grandeur, and Athens was committed to a war of expansion."

pected good fortune are out of place in the context of the Archidamian War. Even though the Athenians are defeated at Delion and Brasidas campaigns in Thrace with formidable success, Thucydides nowhere connects Athenian losses to overconfidence or *pleonexia*. The latter only reappears *in the second half of the work*. Consider the first speech of Nikias. Although it takes place in 415, 10 years later, he leaves the decided impression that little has intervened between Pylos-Sphakteria and the Sicilian expedition — and this in spite of the battle of Mantineia! He states (6.11.5):

> You have yourselves experienced this (contempt) with regard to the Lacedaemonians and their allies, whom your unexpected success (παρὰ γνώμην), as compared with what you feared at first, has made you suddenly despise, tempting you further to aspire to the conquest of Sicily.

Here is a direct link between Pylos and Sicily. The spirit unleashed in 425 is only now asserting itself, as predicted. As if to confirm this link Nikias continues with a warning against "being puffed up by the misfortunes of your adversaries" (11.6: χρὴ δὲ μὴ πρὸς τὰς τύχας τῶν ἐναντίων ἐπαίρεσθαι). But this was years earlier and presumably wiped out by Brasidas' inroads and Mantineia. (See 5.75.3.) There can be no connection now except *in the mind of the historian himself*, if for him fortune, especially unexpected good fortune, *was* a temptress and the Sicilian expedition the predicted disaster.[25] Indeed, the whole *erga-logoi-erga* combination with *tyche* as its *leit motif* and central point is only explicable on this view. Otherwise why introduce *tyche* at all or, in our terms, represent Demosthenes as the type of *tolma alogistos*? The answer is that to provide Demosthenes with a plan or strategy (*pronoia*) would put him on a par with Phormion, who also had the advantage of good luck in addition to *pronoia*, but whose exploits were paradigmatic of Athenian excellence in action. In that incident Thucydides all but eliminated fortuity by allowing Phormion to predict the unpredictable. Here he does just the opposite and eliminates *gnome*, by representing Demosthenes' success as unplanned, unexpected, and fortuitous. Did *this* serve

25. This connection is strengthened by Hermokrates' plea for unity (4.58-65), which immediately precedes the punishment of the three generals for accepting bribes to leave Sicily. It looks forward to the Sicilian expedition in a manner which must impress all but the most obtuse (esp. 60.2 and 61.3).

historical truth? Yes, because the mere fact of Demosthenes' success was of no moment as compared to its aftermath, Kleon's rise to undisputed leadership of the *demos* and the latter's *pleonexia* unleashed. We might even go so far as to say that for Thucydides this *kairos* ended one era and began another, a new cycle of events which culminated in Athens' destruction.[26] And if this was the truth behind the Pylos *erga*, he must make it clear in his usual manner, through the *logoi*. On this view the envoys' speech is truly τὰ δέοντα.

c) In all this the *paradeigma* is most important. It is no mere rhetorical device but a real example for Athens. And if the Athenians will not learn from example, "time and experience" will teach them *what the Spartans now know*. We have already stated that the *logos* mediates the past and future and have demonstrated this *erga-logoi-erga* combination in isolated incidents such as Phormion's victories. Here, however, the *logoi* are at the very heart of the work, its turning-point. One cycle of time has come to a close, the Spartan "experience." Is it now the Athenians' turn? Perhaps just as one incident can be a model for another in future, so a whole cycle of experience can be a model for a second cycle. The question is: will the Athenians repeat the Lakedaimonians' mistakes? We know what they were — errors of judgment or policy (*gnome*), overconfidence, usually based on numbers or Spartan bravery, and a lack of initiative (*tolma*) often manifested by the inability to recognize and take advantage of the *kairos*.[27] On the other hand, we know the qualities which made the Athenians great, that rare combination of *tolma* and *gnome*. Thus we are in a position to understand the fall of Athens *in Thucydides' terms*, if history should repeat itself *in some manner*.[28]

---

26. Gomme 3, p. 463, comments on 4.23.1: ". . . it seems that Thucydides thought that the Athenians were guilty of sharp practice, morally in the wrong. . . ." Thucydides, of course, rarely discusses moral responsibility, but one senses that he felt the Athenians were now in the wrong as the Peloponnesians had earlier been in beginning the war. (See Finley's remarks above, n. 24.) There is some confirmation of this in 7.18.2-3, the motives Thucydides attributes to the Lakedaimonians for fortifying Dekeleia at Alkibiades' urging. They had committed a παρανόμημα in attacking Plataia and refusing arbitration and so deserved their misfortunes (again δυστυχεῖν). But now they decide that "Athens had now committed the very same offence as they had before done, and had become the guilty party. . ." (18.3: τὸ παρανόμημα, ὅπερ καὶ σφίσι πρότερον ἡμάρτητο).

27. This is equally applicable to the "errors" made in the face of the occupation of Pylos.

28. 1.22.4.

The next three chapters will deal with a series of incidents at Syracuse. In them our aim will be twofold:

1) to elucidate Thucydides' own explanation of why Athens failed and

2) in so doing, to establish his methodology securely enough to shed light on his philosophy of history.

Chapter 5
Paradeigma:
Syracusan Thoughts (Thuc. 7.34-41)
🕉🕉🕉

In 413 the Syracusans, hearing of the approach of a second expedition under Demosthenes and Eurymedon, resolve to take the initiative against the Athenians before its arrival. To this end they make the following changes in their fleet (7.36.2):

> they cut down their prows to a smaller compass to make them more solid and made their cheeks stouter, and from these let stays into the vessels' sides for a length of six cubits within and without, in the same way as the Corinthians had altered their prows before engaging the squadron at Naupactus.

There follows a lengthy passage in indirect discourse (36.3-6: ἐνόμισαν γάρ) outlining the motives for these innovations. The passage so impressed Jacqueline de Romilly that she felt compelled to remark: "Aussi Thucydide a-t-il procédé d'une façon exceptionnelle: il a dégagé les conditions générales de la lutte au moyen d'un style indirect. . . ."[1] In actual fact there is nothing unusual about this method. The "thoughts" — or indirect discourse — belong to the same kind of *logoi-erga* combination which is common throughout the *History* and which usually anticipates events. Here the "thoughts" of the Syracusans anticipate the events of 40.5. What *might* call for some comment here is

1. P. 151. This is not to underestimate de Romilly's excellent analysis of the events leading up to the final defeat of the Athenians in the Great Harbour. As she well points out (pp. 154-155), Syracusan tactics are never again described in such detail; not only do conditions, and so the tactics based on them, remain the same, but 7.36 seems to forecast each stage of Athenian decline.

the proportion of "thoughts" to "deeds." What Thucydides later describes in eight lines (40.5) it takes him 24 lines to motivate! And the latter are absolutely essential to the narrative in that the reader can only picture the events of chapter 40 by supplying *for himself* the detailed explanations of chapter 36.

Let us consider the "thoughts" or *logoi* of chapter 36. They consist of a series of statements in the future tense, assumptions and predictions linked together by the connective γάρ and each explaining the one that preceded until every possibility is spelled out and all objections answered. It is a masterpiece of reasoning from εἰκός in which every γάρ implies a question. For example, why did the Syracusans make these innovations? The explanation is (γάρ) that this would give them an advantage over the Athenians whose ships were constructed for mobility and so were slight in the bows. The fact that they were fighting in a restricted area, the great harbour, would also be in their favour. Again why? Because (γάρ) it would (probably) bring about a situation in which by using their newly reinforced ships they could stave in the enemy's bows, and the latter meanwhile would not have sufficient space to make use of their usual manoeuvres. Concretely, how would they be deprived of this *techne*? The explanation offered (γάρ) seems redundant at first, viz., the Syracusans themselves and the στενοχωρία would combine against them, but then goes on to answer two possible objections with further assumptions. Could the Athenians not avoid the ramming tactics either by backing water or by sailing around into the open water? The answer to the first question is that if the Athenians tried to retire, they would have very little space in which to back water, only that in front of their own camp. The rest was hostile. Thus they would (probably) fall foul of one another and be thrown into disorder. As to their sailing around into the open sea, this would (probably) prove impossible, since the Syracusans controlled the harbour mouth, which was not large anyway, and were now also masters of Plemmyrion.

Inevitably, the *erga* correspond to the above. Indeed, part of 40.5 is a repetition of 36.3: "The Syracusans received them, and charging prow to prow *as they had intended*, stove in a great part of the Athenian foreships by the strength of their beaks. . . ." The *italicized* words represent the anticipations of chapter 36. The reader does not need details; he knows what is to happen and supplies them himself, or supplies Thucydides' explanations. For surely that is what they are. Thucydides knew that the Athenians met their first naval setback at this point. And he knew that the Syracusans used ramming tactics to achieve their victory. In effect they turned the encounter into a land-battle on the sea, aided by small boats full of targeteers. These are the facts. But they do not speak for themselves and reveal *why* such "old-fashioned" tactics put the Athenians to flight. Thucydides also knew that the answer lay in the nature of the great harbour, the topographical setting, the στενοχωρία. Thinking out loud, as it were, and using arguments from probability as his logical tool, he reasons back from the Syracusan tactics to this irreversible condition. But in so doing he has turned the problem on its head. For obviously one does not adopt tactics gratuitously and then see if they fit the circumstances. Rather one *starts* from the given, the harbour with its narrow mouth, the recent loss of Plemmyrion to the Syracusans, and the restricted area of the Athenians. The latter suffered from a shortage of sea room. Somehow, one must use this against them by forcing them in on themselves, as Phormion did to the Lakedaimonians (2.84.3). At the same time, one must find a way to keep them from using their usual manoeuvres. The limited nautical ability of the Syracusans must also be taken into account; neither they nor their ships could equal the Athenians for speed. Thus what is necessary is a strategy and tactics commensurate with their naval resources and skill. The answer is to use one's navy to block the harbour, while ramming the enemy back into as constricted an area as possible. Thus the proper sequence of thought is στενοχωρία, topographical conditions, to *dianoia*, strategy, to *techne* or *episteme*, tactics commensurate with skill, to *dynamis*, resources, i.e., ships adapted to all three.

REASONING OF CHAPTER 36	PROPER SEQUENCE OF THOUGHT
36.2 description of changes in construction	*dynamis* — construction — copy example of Corinthians
γάρ 3 explanation — argument from εἰκός showing advantages	
εἰκός a) construction of ships b) στενοχωρία	PRESUPPOSES
γάρ further explanation of a) and b) — εἰκός arguments from εἰκός	*episteme* or *techne* — tactics (to achieve *dianoia*) charge prow to prow
a) assumed result from construction	PRESUPPOSES
4 b) assumed result from στενοχωρία	*dianoia* — strategy (making use of a) b) and c) below)

γάρ   further explanation of loss of *techne*
εἰκός   — argument from εἰκός

γάρ   5 Syracusan tactics and explanation —
εἰκός   argument from εἰκός showing advantages

γάρ   further explanation — arguments
εἰκός   from εἰκός

    a) assumption enemy would have to back water to own territory

6 b) assumption enemy would be crowded together and fall into disorder

    c) assumption they would be unable to reach open water because of Syracusan control of Plemmyrion and the harbour mouth and the size of the latter

a) keep from open water
b) deprive of *techne*
c) put at total disadvantage by forcing into limited space

PRESUPPOSES

στενοχωρία — the great harbour (topography)
a) mouth of harbour not large
b) Plemmyrion now hostile
c) did not have whole harbour, just space in front of camp

Chapter 36 is of course perfectly reasonable, if, as we suggest above, it is Thucydides' *own* reasoning. It is merely his explanation *after the fact* of how the Syracusans might have reasoned in order to achieve their victory. In its fulness, however, 36.3-6 does point up just how much Thucydides depended on the argument from probability and how he made use of it to explain *why* events happened as they did. Starting from the "facts" — in this case the new ramming tactics and their effect on the Athenians — he derived or assumed purposes, in effect a correct plan or strategy. Put in the mouths — or minds — of the Syracusans they represent the ability to αὐτοσχεδιάζειν τὰ δέοντα and are a conquest of futurity by *pronoia*.

What makes possible this conquest of the future is its close connection with the past. For chapter 36 is no more isolated from what preceded than what follows. And the *logoi* or "thoughts," being the intermediary between past and future, reveal wherein knowledge lies, i.e., how men learn. For Thucydides there were two sources of human knowledge, one's own experiences, *empeiria*, or the example of others, the *paradeigma*. The reasoning of chapter 36 makes use of both. From the Syracusan point of view their first encounter with the Athenians represents *empeiria*. Twice Thucydides refers to this sea-battle, pointing out that as a result of it the Syracusans not only made certain improvements to their navy but even felt greater confidence (36.2 and 37.1). In

other words, unlike the Peloponnesians after the battle in the Gulf
of Patrai (2.85 ff.), the Syracusans did learn something from even
this limited experience. At the same time they also had the good
sense to learn from the example of others, in this case the
Corinthians. For major changes in their fleet were modelled after
those made by the latter at Naupaktos. Thus there are two distinct
erga-logoi-erga combinations.

Let us revert to the first sea-fight (7.22-23) and consider
empeiria. Briefly, the Syracusans, encouraged by Gylippos and
Hermokrates, decided to make trial of the Athenians by sea.
(Gylippos, meanwhile, was to assault the forts on Plemmyrion by
land.) Their ships set forth in two groups,. 35 from the great
harbour and 45 others sailing round from the lesser harbour. The
latter were to join the first squadron in the harbour. In effect, for
a time there were two separate battles being waged, one in the
great harbour, where 25 Athenians fought the 35 Syracusans, and
a second in front of the mouth of the harbour, where 35
Athenians had gone out to meet the second group of Syracusans,
whose aim was to force the passage. Inside the harbour the
Syracusans were at first successful, then began to lose. In the end
the Athenians were victorious. Thucydides gives the following
description (7.23.3):

> The Syracusan ships fighting off the mouth of the harbour
> forced their way through the Athenian vessels and sailing in
> without any order fell foul of one another, and transferred
> the victory to the Athenians; who not only routed the
> squadron in question, but also that by which they were at
> first being defeated in the harbour. . . .

What is significant in this brief, factual narrative is how close
the Athenians were to defeat even here. The skirmish in the
harbour was not yet decisively over (οἱ Συρακόσιοι ἐτύγχανον ἤδη
νικώμενοι). What defeated *both* squadrons was lack of skill (due
no doubt to lack of experience), in short, the "error" of the
second group in letting themselves fall into disorder after forcing
the Athenian line. Then they discovered the danger of being
crowded together in a small space. The result was ταραχή,
aggravated by a mobile enemy, for the Athenians still had full use
of the open sea.

Thus in the *erga* are adumbrated all the problems to which the
Syracusans respond in chapter 36, having learned from exper-

ience. Their strategy is to turn the topography, the restrictions imposed by the great harbour, *against* the Athenians and force upon them the same kind of ταραχή they had themselves suffered. They have also witnessed firsthand the kind of manoeuvres for which the Athenians are famous, especially when in the open sea. Most of all then they must deprive them of any opportunity to use this formidable skill by blocking the harbour mouth. With Plemmyrion in their hands and the Athenians at a psychological disadvantage, dismayed and discouraged (24.3: κατάπληξιν παρέσχε καὶ ἀθυμίαν) and anxiously awaiting the second expedition, it is surely an opportunity not to be let go. What better time to take the initiative and test their experience.

The first set of *erga* determines the *logoi* of chapter 36; they lie behind the "thoughts" of the Syracusans and thus the reasoning of the historian. But to understand the past and see possibilities in the present is one thing, to make use of it for the future is another. What gives the Syracusans the opportunity to use their experience is their readiness to learn from example and make innovations, in a word, to use their powers of εἰκάζειν.

Chapter 34 might at first be overlooked. In the first place it is wedged unobtrusively between two chapters describing the slow journey of Demosthenes and Eurymedon towards Syracuse. Secondly, the sea-fight it describes, albeit in some detail, is quite indecisive and irrelevant to the main narrative. It seems to be a classic example of the "objective" reporting for which Thucydides is famous, introduced for no other reason than sheer love of "facts." Closer study reveals, however, that two of these "facts" are quite significant, namely, the topographical setting of the encounter and the tactics employed by the Corinthians. The latter have taken up a station opposite Naupaktos in order to protect the passage of transports to Sicily. At this point they are making ready to engage the Athenians and have anchored off Erineos in Achaia. Thucydides describes the area thus (34.2):

> The place off which they lay being in the form of a crescent, the land forces furnished by the Corinthians and their allies on the spot, came up and ranged themselves upon the projecting headlands on either side, while the fleet, under the command of Polyanthes, a Corinthian, held the intervening space and blocked up the entrance.

How like a harbour, better still the great harbour at Syracuse made hostile with enemy forces! Thucydides does not comment; he gets on with the "facts." In the engagement itself, he states, the Corinthians lose three ships and disable seven of the enemy, "which were struck prow to prow and had their foreships stove in by the Corinthian vessels, whose cheeks had been strengthened for this very purpose" (34.5).

Such is the *paradeigma*. Thucydides does not indicate how many similarities the Syracusans saw in the two situations, for example, whether they thought the hostile, crescent-shaped shore significant. In fact, he does not even state that the Syracusans knew anything about the indecisive battle at Naupaktos. Rather it is implied in the juxtaposition of chapters 34 and 36. The reader makes the connection himself, aided by a reference to the Corinthians (36.2) which recalls the recent battle. The point is that Thucydides *himself* saw and wished to highlight similarities; Thucydides *himself* compared past and present. It was an excellent opportunity to give a lesson in εἰκάζειν. To this end he selected and juxtaposed his material so that the reader would also see similarities and infer a connection which perhaps did not exist. To this end he described the new tactics *three* times, *erga* (34.5) – *logoi* (36.3) – *erga* (40.5).

erga (34.5)

. . . ἑπτὰ δέ τινες ἄπλοι ἐγένοντο ἀντίπρῳροι ἐμβαλλόμεναι

καὶ ἀναρραγεῖσαι τὰς παρεξειρεσίας ὑπὸ τῶν Κορινθίων νεῶν ἐπ' αὐτὸ τοῦτο παχυτέρας τὰς ἐπωτίδας ἐχουσῶν.

logoi (36.3)

ἀντιπρῴροις γὰρ ταῖς ἐμβολαῖς χρώμενοι

ἀναρρήξειν τὰ πρῴραθεν αὐτοῖς, στερίφοις καὶ παχέσι πρὸς κοῖλα καὶ ἀσθενῆ παίοντες τοῖς ἐμβόλοις.

erga (40.5)

. . . ταῖς [τε] ναυσὶν ἀντιπρῴροις χρώμενοι, ὥσπερ διενοήθησαν, τῶν ἐμβόλων τῇ παρασκευῇ

ἀνερρήγνυσαν τὰς τῶν Ἀθηναίων ναῦς ἐπὶ πολὺ τῆς παρεξειρεσίας. . . .

One event thus anticipates and sheds light on another. Earlier we commented on the rather "backward" reasoning of chapter 36. The explanation is at hand. *In Thucydides' account* the adoption of new tactics, the use of εἰκάζειν, is allowed to precipitate a long series of assumptions and predictions so that it is no mere passive response to events but a conscious use of the past as *paradeigma*. *In Thucydides' account* the ability to learn from others' example by means of εἰκάζειν almost surpasses personal experience. For is it not the process of εἰκάζειν which welds these experiences into a meaningful strategy? One is tempted to compare Brasidas' advice to his men in 4.126.3: he exhorted them to learn from experience, i.e., from their previous encounter with the Macedonians, but reserved to himself the right or ability to use his powers of εἰκάζειν. To do this was to go beyond mere personal experience and see the similarities of numerous experiences, even those of others. Thus does the past become the future through the intervention of mind. Εἰκάζειν I would therefore define as the ability to see the truth of past events or *erga* and use it for the future.

If the reader has assumed that the Syracusans learned from the example of the Corinthians, well and good.[2] If not, no matter. Thucydides has achieved his purpose. For the reader the earlier events exist nonetheless as a *paradeigma*, a model situation, the outcome and possibilities of which he knows. By bringing this knowledge of the past with him into the present, he is equipped to compare and judge, even predict.

Chapter 34 raises the question, what is an historical fact? Here is a classic example of that strict, factual narrative that has come to be known as Thucydidean. For us this indecisive battle between Athenians and Corinthians exists as a "fact" of history. And this, we have been led to believe, is what interested Thucydides. It happened; it was a fact; therefore he recorded it. According to this view, Thucydides' history is the accumulation of data which somehow speaks for itself, and the historian is as objective as a sponge transmitting moisture.[3] But is this so? Does this fact exist

---

2. It is not difficult to draw this inference. The Corinthians after all were the first major people to come to the aid of Syracuse (7.2) and it is Ariston the Corinthian, "the ablest helmsman in the Syracusan service," who is responsible for the "breakfast-trick" which catches the Athenians off guard (7.39-40). By the time of Diodoros 13.10.2 there is no longer any doubt where the Syracusans acquired their new tactics. This very Ariston was their adviser. It is interesting to compare the accounts of modern historians. George Grote, *A History of Greece*, Vol. 7, third edition, London, 1855, p. 408, accepts Diodoros' version and makes Ariston their adviser. G. Busolt, *Griechische Geschichte*, Vol. 3.2, Gotha, 1904, p. 1367, states, "Sie hatten . . . ihre Schiffe für die neue korinthische Seetaktik umgestaltet." Finley, p. 238, merely refers to a new type of ship "invented at Corinth and perfected at Syracuse."

3. The idea of facts speaking for themselves permeates Arnold Gomme's chapters

in splendid isolation? We have seen that it does not. Rather it is carefully juxtaposed to later chapters so as to anticipate them; it is the factual antecedent (*erga* or *paradeigma*) of a *logoi-erga* combination. And that is the only reason Thucydides included it: *by his own standards* it was both relevant and meaningful. "Fact" though it was, it might have gone unrecorded, had Thucydides not seen its significance and raised it to the level of history. Just as the latter is an act of mind, so its product, the historical fact, is informed by mind.

What was the status of the fact in Thucydides' eyes? Why did he not merely describe the events of chapter 40, making it clear, as he proceeded, when and where he was adding motives and explanations? Why must there be this significant relationship between *logoi* or "thoughts" and *erga*? Why must the former anticipate the latter? Where some *logoi* are concerned, of course, one might retort, "because this is what Archidamos or Phormion or the Athenians said." Perhaps. But here there is no speech, public or otherwise, there are no names, just Syracusan "thoughts." We have discussed these thoughts at length and decided they were Thucydides' own, as he thought out and assumed motives and purposes after the fact. Is *this* letting the facts speak for themselves? Surely this indicates a far greater preoccupation with the *logoi* or intellectual processes which lay behind them than with the *erga* or facts.[4] This is not to deny Thucydides' interest in facts or his concern for accuracy in recording them. Facts did indeed interest him, because the *erga*, being what actually happened, embody truth[5] and as such may be meaningful for the future, but, this interest in fact is not technical objectivity, since the facts or *erga* must be related to *logoi*. It is

---

on Thucydides in *The Greek Attitude to Poetry and History,* pp. 116-64. The following quotations are also typical: G. F. Abbott, *Thucydides: A Study in Historical Reality,* London, 1925, p. 83: "Unvexed with theories, he was under no obligation or temptation to torture realities into conformity with the subjective exigencies of his own mind." C. N. Cochrane, *Thucydides and the Science of History,* Oxford, 1929, p. 165: "Whatever may be the character of an author's religious and philosophic principles is quite immaterial, so long as he keeps them out of the picture." For a long-overdue criticism of 19th century positivism as it has influenced and distorted the contemporary attitude to Thucydides see Stahl, pp. 12 ff.

4. Cf. Collingwood, p. 31, who describes Thucydides as "an author whose mind cannot be fully concentrated on the events themselves, but is constantly being drawn away from the events to some lesson that lurks behind them. . . ."

5. Cf. Antiphon 5.3, who contrasts the *logoi* with αὐτοῖς τοῖς ἔργοις καὶ τῇ ἀληθείᾳ τῶν πραγμάτων.

the mind that mediates between *erga*, i.e., learns from experience or example. The Syracusans, for instance, learned from both, using εἰκάζειν and εἰκός, and thus converted past truth to future uses. Through the *logoi*, then, past *erga* can achieve the level of *pronoia*, man's only means of intervening in the historical process and his weapon against the future.

Our analysis of 7.34-41, confirmed over and over again by close study of other passages, has led us to the following conclusions about Thucydides' historiographic methods in general and the historical fact in particular. Thucydides' major preoccupation was the *logoi* (speeches or thoughts) as the "exponent of action,"[6] purpose as the precondition of result, the past, whether experience or example, as the key to the future, and everywhere and at all times the intellectual tools of εἰκός and εἰκάζειν. "Prediction" he thought he understood and took pains to represent most *successful* action as the result of careful reasoning in advance. In one sense then facts are merely confirmatory, proof that the reasoning was correct, as, for example, the events of 40.5 confirm that the Syracusan predictions were sound. But facts are also paradigmatic; properly understood, they exist as a body of truth against which to compare the present. Facts therefore can never be ignored. For just as correct reasoning based on past *erga* will ever be necessary, because there will ever be time and futurity, so the *erga* which were today confirmatory may be tomorrow paradigmatic.

---

6 3.42.2 (Diodotos' speech), διδασκάλους τῶν πραγμάτων.

Chapter 6
Pattern:
Demosthenes at Epipolai (Thuc. 7.42-46)

෧෧෧

    Initially, the arrival of Demosthenes and Eurymedon reverses the morale of both parties: the Syracusans are filled with dismay in the face of seemingly endless danger, while the Athenians' confidence revives. At once Demosthenes surveys the situation with his usual vigour, thinking out loud, as it were, in the manner to which we have become accustomed. Thucydides expresses these thoughts by a series of verbs of thinking and feeling (e.g., in 42.3-5: ἰδών, νομίσας, ἀνασκοπῶν, γιγνώσκων, ἐβούλετο, ὁρῶν, ἡγεῖτο). 14 lines of indirect discourse are dependent on them. Generally speaking, there are two parts to Demosthenes' thoughts: He first (42.3) reflects on what has happened up to his arrival, criticizing Nikias' policy and indicating its negative results. On the basis of this analysis he evolves a strategy of his own. Next (42.4-5) he explains how he intends to put the strategy into effect and what he will do if it fails.

    What interests us primarily is 42.3. It is written in a kind of ring composition. First Demosthenes' thoughts are presented in a general way. "Demosthenes, seeing how matters stood, felt that he could not drag on and fare as Nicias had done. . . ." Next follows a parenthesis explaining just what Nikias had experienced. Then with ταῦτα οὖν ἀνασκοπῶν there is a return to the original reflections, only now applying the lesson of Nikias' experience to the present *kairos*:

> well aware that it was now on the first day after his arrival that he like Nicias was most formidable to the enemy, Demosthenes determined to lose no time in drawing the

utmost profit from the consternation at the moment inspired
by his army.

Note here the same reasoning we have observed throughout the
speeches: statement, explanation, and conclusion or application,
in this case based on a psychological assumption, in effect an
argument from εἰκός.

What is interesting about this passage is that the explanation
attributed to Demosthenes is clearly that of the historian himself,
for unlike the rest of Demosthenes' thoughts it is in direct
discourse.[1] It states the following:

> (Nikias) by wintering in Catana instead of at once attacking
> Syracuse had allowed the terror of his first arrival to
> evaporate in contempt, and had given time to Gylippus to
> arrive with a force from Peloponnese, which the Syracusans
> would never have sent for if he had attacked immediately; for
> they fancied that they were a match for him by themselves,
> and would not have discovered their inferiority until they
> were already invested, and even if they then sent for
> succours, they would no longer have been equally able to
> profit by their arrival.

The careful reader knows all this already. It was anticipated in
Book 6 by Lamachos in his discussion of strategy with Nikias and
Alkibiades (47-49). In a sense what was presented there in indirect
discourse was an *antilogia* of three conflicting *gnomai*. In *one*
sense it might even be considered an example of *dissoi logoi* in
that Nikias' opinion is in obvious contradiction with the stated
aim of the expedition, the conquest of Sicily (6.6.1, 8.4, 15.2,
18.4, and 24.3). As Thucydides presents Nikias, he is rather naive
in persisting with the "ostensible" object, to help Egesta against
Selinous. In terms of confronting Syracuse then there are only two
opinions: Alkibiades proposes delay and Lamachos immediate
attack.

As opposed to Alkibiades' policy of winning friends and allies
before attacking, Lamachos' *gnome* is as follows (6.49): They
ought to sail against Syracuse with all speed while its people "were
still unprepared, and the panic at its height." Why? He explains

---

1. See Appendix to Chapter 6. See K. J. Dover's thorough discussion of this
passage in Gomme 4, pp. 419 ff. He also believes that the parenthesis expresses
Thucydides' own judgment.

the above with a psychological generalization. "Every armament was most terrible at first; if it allowed time to run on without showing itself, men's courage revived, and they saw it appear at last almost with indifference." To apply this psychology to the present, if they attacked suddenly while the Syracusans were full of fear, they would have the best chance of success and of terrifying the enemy "by the aspect of their numbers – which would never appear so considerable as at present – by the anticipation of coming disaster, and above all by the immediate danger of the engagement."

Demosthenes' reflections (or Thucydides' explanation) parallel Lamachos' *gnome* in every respect. Both stress speed and immediacy (Lamachos, ὡς τάχιστα, τὸ πρῶτον, αἰφνίδιοι; Demosthenes, εὐθύς, τῇ πρώτῃ ἡμέρᾳ, ὅτι τάχος) and fear on the Syracusans' part (L., ἐκπεπληγμένοι, δεινότατον, περιδεεῖς; D., φοβερός, δεινότατος) resulting in panic (L., ἐκφοβῆσαι; D., ἐκπλήξει) *or*, if they wait, contempt (L., καταφρονεῖν; D., ὑπερώφθη).

There is then an obvious correspondence between these *logoi*. But even more significant, the intervening *erga* also *correspond precisely with Lamachos' predictions*.

For some reason Lamachos supports Alkibiades against Nikias with the result that apart from a display and proclamation in the great harbour of Syracuse the rest of the summer is spent in seeking out allies and money. With winter coming on the Athenians finally prepare to attack Syracuse. At this point Thucydides describes the psychology of the Syracusans (6.63.2):

From the moment when the Athenians failed to attack them instantly as they at first feared and expected, every day that passed did something to revive their courage; and when they saw them sailing far away from them on the other side of Sicily . . . they thought less of them than ever. . . .

logoi (6.49.2)

τὸ γὰρ πρῶτον πᾶν στράτευμα δεινότατον εἶναι· ἢν δὲ χρονίσῃ πρὶν ἐς ὄψιν ἐλθεῖν, τῇ γνώμῃ ἀναθαρσοῦντας ἀνθρώπους καὶ τῇ ὄψει καταφρονεῖν μᾶλλον.

αἰφνίδιοι δὲ ἢν προσπέσωσιν, ἕως ἔτι περιδεεῖς προσδέχονται, μάλιστ᾽ ἂν σφεῖς περιγενέσθαι καὶ πάντα ἂν αὐτοὺς ἐκφοβῆσαι, τῇ τε ὄψει . . . καὶ τῇ προσδοκίᾳ ὧν πείσονται. . . .

erga (6.63.2)

ἐπειδὴ γὰρ αὐτοῖς πρὸς τὸν πρῶτον φόβον καὶ τὴν προσδοκίαν οἱ Ἀθηναῖοι οὐκ εὐθὺς ἐπέκειντο, κατά τε τὴν ἡμέραν ἑκάστην προϊοῦσαν ἀνεθάρσουν μᾶλλον καὶ ἐπειδὴ . . . ἔτι πλέον κατεφρόνησαν. . . .

logoi (7.42.3)

ἀφικόμενος γὰρ τὸ πρῶτον ὁ Νικίας φοβερός, ὡς οὐκ εὐθὺς προσέκειτο ταῖς Συρακούσαις, ἀλλ' ἐν Κατάνῃ διεχείμαξεν, ὑπερώφθη. . . .

γιγνώσκων ὅτι καὶ αὐτὸς ἐν τῷ παρόντι τῇ πρώτῃ ἡμέρᾳ μάλιστα δεινότατός ἐστι τοῖς ἐναντίοις, ἐβούλετο ὅτι τάχος ἀποχρήσασθαι τῇ παρούσῃ τοῦ στρατεύματος ἐκπλήξει·

Pp. 97-98 illustrate best just how closely the above corresponds with both Lamachos' predictions and Demosthenes' reflections not only in the mood it describes but also in the very vocabulary used to describe it.

Once again "anticipation" proves correct. And once again the close correspondence between *logoi* and *erga* can be no mere coincidence. Thucydides knew that Lamachos was the exponent of a swift and immediate attack on Syracuse and evidently later came to the conclusion that this was the best strategy of the three proposed at the time.[2] He therefore consciously formulated arguments for Lamachos which were based on *pronoia* and under the circumstances τὰ δέοντα. But, just as we concluded earlier about Phormion's *logos*, Lamachos' *gnome* "was only tentatively the stronger until events conformed to it. Then it *was* the stronger. Then truth was established, truth *for that particular situation*, and *perhaps* truth of value for the future."[3] Conversely, the reader might very well miss his truth and find himself lost in a maze of "facts," had not the *logoi* clearly distinguished three conflicting viewpoints and thus given him clues to look for in his reading. He can now follow, knowing *before it happens* what may happen and thus be led inexorably to recognize truth when it actually does happen as predicted. Indeed, the careful reader should be fully prepared for Demosthenes' reflections in 42.3, for they merely generalize what he already knows.

We have referred to Phormion's *logos* with good reason, for

2. See Appendix to Chapter 6. As K. J. Dover points out in Gomme 4, p. 315, many readers of Thucydides have felt that Lamachos' plan was correct and it is "a fair inference" from 7.42.3 "that Thucydides himself thought so."
3. Chapter 3, p. 56.

here we find, albeit on a larger scale, the same *logoi-erga-logoi* combination we have observed in the account of his exploits (2.83-92). In 84.2 Phormion's "thoughts" anticipate the first encounter, which in turn confirms his predictions as truth. On the basis of this experience and the knowledge gained from it he then proceeds to formulate a new *logos*, his speech in answer to the Peloponnesians (2.89). A similar relationship exists between *logoi* and *erga* here; the second *logos*, Demosthenes' thoughts, incorporates Lamachos' predictions, now confirmed as "truth."

In chapter 3 we also made the suggestion that "some *logoi*, major debates, foreshadow whole periods."[4] Such were the debates of Book 1. Who was correct, events themselves ultimately decided, as the war proceeded. So this three-sided discussion or council of war foreshadows the whole first phase of the expedition. Before long the *erga* reveal that Lamachos, like Archidamos, who was similarly ignored, was correct in his predictions not only about the changing psychology of the Syracusans, but also about the vacillation of the allies. We have selected 6.49.1-2 as our example and shown its confirmation in 6.63.2 and ultimate reappearance in 7.42.3. We might equally well have demonstrated our point with 49.4. Kamarina is typical, a kind of *paradeigma* of the uncertain smaller powers which might have joined Athens. For a time she chose neutrality "waiting to see which were the strongest" (49.4; cf. 6.88.1-2). Even before the arrival of the second expedition from Athens her active support of Syracuse symbolized the beginning of the end. For then not just Kamarina but "almost the whole of Sicily . . . now ceased merely to watch events as it had hitherto done, and actively joined Syracuse against the Athenians" (7.33.2). Thus, Lamachos was also correct in foreseeing the uncertainty of the allies in Sicily and their ultimate adherence to the stronger power.

In other words, *through the logoi-erga-logoi technique* Lamachos' predictions anticipate not merely an isolated incident but the whole course of events up to Demosthenes' arrival. The latter, by confirming the correctness of these predictions, *seems* to wipe the slate clean.

Earlier we stated that the *logos* mediates between past and future. Or so it did for Phormion and for the Syracusans. To put it another way, correct prediction is based on past experience. One

4. Chapter 3, p. 57.

cannot *begin* with *logoi*. Thus it is wrong to isolate combinations of *logoi-erga-logoi*. Rather *erga*, either *empeiria* or *paradeigma*, must begin the process. Although we did not ask the question in the case of Phormion or Archidamos, we are now led to enquire if it is possible to discover earlier *erga* from which Lamachos might have learned and so be able to predict.

Consider 6.49.3, a continuation of Lamachos' predictions and a further argument for immediate attack. It is an argument from probability. "They might also (εἰκός) count upon surprising many in the fields outside, incredulous of their coming; and at the moment that the enemy was carrying in his property the army would not want for booty if it sat down in force before the city." One knows at once that Lamachos is probably right. After all there has just been a debate at Syracuse between Hermokrates and Athenagoras on this very question. Led by the latter the majority of Syracusans refused to believe there even was an expedition (6.32.3 and 35.1), and though the generals made a half-hearted effort to get preparations underway (6.41), it was not until the Athenians were at Rhegion that "they laid aside their incredulity and threw themselves heart and soul into the work of preparation" (6.45). One would therefore not be in the least surprised to find the Syracusans in the chaotic state which Lamachos predicts.

Though the reader knows this well, note that Lamachos does not have accurate information or express himself with certainty on this point. His main prediction is based on the psychological generalization of 49.2. It is only an assumption, even as his second point is termed a "probability." Lamachos must have predicted from past experience, and we believe that experience can be found in the pages of the *History*. If one senses an aura of *déjà vu* about the Syracusan response to invasion, the reason is that it is a repetition of the Athenian response to the first Peloponnesian invasion. Lamachos' predictions are the very ones one might *assume* of a man who had experienced this invasion and learned from it.

Three significant points stand out in that first invasion of Attika.

a) The Athenians were deeply discontented and reluctant to abandon their homes in the country. They were quite unprepared for the Peloponnesian invasion and were still in the process of moving when Archidamos reached Oinoe. Thucydides, be it recalled, was at great pains to explain Archidamos' delay there.

(See 2.18-21 and Chapter 1.) Some considered it a fatal error, for he pointed out (2.18.4): "During this interval the Athenians were carrying in their property; and it was the belief of the Peloponnesians that a quick advance would have found everything still out, had it not been for his procrastination."

b) To the very end the Athenians refused to believe that the Peloponnesians actually would advance as far as Athens, and hoped they would not go beyond Eleusis and Thria (2.21.1). Thus, being psychologically unprepared they were shocked and indignant at the sight of an army at Acharnai. (Note the stress on seeing the unexpected *before one's very eyes* in 2.21.2; cf. 2.11.7.) Their reaction was wholly emotional and undisciplined. Only Perikles prevented possible disaster.

c) Frightened as they were of the Spartans by land, their fear later turned to contempt. (See Nikias' remarks in 6.11.5: καταφρονήσαντες.) First they grew used to the invasions and realized their ineffectiveness; later they saw the allegedly invincible Spartans defeated at Pylos-Sphakteria.

At Syracuse the same pattern can be discerned, only now Lamachos predicts it in advance. His main concern is that he not repeat Archidamos' error, i.e., let opportunities pass and so miss the *kairos*. If the Syracusans are as unprepared, as slow and reluctant to move as the Athenians were, there will be booty to pick up. If they are as psychologically unready, they will react with emotion from surprise or shock. However, since they face the greatest naval power in the world, their reaction will probably be somewhat different from that of the Athenians, not so much indignation, as panic. If, on the other hand, the present expedition should miss this *kairos* and not take advantage of the terror caused by first sight (here ὄψις), then they must expect the same kind of disdain the Athenians later felt for the Lakedaimonians, especially if, seemingly invincible, they suffer defeats.

If we assume that Thucydides did witness the events in Athens in 431 and did see certain similarities in the expedition against Syracuse, is it not reasonable that he base Lamachos' (i.e., his own) assumptions on this experience, and that in describing the Syracusan response he use language and psychology derived from the previous incident, thus creating a patterned situation?

And this is no small matter, for it raises the question of schema in the *History*, a subject certainly worth pursuing.[5]

5. This will be the subject of Chapters 7 and 8.

Let us return to Demosthenes at Syracuse. Having criticized Nikias, he determines to take advantage of the enemy's terror. His strategy is simple, a swift attack on the counterwall which kept the Athenians from investing Syracuse, his aim being either to take the city at once or lead the expedition home.

Chapter 43 describes the attack. First he decides to attempt the counterwall with engines. When that proves ineffective, he decides to stop wasting time and make a direct assault on Epipolai. Since he believes it impossible to avoid detection by day, he sets out by night with Eurymedon and Menander, leaving Nikias behind in the lines. At first they carry all before them, surprising the enemy with their speed and daring (43.6: ἀδοκήτου τοῦ τολμήματος). Indeed, speed is what characterizes the enterprise from the outset. The tone is established at once when "Demosthenes determined to lose no time (42.3) in drawing the utmost profit from the consternation at the moment inspired by his army; and . . . made all haste (42.5) to attempt the enterprise." Although his first efforts fail, he remains undaunted and decides "to delay no longer" (43.1) and make a direct assault. The description which follows again emphasizes speed. After routing their opponents the Athenians push on (43.5), "eager to achieve the objects of the attack without giving time for their ardour to cool. . . ." When the Syracusans are compelled to retreat, their aim is "to make their way as quickly as possible (43.7) through the whole force of the enemy not yet engaged. . . ."

But then their very speed turns against them, for it leads to disorder. Left vulnerable, they are routed by the first attack. Immediately the scene is one of total confusion, aggravated by darkness and noise. Thucydides asks the question, "how could any one know anything for certain (44.1)?" But he does attempt a description. It is much like the ταραχή suffered by the Peloponnesians at Naupaktos. In both accounts the reversal comes when the victors fall into disorder in their overconfidence. (43.7: ἐν ἀταξίᾳ μᾶλλον ἤδη ὡς κεκρατηκότων; cf. 2.91.4: ἅμα ἀτάκτως διώκοντες διὰ τὸ κρατεῖν.) Then because they are hemmed into a small area (44.2: ἐν στενοχωρίᾳ), they are thrown into utter confusion. The *leit motif* is ταραχή, though Thucydides uses a number of other expressions: 44.1, ἐν πολλῇ ταραχῇ καὶ ἀπορίᾳ; 44.3, ἐτετάρακτο; 44.4, θόρυβον; 44.6, ἀπορίαν and φόβον; 44.7, ἐταράχθησαν and φόβον. (Cf. the ταραχή of 2.84.2-3.)

What first strikes one about this episode is the absence of any speech of advice and encouragement given by Demosthenes. This, of course, may merely indicate that there *was* no speech. But is a speech *always* necessary to present a *dianoia*, a plan spelling out one's tactics step-by-step and the enemy's possible response to them? No, sometimes "thoughts" in indirect discourse are sufficient (e.g., 2.84.2: Phormion; 7.36.3-6: the Syracusans). Demosthenes does not have such "thoughts." I.e., Thucydides does not allow Demosthenes to anticipate the action by employing his usual *logoi-erga* technique. And this cannot be mere oversight because he has just spent 14 lines presenting in some detail Demosthenes' criticisms of his predecessors and his own general intentions. Then apparently he stops thinking ahead. The reason is obvious. How is Thucydides to represent Demosthenes as predicting what will happen when the affair is a complete fiasco? How is Thucydides to derive purposes from results when an action is non-effective? Plan and effect obviously do *not* correspond. Therefore, it would be pointless to present a plan. But that does not stop him from assuming motives on Demosthenes' part. But they are different from the usual motivations, more in the nature of explanations concurrent with the action. In other words, he represents Demosthenes not as anticipating but as reacting to events *just as he did at Pylos*. Ἐδόκει repeated three times gives the impression of decisions taken on the spot. There is no *logismos* in the Thucydidean sense.

As we have seen, what Demosthenes depends on is speed and *tolma*. And though Thucydides makes no criticism, it is obvious that this is what leads to defeat. *Logismos* would have included some attempt to reconnoître, to know and ensure that the men knew the kind of terrain into which they were going, especially if the action was to be at night. Apparently Demosthenes was in too much of a hurry to seek out this information for himself. Indirectly Thucydides makes it clear that this was a major error, by describing how the newcomers got lost as they fled, because they did not know the country (44.8). Secondly, διδαχὴ ἀληθής, if such there had been, might have followed the lines of Phormion's advice (2.89.9), ". . . in action think order and silence all-important — qualities useful in war generally. . . ." Indeed, if *pronoia* is the part of the leader, order and silence are the duty of the men. Then they might not have scattered and might have heard whatever orders were given. (Cf. again 2.84.3: the noise and lack of order of the Peloponnesians in the Gulf of Patrai.) We could go on. The point is that for Thucydides the basic ingredient of success is correct forecast, and of confidence in action, διδαχή. The leader must transcend the emotions (θυμός) of the ordinary man by means of intellect (γνώμη, πρόνοια, ξύνεσις). He must direct these emotions (courage, for example) along proper lines. This he does by informing them with διδαχή. The result is a kind of *tolma* which is not mere emotion but a combination of θυμός and intellect.[6] This alone keeps men's courage up, for they see events unfolding as predicted and do not panic.[7] Conversely, where action fails, there can be no διδαχή. So Demosthenes has none to offer, in fact, makes no forecasts at all, even to himself.

But surely by now one's suspicions are becoming aroused. Does it not seem rather too much of a coincidence that Demosthenes is *always* playing the same role? Thucydides obviously thought such behaviour typical of him. Earlier we called him the type of *tolma alogistos*. This epithet is even more appropriate here. Only now it begins to seem that Demosthenes is acting out a definite pattern of behaviour. He does not look ahead – calculate or predict – but rushes into action on the spur of the moment, boldly and vigourously confronting what are often tremendous odds. One need only recall his "adventure" at Pylos; there he took his chances and ended up with only hope and sheer tenacity to depend on. But he was "lucky" that time, luckier than he was in Aitolia, where he acted with the same impetuosity. There, in fact, he was so impatient that he would not even wait for light-armed reinforcements, much as he needed them. "Led on by his advisers and trusting in his fortune" (3.97.2: τῇ τύχῃ ἐλπίσας), he plunged right in. The result was somewhat the same as at Epipolai. At a disadvantage to begin with his men suffered doubly because they did not know the country. They perished in "pathless gullies and places that they were unacquainted with" (98.1).[8]

6. This kind of *tolma* Perikles attributed to the Athenians (1.144.4 and 2.62.5); it is the result of reflection. Thus it is very different from the *tolma alogistos* of 3.82.4. Cf. too the *tolma* "of necessity (ἀνάγκῃ)" inspired by poverty (3.45.4).

7. *Tolma* (or θάρσος) was the aim of most of the exhortations studied so far (Phormion, 2.88.1 and 3; Brasidas, 4.126.4 and 5.9.2).

8. Cf. de Romilly, pp. 169-172, where she brings together all the passages in which ταραχή or θόρυβος is the central point in order to demonstrate Thucydides' descriptive powers and his concern with the irrational. "L'évocation concrète de la bataille, avec ses éléments visuels et auditifs suggérant une réalité psychologique, rejoint donc ce qui en fait le pathétique. Le θόρυβος, dans lequel les angoisses individuelles prennent le pas sur la discipline, marque le moment où Thucydide ne peut se contenter

Did Demosthenes really always act this way? Of course not; we decided earlier that it was he who planned in advance and executed the brilliant coup at Pylos. But we also know that even that exploit, *as Thucydides described it*, conformed to the same "pattern." There too the historian succeeded in representing Demosthenes as a "daredevil" by refusing to motivate him as he did Phormion or Brasidas *even though he was successful*. We begin to suspect that the "pattern" to which these three events conform existed in the mind of the historian. Perhaps by seeking out in all honesty the typical and recurrent in history, he imposed such patterns on events.

We shall return later to pattern. For the present let us make just one observation. As Thucydides presents them, Lamachos and Demosthenes play opposite roles in the *History*. The former learns from experience and uses his knowledge to formulate a correct *logos*. Because he can see the similarities in a new situation, he is able to predict what will probably happen and thus mediate past and future. Demosthenes, on the other hand, in spite of a wealth of experience does not learn, does not see similarities between past and future and so cannot and does not anticipate the future by means of *logoi*. He is doomed to repeat his own errors.

de pure stratégie ou de pure intelligence (172)." De Romilly also points out the similarities of Demosthenes' predicament in Aitolia and at Pylos (p. 169). Throughout her account she makes frequent references to Phormion's victories and the *tarache* suffered by the Peloponnesians. See above, p. 102 and de Romilly, pp. 153 and 172, n. 1. Phormion seems always to have been at the back of the historian's mind.

Chapter 7
Inevitability:
The Final Encounter (Thuc. 7.60-71)

ⓑⓑⓑ

In attempting to relate the action of the *History* to its prognostic purpose John Finley states:

> For if Thucydides detected what he thought would be a recurrent pattern beneath the events of his time, it follows that, though the speeches might be one way of setting forth the elements in that pattern, the mere movement of events in themselves would also illustrate it.[1]

Finley does not explain what methods Thucydides used to achieve this. What this chapter will attempt to do is trace out this process right in the *History*, thereby demonstrating such pattern and recurrence in the very movement of events. It will do so by analyzing Thuc. 7.60-71.

Having suffered three decisive defeats, two by sea and one at Epipolai, the Athenians face a third naval encounter. Previously real alternatives had faced them at every juncture. But now the situation is much worse, for the Syracusans have closed up the great harbour. They have little choice but to try to force their way out or, if that fails, retreat by land. It is no wonder then that the men are demoralized (60.5: ἀθυμοῦντας): they are not used to defeat by sea and besides provisions are low. With this in mind Nikias comes forward to address them in an attempt to dispel their paralyzing ἀθυμία. His speech is an exhortation in three main parts: a) a frank statement of what is at stake and some general advice, b) a plan or *dianoia*, c) a lengthy exhortation.

1. Finley, p. 295.

a) General advice (61). The Athenians are on the defensive, that is clear. Nikias makes no reference to glory or even conquest. The issue is self-preservation and return home. This being so, he argues by means of a *paradeigma* or example. They must not be discouraged or act like men without any experience, who fail in a first try and ever afterwards expect the future to hold similar disasters. Being experienced they should "remember the surprises of war (τῶν δὲ ἐν τοῖς πολέμοις παραλόγων), and with the hope that fortune will not be always against us (τὸ τῆς τύχης), prepare to fight again in a manner worthy of the number which you see yourselves to be."

b) *Dianoia* (62). Earlier Thucydides referred to their plan as imposed by necessity (60.4: ἐξ ἀναγκαίου . . . διανοίας). Forms of that word reappear ominously throughout this chapter. Twice Nikias asserts that they are "absolutely compelled to fight a land battle from the fleet" (62.2: ἐν δὲ τῇ ἐνθάδε ἠναγκασμένῃ ἀπὸ τῶν νεῶν πεζομαχιᾷ; 62.4: ἠναγκάσμεθα). Thus their tactics are defensive, a response to Syracusan innovations. Against the forces on the latter's decks archers and darters will go on board, a multitude useful in a land-fight, though admittedly disastrous in the open sea, "where our science (τὸ τῆς ἐπιστήμης) would be crippled by the weight of the vessels." Secondly, against the thicker cheeks of the enemy's ships they have provided grappling-irons to prevent their backing water, and thus hope to give their own marines a chance to fight it out. And this they must do rather than back water, since so much of the shore is hostile.

c) Exhortation (63-64). All the rest is exhortation, to three groups in turn, the hoplites, the sailors, and the Athenians. On the hoplites everything now depends, for it is their responsibility to sweep the enemy from the decks. As for the sailors, (presumably left no opportunity to use their skill), they must not panic, as their armament has been improved and they have the larger fleet (63.3). With that Nikias launches into an emotional appeal rather reminiscent of the Funeral Oration. He reminds the sailors of their lofty position and privileges vis-à-vis the Athenians and their subjects; it is not something to cast aside lightly.[2] He ends thus: ". . . we ask you to repel them, and to show that even in sickness

---

2. From the context the *nautai* must be primarily metics. For corroboration see, e.g., the pseudo-Xenophon, *Constitution of the Athenians* 1.12: δεῖται ἡ πόλις μετοίκων διὰ . . . τὸ ναυτικόν. In any case Nikias' letter (7.13.2) indicated that by this time the Athenians had lost many of the *xenoi* through defections.

THE FINAL ENCOUNTER 109

and disaster your skill is more than a match for the fortune and vigour of any other" (63.4). Finally, the Athenians. Again the appeal is emotional and, in a sense, the counsel of despair. There is no alternative; everything, Athens herself and her glorious name, depends on them. Whatever they possess of skill or courage let them now use on her behalf.

Nikias' speech does not go unanswered; Gylippos and the generals present a counter *logos*. The two speeches constitute an *antilogia* very like that between Phormion and the Peloponnesians before the battle of Naupaktos in Book 2. Analysis of 2.87-92 revealed that the *erga* which follow, i.e., the battle itself, demonstrated the superiority of Phormion's evaluation and predictions. His *logos* we therefore called the stronger ($\kappa\rho\epsilon\acute{\iota}\tau\tau\omega\nu$) on the principle that life itself, the *erga*, confirmed it as true. On the same principle the Peloponnesians' *logos* was the weaker ($\mathring{\eta}\tau\tau\omega\nu$).[3] In analyzing the *antilogia* between Nikias and Gylippos we suspect at once that it too will evince this Thucydidean opposition between stronger and weaker argument and that it may be possible to distinguish one from the other even before the *erga* provide confirmation. At the same time it is surely no coincidence that the debate between Phormion and the Peloponnesians comes to mind. The Athenians, having confronted a daring adversary and lost, are in a position very similar to that of the latter; they must face him again. What have they learned from their previous errors? The aura of *déjà vu* does not end here, however. Throughout the present *antilogia* there are numerous echoes of the previous debate. In fact, the latter can be considered a kind of *paradeigma*, a model against which to compare the present *logoi*.[4] With this *paradeigma* in mind then, let us attempt to discover wherein Nikias has left himself open to criticism even before analyzing Gylippos' counter *logos*.

Nikias appeals to his men's experience in war (61.3). It is this and the skill which is its concomitant which will be their salvation against the enemy's vigour (63.4). *Episteme* must combine with *eupsychia* in defence of Athens (64.2). To be sure, one need only consult the earlier *antilogia* between Phormion and the Peloponnesians to know that *episteme* and *empeiria* are characteristic of the Athenians (cf. 2.87.4 and 89.3). However, Nikias has forgotten

3. See Chapter 3, pp. 52 ff.
4. See Chapter 4, n. 20.

or ignored the fact that these specifically nautical qualities will be of no advantage in the coming encounter. It is to be a πεζομαχία in which everything will depend on the hoplites, *not* the sailors. The στενοχωρία, as Phormion once predicted so graphically (2.89.8), has deprived them of all opportunity to display their characteristic manoeuvres, their *episteme*. Thus, just as in 429 the Peloponnesians trusted in their land-experience to support them at sea (2.89.2), so Nikias here trusts in the nautical skill and experience of the Athenians to support them in what is virtually a land-battle.

Of course, leadership too is important. How does Nikias' *dianoia* stand up in this respect? First, it is totally unimaginative. Far from using his men's ability or attempting to find the enemy's weaknesses, he is to fight on the latter's terms, relegating himself to mere brute force. Even the projected grappling-irons as necessary to force the Athenians to fight on the enemy's terms seem to be a counsel of despair. Worse still, he makes no attempt to spell out in advance what the men may expect from the enemy. Rather than forecast the possibilities in advance, he depends on emotional appeal and fear of the consequences (cf. 2.87.8-9).

If this bodes ill, so does his obvious underestimation of the Syracusans. Theirs is a "lucky energy" (63.4 – my translation of εὐτυχούσης ρώμης). This is just like the excuse of the Peloponnesians after the battle in the Gulf of Patrai, that *tyche* has had something to do with the reverses they have suffered (cf. 2.87.2-3). The reader knows, however, that this is not entirely the case.[5] One need only consult the *erga* to discern the errors and lost opportunities on one side, the initiative, innovation, and growing confidence on the other. One is tempted to compare Nikias' plea that the Athenians scorn the Corinthians and Sicilians (63.4: κατα-φρονήσαντες) with Perikles' statement (2.62.4): ". . . disdain (καταφρόνησις) is the privilege of those who, like us, have been assured by reflection (γνώμη) of their superiority to their adversary." Has Nikias a right to disdain? We suspect that such feelings belong more rightfully to the Syracusans. (See especially 7.56.2.)

---

5. This does not mean that in addition to human error there is not an element of "misfortune" in the events leading up to the final encounter. The eclipse of the moon which keeps the Athenians from leaving Sicily (7.50.4) was certainly a stroke of bad luck, though presumably with more determined leadership the men might have been persuaded to leave.

Nikias must offer some encouragement to his men, and he does — "chance" and numbers. Three times Nikias refers to their numerical superiority. They must fight in a manner worthy of their number (61.3), for their land-forces are the stronger (63.2) and they have the larger fleet (63.3). But is this not just what the Peloponnesians once depended on to their sorrow (2.87.6)? Phormion proved them wrong: numbers are not always determinant. He stated (2.89.6): "An adversary numerically superior, like the one before us, comes into action trusting more to strength (δυνάμει) than to resolution (γνώμῃ). . . ." Surely this is what the Athenians are doing. And if the Peloponnesians blamed the "chances of war" for their previous defeat (2.85.2 and 87.2-3), Nikias also appeals to the same forces (61.3); he calls for that against which Perikles ever warned, "hope, which is the prop of the desperate (2.62.5)," and worse still, hope based on a change of fortune. Thus have *elpis* and *tyche* become a substitute for *pronoia* and *gnome*. Thus are the Athenians all but reduced to those straits to which they once brought the Melians (cf. especially 5.102-104). Thus has come about the ultimate reversal, for Athens now depends on *tyche* and *dynamis* (1.144.4).

Gylippos' παρακέλευσις follows, significantly, with no mention of demoralization or even fear on the Syracusans' part. This second *logos* closely parallels the first in structure and can be roughly divided into three similar parts: a) the issue at stake and some general words of encouragement, b) a *dianoia*, and c) the exhortation proper. There is, however, more than just a formal similarity between them; the second speech, being the counter *logos* in an *antilogia*, presents arguments which answer or even refute the first *logos*. Summarizing these arguments will show the relationship between the two speeches.

a) Encouragement (66-67.1). Gylippos' opening sentence echoes Nikias' words. For the Syracusans, however, the issue is very different, not self-defence as it once was and now is for the Athenians but glory. This presumably is the source of their ardour (προθύμως, again in contrast to Athenian ἀθυμία). After all, having already defeated the greatest empire of all times, the veritable masters of the sea, there is every probability (ἐκ τοῦ εἰκότος) they will do so again. This prediction Gylippos reinforces with a *gnome*, in effect an answer to Nikias' *paradeigma* of men without experience. That very experience may well prove to be a disadvantage, for:

When men are once checked in what they consider their special excellence, their whole opinion of themselves suffers more than if they had not at first believed in their superiority, the unexpected shock to their pride causing them to give way more than their real strength warrants. . . (66.3).

This is probably just what the Athenians are suffering. As for themselves, Gylippos ends on a note of hope, once again following Nikias' example. But the hope is less vague, based as it is not on "fortune" but past achievements. Since they have dared and defeated the best, they must be the best seamen of their times. And so it is a double hope which lies behind their προθυμία.

b) *Dianoia* (67.2-4). Gylippos' *dianoia* deals only cursorily with his own strategy. Presumably it will be the same as in previous battles. Even the recent Athenian innovation causes him no concern; it will "be met by proper provisions." (The *erga*, 65.2, have already described how the Syracusans stretched hides over their prows against Nikias' grappling-irons.) Confident in his own strategy then, Gylippos concentrates on what they might expect from the enemy, thereby pointing up the weaknesses of Nikias' *logos* and anticipating Athenian defeat. His arguments are based on probability and concern three matters, the πεζομαχία, numbers, and morale.

i) Nikias deployed all his forces for a πεζομαχία. But surely this will prove his undoing. For the number of hoplites fighting on deck is unprecedented and so are the darters. The latter, being landsmen (e.g., Akarnanians), will not have the same control over their weapons, when their mobility is hampered. Like Phormion (2.84.2) he predicts ταραχή. They will fall "all into confusion (ταράξονται) among themselves through fighting not according to their own tactics."

ii) As for their superior numbers the στενοχωρία will turn that into a disadvantage. Being unable to manoeuvre from lack of space, they will be more liable to injury from the Syracusan armament (presumably using ramming tactics).

iii) If the truth be known, the Athenians are utterly demoralized from hardship and scarcity. It is *tyche* alone to which they trust — the "chance" that they may force their way out, since they cannot be worse off. The remark made by Brasidas when confronted by the Lynkestians comes to mind (4.126.4): "Where an enemy seems strong but is really weak, a true knowledge of the facts makes his adversary the bolder. . . ." For Gylippos like Brasidas instils confidence in his own men by forecasting in detail the probable results of the enemy's weaknesses. Surely by now καταφρόνησις is their "privilege."

c) Exhortation (68). Gylippos' exhortation complements Nikias' by confirming his worst fears. The latter merely hinted at the fate which would be theirs and even that of Athens herself if they should fail. And now Gylippos exhorts the Syracusans to fight in anger (ὀργῇ) with vengeance as a legitimate motive, since they are well aware what might have been their fate had the Athenians won. To be sure, Nikias' cryptic reference to "the intentions with which you attacked them" (64.1) and the cruel punishment of the Melians seem to give substance to Gylippos' suspicions and justify his desire for complete victory. He ends on a note of optimism, predicting success (ἐκ τοῦ εἰκότος) and, in preserving Sicily's freedom, glory.

Compared to Nikias' *logos* Gylippos' answer is all but unassail-able. One senses immediately it is κρείττων. And much as the reader may hope for that "stroke of luck" to save the Athenians, somehow he knows defeat is inevitable. A curious premonition, and one which the *erga* confirm. Here, however, it would be insufficient to offer the explanation that since Thucydides derived purposes from results, *logoi* from *erga*, it is neither novel nor startling for Gylippos to make correct predictions and thus anticipate the Athenian defeat, while Nikias, who was to lose, could hardly present a masterful strategy. This is all true, but here more is involved. Somehow the *erga* themselves sustain and strengthen the feeling of inevitability. The question is, how and why?

Chapters 70-71 are masterly drama. Ever concerned with psychology, Thucydides now brings all his powers of description to bear on the fluctuating emotions of both participants and spectators. Close analysis suggests that it was this — emotion, mood, psychology — which captured his imagination, not the bare facts of the matter, details of individual encounters, manoeuvres, etc. The latter are there, yes, but in a most general way, as a kind of backdrop against which the historian performs a *tour de force* with pathos and suspense as his real aim.

The Syracusans won, that we know; 71.5 describes how "at last the Syracusans and their allies, after the battle had lasted a long while, put the Athenians to flight, and with much shouting and cheering chased them in open rout to the shore." Brief in the extreme, less than 4 lines, and all the more surprising because Thucydides has never given the slightest indication that the Syracusans had the upper hand, or indeed what exploits they performed to gain it and what, if any, individual encounters were significant. All the usual details of the conventional battle narrative are lacking; the facts fail to reveal how and when the Syracusans turned the tide.

But, one might retort, there *are* details. We can picture very well what happened. Once the Athenians failed to break the barrier and were forced to fight in the harbour (70.2), an unprecedented number of ships were crowded together in a small area. Thucydides is emphatic about this: ". . . these were the largest fleets fighting in the narrowest space ever known, being together little short of two hundred. . . " (70.4). And so those clever Athenian manoeuvres of Phormion's day were out of the question. Instead there were "collisions" and a πεζομαχία on board ship. Two groups bore the brunt of the fighting, the light-armed with their darts, arrows, and stones and, when ships came together, the hoplites (70.5). We also know that the hostile shore forced the Athenians to fight on rather than back water (70.8). Are these not details? In any case, Thucydides described the scene as it might have appeared to one on the shore. It was a scene of total confusion (ταραχή), aggravated by noise of every kind from human cries to crashing prows. In shifting from theme to theme, group to group, Thucydides has reproduced this and the mood it induced.[6]

All this is true, and, we grant, Thucydides was perfectly within his rights to emphasize confusion and noise, if this is what happened, i.e., as he heard it from his informants. We do not intend to convict him of "omissions." Rather we would hope to explain why he was able to concentrate on mood to the exclusion of lengthy accounts of motive and reason or even explanations of tactics. To this end we deliberately isolated the main elements of his narrative, which, by the way, gives only a general picture and not a blow-by-blow description of the battle, the στενοχωρία, the ramming tactics, the hostile shore, and the πεζομαχία. Anyone

---

6. 71.3, for instance, describes the varied emotions of the Athenians on shore by moving swiftly from one group to another, each of which witnesses the struggle from a different point of view (τινες . . . οἱ δὲ . . . ἄλλοι δὲ). Victory, defeat, and indecision are all represented.

who has been following the *History* up to this point, the victim of a kind of "subliminal persuasion,"[7] responds predictably to these four themes. He seizes upon them and instantly fills in the gaps himself. For in his own mind he finds a wealth of details and explanations indicating who will win, how and why. So securely has Thucydides the reader in his grasp. He has anticipated everything. For the final battle has been foreshadowed not just once by the *antilogia* but a number of times throughout Book 7, one might even say from the beginning of the *History*.

How does Thucydides make the final defeat inevitable? Primarily through the juxtaposition of *erga* and *logoi*. But here it will be necessary to untangle two separate threads of the *History*, two concurrent preoccupations of the historian, which combine effectively for the final disaster. The first we shall call for want of a better name "military science"; it includes both physical resources, men and ships, *dynamis* in the broadest sense of the word, though often referred to as παρασκευή, as well as the skill, knowledge, and experience necessary to make use of this *dynamis*, in a word, *techne*, *episteme*, or *empeiria*. The second stream of the narrative is morale, especially the psychology of victor and vanquished and their relationship to action. Fear and demoralization, on the one hand, ardour, confidence, and disdain on the other are all a part of morale.

First, "military science." Hovering over the final encounter are the *logoi* of 7.36, the "thoughts" of the Syracusans as they reason out and explain their strategy and tactics. In this early chapter three major themes of 70-71 are already adumbrated, the στενοχωρία and its effects, ramming tactics, the hostile shore, as well as the end result of all three, ταραχή. Never again are these tactics explained; Gylippos takes them for granted in his *logos* and so do the *erga* which follow. The reader must retain and apply for himself what he learned in 7.36. But there is more to it than that, for these same themes first appeared in even earlier *erga*. In 7.22-23, the first naval confrontation, the Syracusans learned through personal experience, *empeiria*, the effects of the

---

7. The words of W. P. Wallace, p. 258. In the same article he makes the following comment on inevitability (p. 252): "Thucydides himself makes hardly any comments, and yet the reader feels deeply convinced at every stage that he understands exactly what is happening, that, like the spectator of a great drama, he sees events rushing to their only possible conclusion; he feels that he knows, where those who took part in the events could only guess."

στενοχωρία, ταραχή. Then, following the example of the Corinthians, *paradeigma* (7.34), they decided to adopt ramming tactics and make use of their curved shore-line by filling it with troops. These past *erga* became useful through the *logoi*, *logoi* which in turn achieved the status of empiric truth through a second set of *erga*, two new experiences. 7.40.5 confirmed what the Syracusans had predicted about the στενοχωρία and the efficacy of ramming tactics. Then a second successful encounter (7.52), in which Eurymedon was killed, by revealing how the Athenians were forced ashore on enemy territory and were only narrowly saved by the Tyrrhenians, proved conclusively the effectiveness of a hostile, crescent-shaped shore.[8] Moreover, in this second set of *erga* the fourth theme, the πεζομαχία appears unheralded as an innovation of the Syracusans (7.40.5). It is at once deleterious to the Athenians and from then on recurs until its final reappearance is 7.70. (See p. 117.)

The final *logoi* presuppose all the *logoi* and *erga* which preceded. In his *dianoia*, for example, Nikias is forced to consider all four circumstances outlined above and adjust to them. In so doing, he adopts a completely defensive strategy, thus foreshadowing the Athenian role in the coming encounter. Gylippos, on the other hand, having tried his tactics in life and found them adequate, has no need to evolve a new *dianoia* but merely adapts the successes of the past to the present. Seeing that the coming encounter will be similar to those which preceded, a repetition of the past, he is free to concentrate his powers of εἰκός and εἰκάζειν on what will probably be the results of the enemy's weaknesses. In predicting ταραχή, he — and the reader with him — bears in mind all the previous encounters.

Thus, following the account of the final battle, the reader carries forward with him both sets of *logoi*. The first motivates and explains the Syracusan tactics, the second motivates and criticizes the Athenians. None of this the *erga* need repeat. At the same time the three former sea-battles, each demonstrating some

---

8. Cf. de Romilly, p. 155 for whom "le récit montre tout à la fois la justesse de leurs prévisions et la raison qui empêche leur victoire définitive." She points out the verbal echo in 52.2 (ἐξεώθουν ἐς τὴν γῆν) of 36.5 (ἐξωθουμένοις . . . ἐς τὴν γῆν). In the same passage de Romilly also stresses the importance of 7.36 to the narrative which follows. "Les conditions étant donc les mêmes, Thucydide ne fournit, avant la bataille, aucune nouvelle explication de tactique navale. . . ." More important for our account, she distinguishes the two threads of the narrative, "l'analyse des dispositions morales" and "celle des groupements de forces en présence" (p. 160).

erga	logoi	erga	logoi	erga
7.22-23 – empeiria	7.36 – Syracusan "thoughts"	7.40.5 – empeiria	7.62 – Nikias' dianoia from ἀνάγκη responds to:	7.70 – empeiria
a) στενοχωρία = ταραχή 7.34 – paradeigma	a) στενοχωρία	a) στενοχωρία	a) στενοχωρία	a) στενοχωρία (70.4)
b) ramming tactics	b) ramming tactics	b) ramming tactics confirmed by success 7.52 – empeiria	b) ramming tactics	b) ramming tactics (70.4)
c) hostile shore	c) hostile shore = ταραχή	c) hostile shore confirmed by success	c) hostile shore	c) hostile shore (70.8)
		d) 7.40.5 – πεξομαχία – darters and small boats	d) πεξομαχία 7.67 – Gylippos basing himself on previous empeiria predicts ταραχή	d) πεξομαχία (70.5) = ταραχή
empeiria and paradeigma	gnome	confirmation through experience = truth	διδαχή	confirmation through experience

point of war, provide, as a group, a model against which to set the final encounter.

But it is not just in "military science" that there is a reversal of roles; a similar change takes place in "morale." Earlier we referred to Athenian demoralization before the final battle, very much in contrast to Syracusan ardour (66.1 and 67.1: προθυμία). The contrast does not begin here; it has been developing all throughout Book 7, ever since the arrival of Gylippos. From that moment ἀθυμία becomes increasingly characteristic of the Athenians and ῥώμη of the Syracusans. In most cases when Thucydides indicates a deterioration in morale on one side, he balances it with an increase in confidence on the other. The following turning-points will make this changing relationship clear:

Syracusans	*Athenians*

News of Gylippos' approach (7.2.1)

7.2.2: καὶ οἱ μὲν Συρακόσιοι ἐπερρώσθησαν. . . .

7.3.1: οἱ δὲ Ἀθηναῖοι. . . ἐθορυβήθησαν. . . .

Athenians miss *kairos* (7.2.4) and Syracusans build counterwall (7.6.4)

7.7.4: οἵ τε Συρακόσιοι. . . πολὺ ἐπέρρωντο.

7.8-15: Nikias' letter explaining Athenian ἀπορία.

Capture of Plemmyrion (7.24.1)

7.25.1: Syracusans ἐν ἐλπίσιν εἰσί.

7.24.3: Athenians experience κατάπληξιν and ἀθυμίαν.

Battle of Epipolai (7.43-44)

7.46: Syracusans πάλιν αὖ ἀναρρωσθέντες.

7.47.1-2: Athenian soldiers ἀχθομένους and affairs ἀνέλπιστα.

Second naval defeat (7.52.2)

7.56.1-2: Syracusan aim becomes not mere self-defence but glory καλὸν . . . τὸ ἀγώνισμα.

7.55.1-2: Complete demoralization — Athenians ἐν παντὶ δὴ ἀθυμίας ἦσαν καὶ ὁ παράλογος αὐτοῖς μέγας ἦν. . . .

In this subtle reversal of morale we are led to feel a premonition of Athenian defeat. And something more. For surely once again there is about these respective moods an aura of *déjà vu* which demands explanation. Surely it is significant that Gylippos, a Spartan, predicts the outcome of Athenian demoralization. His predictions are the very ones one might assume of a man who had experienced Spartan demoralization at and after Sphakteria. For, while the Athenians felt a growing disdain for their enemy in that first war, the Spartans suffered a total paralysis as a result of unexpected defeats. Two significant passages make this clear:

a) Reread carefully the account of the battle of Sphakteria. The Athenians were clever enough there to deprive the Spartans of their superior skill and experience (4.33.2: τῇ σφετέρᾳ ἐμπειρίᾳ). In a word, they forced them to fight "not according to their own tactics" (Gylippos – 7.67.2). Their light-armed assailants soon gained in confidence (τοῦ θαρσεῖν). They became used to the Spartans and found them not so formidable, "the result not having justified the apprehensions which they had suffered, when they first landed in slavish dismay at the idea of attacking Lacedae-monians; and accordingly their fear changing to disdain (καταφρονήσαντες), they now rushed all together. . ." (4.34.1). The Spartans, unaccustomed to this mode of fighting, were utterly confounded. Plagued by noise and dust and unable to see, they were soon forced to retreat. The above is, of course, only the culmination of a growing contempt on the part of the Athenians. Finally come face to face with the dreaded Spartan hoplite they find him not at all invincible.[9]

b) What is more important is the psychology of defeat as it now applies to the Athenians. Surely they can be expected to feel and react as the Spartans did at Sphakteria, deprived of the benefits of skill and experience. But worse still, since they have already suffered two defeats on their own element contrary to their expectation (7.60.5), they may well experience the complete paralysis of the Spartans after Pylos-Sphakteria. For the psycho-logical pattern one need only reread 4.55. Two points stand out. What happened at Sphakteria was totally unexpected (4.55.1 and 55.3), and the Spartans subsequently "became more timid than ever in military matters" (55.2). Thoroughly unnerved (ἀτολμότεροι)

> they were always afraid of a second disaster like that on the island, and thus scarcely dared to take the field, but fancied that they could not stir without a blunder, for being new to the experience of adversity they had lost all confidence in themselves (55.4).

9. For the Syracusans to experience in actual combat what the Athenians and their light-armed allies felt at Sphakteria is, of course, nothing more than a logical extension of Lamachos' *gnome* in the first council of war (6.49.1-2). He anticipated Syracusan disdain once the Athenians failed to attack at once (6.63.2: κατεφρόνησαν).

In effect

> once checked in what they consider their special excellence,
> their whole opinion of themselves suffers more than if they
> had not at first believed in their superiority, the unexpected
> shock to their pride causing them to give way more than their
> real strength warrants. . . .

The latter is Gylippos (7.66.3). But surely it describes what
happened to the Spartans; they did not oppose the Athenians in
force, "stood very much upon the defensive," and "allowed the
Athenians to ravage their seaboard." It is easy to see the source of
Gylippos' psychology. He has learned enough from past experiences (*erga*) to see similarities in the present (*logoi*) and so predict
the future (*erga*).

Combining both the defensive strategy of the Athenians which
fails to make use of *empeiria* or *episteme*, as contrasted to the
successful innovations of the Syracusans, "military science" and
the patterns of behaviour retained by the careful reader and now
recalled by Gylippos — morale and its effect, and keeping in mind
the original *paradeigma* of Athenian nautical skill, Phormion's
exploits, we can now see that every aspect of the final battle has
been anticipated a number of times and on a number of levels. We
begin to understand why Thucydides does not need to describe
the encounter but can concentrate on the emotions of the
spectators, on pathos and suspense. We begin to understand why
the *erga* seem inevitable. In fact, they are nothing more than the
confirmation of truths we have known for a long time.[10] History
thus repeats itself, though with a difference (1.22.4: τοιούτων καὶ
παραπλησίων). But for human beings to intervene in and take
advantage of this process they require a leader who not only
understands men's psychology but can read the message of the
past, one who can combine his own and others' experiences with
the intellectual tools of εἰκός and εἰκάζειν to predict and so
conquer the future. In this instance Gylippos is such a man.

What is the relationship between leader and men, whether
strategos and soldiers such as Brasidas and Phormion or statesman
and citizens such as Perikles and Hermokrates? It is possible to

---

10. De Romilly, p. 161 expresses a somewhat similar view: "Rien n'apparaît dans
les événements que la confirmation ou l'infirmation des calculs élaborés par l'intelligence; rien ne s'y montre qui n'ait reçu de l'intelligence sa forme et son armature, qui
ne soit transposé, qui ne soit idée."

isolate the three major qualities of the former: *pronoia*, correct forecast with all that implies of past experience; *gnome*, the application of *pronoia* to a concrete situation through the formulation of a plan or strategy; διδαχή, the ability to communicate this *gnome* to one's men so that they do not give in to emotions such as fear, anger, indignation, or demoralization. Often the leader does this by reminding them of their skill and experience or their past successes; always he forewarns them by anticipating every possibility they may face. He thus informs their spirit with διδαχή. The result is a kind of *tolma* which is not mere emotion but a combination of θυμός and intellect. What else is this but Perikles' *tolma* and *gnome* (1.144.4)? [11] And this combination, representing the two threads of the narrative, "military science" and "morale," is what now characterizes the Syracusans, in contrast to *tyche* and *dynamis* upon which Nikias depended and lost. This is the ultimate reversal. In Themistokles' day the Persian empire suffered the same fate. And this was also the fate of the Peloponnesians — though on a smaller scale — when men like Perikles and Phormion were in command. What we have been witness to then is the decline of empire through the loss of these qualities in one people and their development in another. A major theme of the *History* is thus drawing to a close.

To return to Finley and the "recurrent pattern beneath the events" of Thucydides' time. We began by isolating one *logoi-erga* combination, the *antilogia* of Nikias and Gylippos and the events which followed it. It would seem however that such combinations are infinitely extensible. History is a continuum of experience, not just a series of isolated events. Indeed, the theory of knowledge we have propounded for Thucydides, past experiences as a source of truth and means of conquering the future, in a word, *prognosis*, implies that events will happen in the future much as they did in the past. This assumption also lies behind the concept of εἰκάζειν or, for that matter, probability itself. Though Thucydides states as much (1.22.4 and 3.82.2), no one has really taken him at his

---

11. See Chapter 3, p. 59, and Woodhead, *Thucydides on the Nature of Power,* pp. 108-109, where he speaks of "a breakdown of the five essential elements which compose it (power) — *kratos, dynamis, gnome, perousia,* and *tharsos*." Again he is not clear about the relationship of these factors or characteristics to one another in the breakdown. The present chapter should indicate where and how this reversal took place. Woodhead, (p. 120), also has some interesting comments on Spartan loss of *tharsos* (or *tolma*) in the Archidamian War. See above, p. 82 for Sparta's lack of *gnome* and *tolma*. Chapter 8 will elucidate these points further.

word. But surely this is what we have demonstrated in this chapter, pattern and recurrence in the very movement of events, patterns which men may recognize and use as a guide to the future.

We begin to suspect that time spans were for Thucydides very different than for ourselves, who, with thousands of years behind us, cannot help but think in terms of linear history. Thucydidean "time" we will return to along with two other points. Is there some thread of unity to the patterns which recur in the *History*? If so, what significance might this have for Thucydides' standards of relevance?

Chapter 8
Κατὰ τὸ Ἀνθρώπινον:
Nikias' Warnings (Thuc. 6.8-24)

ରରର

Recurrences of patterns in battles are easy to see; striking events are easy to remember, particularly when recalled by verbal repetitions in *erga-logoi-erga* combinations. The specific events in Sicily, recalling those at Sphakteria and the successes of Phormion, show, in a segment of the work, the "recurrent pattern" of Finley, and the Thucydidean view that men may recognize and use patterns. But this view is not limited to the acknowledged *empeiria* in planning tactics in specific situations; it extends to long-term political and military strategies as well, and shows up in Thucydides' work when whole sections of the *History* are considered, as we have considered specific and limited narratives. Turning back to the debate which preceded the dispatching of the Sicilian expedition, we find the same characteristics of anticipation which we saw in the exhortations of generals before battles.

When, in 415 the Athenians voted to send 60 ships to Sicily under the command of Alkibiades, Nikias, and Lamachos, their aim was "to help the Egestaeans against the Selinuntines, to restore Leontini . . . and to order all other matters in Sicily as they should deem best for the interests of Athens" (6.8.2). Soon after a second assembly is held to consider logistics. At this point Nikias, who has been chosen against his will and who believes that the above aims are a mere pretext for the conquest of Sicily, comes forward in an attempt to divert the Athenians from this course. His speech has three main parts: a) a preamble setting forth his object in speaking and his right to offer advice, b) a realistic statement of the facts, in effect a series of arguments from εἰκός predicting probable difficulties both in Greece and Sicily, c) an epilogue in three sections, advice of a general nature, a concrete program addressed to the older citizens, and an appeal to the Prytanis.

a) The Preamble (6.9). Two familiar terms appear at once, ἐν καιρῷ and διδάξω (9.3). The speech will be διδαχή, its aim to consider the advisability of sending the expedition at all. Such reconsideration is justified on two counts: they have made a hasty decision about matters of very great importance and they have let themselves be persuaded by outsiders to undertake a war which does not concern them. Note, however, that Nikias refuses — admits in fact his incapacity — to confront the issue head-on. Though he would like to be able to convince them that it is folly to risk what is "secure" for what is "out of sight and in the future,"[1] he quails before the Athenian temperament, confessing his inadequacy as a speaker. Thus he addresses himself to the practicability of the venture. In other words, he will not raise the question of moral responsibility, i.e., whether it is right (δίκαιον) for Athens to attack Sicily, nor presumably, will he argue in the manner of the Spartan envoys. They, be it remembered, warned against those μεταβολαί which are somehow in the nature of things: those who overextend themselves usually court disaster. Instead Nikias bases his argument on expediency (ξύμφορον). Are the circumstances favourable for such an expedition? In a word, is it the "right thing at the right moment" (καιρός)?

b) Prognostications (6.10-11.5, including two further predictions in 12 and 13). Nikias makes five main predictions: 1) In the event of a serious reverse their enemies at home (the Lakedaimonians)[2] will attack at once (10.2). 2) Other Greek states already at war with them or restrained only by truces renewed every ten days will join the Sicilian side on seeing Athens' power divided (10.3). 3) Although the Syracusans fear them from afar, if they should suffer the least reverse in Sicily, this fear will straightway turn to contempt (11.4-5). 4) The Egestaians are not to be trusted — in fact, are liars (12.1). 5) The Athenians face the greatest danger in their history (13.1).

---

1. My translation. Cf. the Athenians' final warning to the Melians (5.113): "Well, you alone, as it seems to us, judging from these resolutions, regard what is future (τὰ μὲν μέλλοντα) as more certain than what is before your eyes, and what is out of sight (τὰ δὲ ἀφανῆ), in your eagerness, as already coming to pass. . . ."

2. This is surely whom he means. The terminology of Pylos-Sphakteria recurs: ". . . the convention was forced upon them by disaster and was less honourable to them than to us. . . ."

It is not the aim of this chapter to discuss anticipations. It is sufficient to state that Nikias' several predictions find confirmation in later *erga*. Like the anticipations studied earlier they are reasoning after the fact. Moreover, careful analysis reveals that most of them fit into *erga-logoi-erga* patterns. The third prognostication above, for example, is an assumption about psychology already familiar to us; it is a variation on Lamachos' predictions (6.49.2) discussed at length in Chapter 6. Both predictions are confirmed in 6.63.2, where Syracusan fear turns to contempt. Earlier we suggested that Lamachos, as Thucydides represents him, might well have acquired this knowledge of psychology from his own experience. For what he assumes about the Syracusans is exactly what the Athenians felt towards the Spartans after Pylos-Sphakteria. Indeed, it is this very experience drawn from the first war that Nikias offers his listeners as a *paradeigma* to support his prediction about the probable pattern of Syracusan behaviour. He states: "You have yourselves experienced this with regard to the Lacedaemonians and their allies, whom your unexpected success, as compared with what you feared at first, has made you suddenly despise. . . ." Obviously Thucydides saw similarities in the two situations.

In the same way the duplicity of the Egestaians, suggested in 6.8.3, is confirmed in 6.46, a lengthy description of the stratagem they employed when the envoys from Athens came to inspect their resources. Implicit are earlier *erga*, the *paradeigma* of the Kerkyraians, also "outsiders" who persuaded Athens to involve herself in a war "which did not concern her" but which led inexorably to a confrontation between Athens and Sparta. Then Kerkyra, in spite of her talk of gratitude, proved a less than enthusiastic ally.[3]

Little need be said about Athens' enemies in Greece. Corinth, always hostile, was quick to answer a Syracusan appeal for aid (6.88.8). And soon after Sparta herself agreed to send Gylippos to take over the leadership (6.93.2). But it was only in 413 after the Athenians' first real reverse (7.6) that the Spartans threw themselves heart and soul into the war with the fortification of Dekeleia. According to Thucydides, it was at this point that they decided that Athens was legally in the wrong (7.18). The muster-roll before the final encounter also lists Leukas, Ambrakia,

3. See Gomme 1, p. 168, "in fact Kerkyra did little for Athens in the war." He reviews her record.

and Boeotia as fighting for Syracuse (7.58).[4]

Nikias' prediction about the magnitude of the danger (μέγιστον δὴ τῶν πρὶν κίνδυνον) – glaringly *post eventum* – is echoed after the final defeat in the harbour (7.75.7: μέγιστον γὰρ δὴ τὸ διάφορον) and again in Thucydides' own evaluation of the disaster. "This was the greatest Hellenic achievement (μέγιστον) of any in this war, or, in my opinion, in Hellenic history. . . ." (7.87.5).[5]

c) Advice (11.6-end). Nikias' advice is threefold: 1) The Athenians have underestimated not only the instability of affairs in Greece, but also the capacity of their enemies. Because of their longstanding contempt for the Lakedaimonians they have become overconfident, "puffed up by the misfortunes of your adversaries." But only superior policy (*dianoia*) should inspire confidence. Therefore, if they are wise, they will attend to problems at home. Or, as he stated earlier, they ought not to think of "grasping at another empire" (10.5), before securing the one they have.[6] 2) Their concern should be the preservation of that prosperity they have only lately recovered. After referring to the Egestaian "exiles," Nikias launches into a diatribe against Alkibiades wherein not only old and young but public and private interests are set against one another. Private pressures come from two sources, externally the Egestaians, "outsiders" and "barbarians" and internally, Alkibiades, the spendthrift. 3) Nikias next appeals to the older men in the audience not to be intimidated by Alkibiades and his supporters but to avoid their "mad dream of conquest." Mere desire rarely determines the success of an enterprise; it is foresight that counts. Having thus characterized

4. Note that the *erga* which precede are also important. The reader need only consult Book 5 to verify Nikias' remarks about the unsettled state of affairs in Greece since the Peace of Nikias. See especially 5.26.2, Thucydides' own judgment: it could hardly be considered peace. It is becoming increasingly evident that there is very little in the *logoi* which is not integrally connected to both the *erga* which precede and those which follow. While the latter confirm the truth of the *logoi*, the former allow one to judge of the soundness of statements which a speaker may use as a basis for prediction. In other words, the *erga-logoi-erga* technique is omnipresent.

5. Finley, "The Unity of Thucydides' *History*," *Three Essays on Thucydides*, pp. 129-140, has used Thucydides' remarks on the magnitude of the war as an argument for unity: they are but "one part of that recurrent and interwoven complex of ideas around which the *History* is built. . ." (p. 132). In the above analysis we have not dealt with *every* prediction Nikias makes. Some cannot be judged bacause the Athenians did not follow his advice.

6. Note the terminology of Pylos-Sphakteria (τὰς τύχας, τὸ αἰσχρόν, σφήλαντες). See Chapter 4, pp. 80-81, where it is shown that this passage establishes a direct link between Pylos and Sicily.

the Athenian aims as based on emotion rather than reason, he proceeds to a concrete program. In brief, keep out of Sicily.

Nikias' speech is, of course, only one side of an *antilogia*. Alkibiades presents a counter *logos* immediately. Again this is one of those major debates which foreshadow a whole period. Which argument is κρείττων events themselves will ultimately decide as the war proceeds. Thus it is not unlike the discussion of strategy held at Rhegion soon after the departure of the expedition for Sicily. Of the three opposing views presented there later events showed that in Thucydides' view Lamachos' *gnome* was correct, for the *erga* corresponded precisely to his predictions. To repeat the comment of Chapter 6 (p. 98):

> the reader might very well miss this truth and find himself lost in a maze of "facts," had not the *logoi* clearly distinguished three conflicting viewpoints and thus given him clues to look for in his reading. He can now follow, knowing *before it happens* what may happen and thus be led inexorably to recognize truth when it actually does happen as predicted.

In the same way, as we have demonstrated, Nikias' predictions are also confirmed by the *erga*, proving his *logos* κρείττων. But this is later. In 415 the Athenians do not take his warnings any more seriously than they did those of the Spartan envoys 10 years earlier. The latter we called tragic warners. And this, it seems, is also Nikias' role, to predict correctly but be ignored.

But there is an even better parallel in the *History* than Lamachos or the Spartan envoys. Surely one thinks immediately of Archidamos' warnings to the Spartans, part of the great debate held at the first congress at Lakedaimon in 432 (1.79-85). The similarities between his and Nikias' role can hardly be accidental. Like Nikias, Archidamos aims to divert the Spartans from an all but inevitable course, in this case, the immediate declaration of war. The major part of his *logos* is also a realistic appraisal of the facts — a comparison of the resources and experience of the two great powers. Based on this thorough analysis he too makes a series of predictions from εἰκός. Once again the content of these predictions will not concern us primarily. It is sufficient to state that Archidamos, as Thucydides portrays him, anticipates Perikles in foreseeing the probable course of the war, in sum, the ineffectiveness of Spartan land-power against a state which controlled the sea (1.81 and 1.143.3-5). Thus Archidamos urges the Spartans *not* to underestimate the nature of Athens' power, her resources in ships and money, her naval experience, and her determination (1.80-81 and 83).[7] But Corinth prevails and the result is a long war ending in disgrace for the Peloponnese.[8] Though ignored, Archidamos' *logos* later proves correct to the smallest detail. Thus, different as are his particular predictions, Archidamos plays the same role vis-à-vis the Corinthians as Nikias does in opposing Alkibiades. Both anticipate the entire war and the failure of the enterprise against which they warn.

But the parallel does not stop there. Consider the following similarities between their respective *logoi*:

What especially worries Archidamos is the haste of the Spartan decision in dealing with matters of such tremendous importance (85.1). He also feels they are being hurried into such a decision by private interests. And yet, if war is begun, it is they who will have the largest share of the responsibility (82.5; 82.6; 83.3). Then, too, they must avoid a decision based not on reason but emotion. Out of inexperience most of them desire war (80.1). But they ought not to be elated by their hopes, either that the war will end quickly or that the enemy will make mistakes (81.6; 84.4). Thus, he makes a special appeal to men of his own generation, who share his experience and so should know better (80.1). Finally, what he advises is moderation and in place of hope foresight which is more dependable (80.2 and 84 *passim*).

P. 129 illustrates these parallels and points out verbal echoes where they occur.

---

7. See especially Perikles' first speech (1.140-144), a counter *logos* to the optimistic predictions of the Corinthians (1.120-124). Both in its assessment of their respective resources and its anticipation of the probable course of the war, it is identical to Archidamos' analysis. Cf., e.g., their views on the Spartans' lack of ships, experience, and money (1.80.4 — 141.3-4 and 142.6-9) and the futility of the land invasions against an imperial city (81.1 — 143.4-5). Athens' wealth of resources is confirmed by 2.13.2-9 and the advantage of experience by Phormion's exploits. (See Chapter 3.) See too Thucydides' own judgment on Perikles' policy in so far as it was carried out (2.65.5-7 and 13) and by implication Archidamos' predictions.

8. "Disgrace" is a constant theme. First predicted by Archidamos (1.82.5: αἴσχιον), referred to as impending by the Spartan envoys (4.20.2: πρὸ αἰσχροῦ τινός), commented on by Thucydides himself (5.28.2), it finally reappears in Nikias' *logos* (6.11.6: διὰ τὸ αἰσχρόν).

Archidamos (1.79-85)   Nikias (6.8-14)

The Decision

85.1: ἐν βραχεῖ μορίῳ ἡμέρας περὶ   9.1: βραχείᾳ βουλῇ περὶ μεγάλων
πολλῶν σωμάτων καὶ χρημάτων καὶ   πραγμάτων.
πόλεων καὶ δόξης.
                                                           12.1: καὶ χρήμασι καὶ τοῖς σώμασιν
                                                           ηὐξῆσθαι.

The Private Interests Involved

Sparta's allies   the Egestaians and Alkibiades

82.5: τοῖς τῶν ξυμμάχων ἐγκλήμασιν   9.1: ἀνδράσιν ἀλλοφύλοις πειθομένους.
ἐπειχθέντες.
                                                           11.7: ἀνδρῶν βαρβάρων.
83.3: μὴ τοῖς τῶν ξυμμάχων λόγοις
πρότερον ἐπαιρώμεθα.   12.2: ἰδίᾳ, τὰ ἴδια.

82.6: ἕνεκα τῶν ἰδίων.

The Emotions which Substitute for Careful Calculation

Desire and Hope   Desire and Cupidity

80.1: ἐπιθυμῆσαι ... ὅπερ ἂν οἱ πολλοὶ   13.1: ὅπερ ἂν αὐτοὶ πάθοιεν, δυσέρωτας
πάθοιεν.   εἶναι τῶν ἀπόντων and ἐπιθυμίᾳ.

81.6: μὴ γὰρ δὴ ἐκείνῃ γε τῇ ἐλπίδι   11.6: χρὴ δὲ μὴ πρὸς τὰς τύχας τῶν
ἐπαιρώμεθα (quick end to war).   ἐναντίων ἐπαίρεσθαι (basing selves on
                                                           enemy's misfortunes).
84.4: οὐκ ... δεῖ τὰς ἐλπίδας (basing
selves on enemy's possible errors).

Appeal to Older Men

80.1: τοὺς ἐν τῇ αὐτῇ ἡλικίᾳ.   13.1: τοῖς πρεσβυτέροις.

Advice: Moderation and Foresight

80.2: εἰ σωφρόνως τις αὐτὸν ἐκλογίζοιτο.   11.7: εἰ σωφρονοῦμεν.

84 passim: σωφροσύνη.   13.1: ἐπιθυμίᾳ μὲν ἐλάχιστα κατορθοῦνται,
                                                           προνοίᾳ δὲ πλεῖστα.
84.4: ὡς ἡμῶν αὐτῶν ἀσφαλῶς
προνοουμένων.

What we have then is a pattern, which by now should not surprise the reader. For in Chapters 6 and 7 we already demonstrated "pattern and recurrence in the very movement of events, patterns which man may recognize and use as a guide to the future" (p. 122). Noting an aura of déjà vu about the Syracusan response to invasion, we suggested that this impression arose because the Syracusan reaction was a repetition of the Athenian response to the Peloponnesian invasion (p. 100). Similarly, Gylippos had no difficulty predicting the total demoralization of the Athenians, since it was a repetition of Spartan demoralization at and after Sphakteria. *Both* leaders' predictions were the very ones that might be *assumed* of men who had experienced these earlier events. Thus, as Thucydides presents them, both men had learned enough from experience to see the similarities in a new situation (εἰκάζειν) and so be able to predict what would probably happen in the future (εἰκός).

Is this also true in Nikias' case? He must, of course, have learned something from the first war. But more is involved. It is not just Nikias' reaction and advice which approximate those of Archidamos, for as a tragic warner he is only part of a total situation which repeats itself. A parallel also exists in Thucydides' treatment of Demosthenes. We called him the type of *tolma alogistos* because his behaviour usually followed the same pattern, that of the daredevil. But we also recognized that his brilliant coup at Pylos was in no sense *alogistos* except in so far as *Thucydides described it in that way*. In other words, we began to suspect that the pattern to which Demosthenes' role in three different events conformed existed in the mind of the historian.

This we suggest is also true here. The pattern is the historian's own. Moreover, while patterns discussed in previous chapters were isolated, it now appears that such patterns are not discrete but belong to *successions* of events. To use the analogy of the plague, symptoms do not occur in isolation; they form a syndrome. If they did not occur together or in sequence, how else could the physician make his prognosis? Thus the two tragic warners together with the errors and dangers they recognize are *paradeigmata* of a common pattern.

Surely by now the parallels which exist between human responses, type-characters, and whole situations have become numerous enough to demand some explanation. And there is an explanation. Careful analysis reveals that it is not merely isolated patterns or even complex successions of events which recur, but a whole cycle of experience is repeated a second time. Between the two cycles the following parallels may be noted:

1) The cycle begins with a small independent nation seeking aid against a more powerful state (Kerkyra – Egesta).

2) From this arise *aitiai* which serve as a pretext for a war involving the great powers (Kerkyra – *Athens* – Corinth – *Sparta*: Egesta – *Athens* – Selinous – *Syracuse*).

3) But the real reason for the conflict is deep-rooted human emotions (fear – greed).

4) Inexperience and/or ignorance also serve to increase the enthusiasm of the masses for war.

5) Two sets of tragic warners attempt to prevent irremediable acts which are bound to have dire consequences: a) arguing on principle (Athenian envoys — Spartan envoys) and b) arguing on practicability (Archidamos — Nikias).

6) On one side (Sparta — Athens) a policy is adopted which is mistaken from the outset because it is based on inexperience or ignorance and so underestimates the enemy and the magnitude of the war. Private interests urge this course.

7) Ironically the warner becomes reluctant leader of the expedition.

8) Right at the beginning the invaders do not seize the *kairos* (Archidamos' delay — Alkibiades' *gnome*). As a result the defenders' attitude changes from fear to contempt.

9) Because their *gnome* is basically erroneous, the invaders underestimate the enemy and depend overmuch on *dynamis*. From this arise fatal errors.

10) *Tyche* acts against the side which began the war.

11) The final defeat is a *paralogos*.

12) There follow retreat, encirclement, and in the end, surrender.

13) By coincidence the side which began the war, technically the aggressors and thus morally responsible, also suffers defeat. One might construe this defeat as a punishment.

Pp. 145-48 serve to illustrate these parallels and for some will suffice without further comment. (See end of chapter.) Others, more complex patterns (e.g., the tragic warner and invasion and response), have already been discussed at length in this or earlier chapters: the reader will be referred to these discussions. Clearly it would be impossible to subject all 13 points to the same degree of study without reconsidering the entire *History*; therefore, we will content ourselves with analyzing two further parallels (5a and 6), both of which seem to require elaboration.

5a) The first set of tragic warners.

The speech of the Athenians to the Peloponnesians assembled at Lakedaimon in 432 (1.72-78) is part of the same debate to which Archidamos contributed and follows that of the Corinthians, who have heatedly urged war on the Spartans. In offering a counter *logos* their aim is twofold (1.72.1), first, to prevent a hasty decision and second, to enlighten the Lakedaimonians, (especially the young, who are ἄπειροι), about the nature of Athens' power (δύναμιν).

The description of Athens constitutes the major part of the speech (73.2-77) and is a vigorous defence of the Athenian empire. Its details will not concern us but rather its effect as a whole. By making it clear to the Spartans the kind of opponent (75.1: καὶ προθυμίας ἕνεκα τῆς τότε καὶ γνώμης ξυνέσεως)[9] and so the kind of struggle they must expect, it provides a valid reason for their *not* "taking the wrong course on matters of great importance by yielding too readily to the persuasions of your allies" (73.1).[10] Thus it adds substance to the warnings of the peroration (78), which do interest us directly.

The reasoning of the peroration follows the familiar pattern, statement, explanation, and application. It begins by repeating the original advice. Go slowly and do not be rushed into war by allies. Instead, consider in advance the "vast influence of accident in war" (τοῦ δὲ πολέμου τὸν παράλογον). The latter they explain by a *gnome*. "As it continues, it generally becomes an affair of chances (*tychai*), chances from which neither of us is exempt, and whose event we must risk in the dark." A second generalization follows, this time about human nature. Men usually begin at the wrong end: they act first and discuss later, having suffered disaster (κακοπαθοῦντες). To apply this to themselves, since neither is yet so misguided (ἐν οὐδεμιᾷ πω τοιαύτῃ ἁμαρτίᾳ ὄντες) and they are free to choose discussion, let them settle their differences by arbitration (δίκῃ) in accordance with their agreement. Otherwise, the Athenians swear to repel those who begin hostilities.

The above speech, though a warning, differs basically from that of Archidamos. The latter more or less accepts the fact that war is inevitable and, while urging the Spartans to negotiate, advises simultaneous preparation for war. What they need most is time (82.1 and 85.2). I.e., his main concern is the consequences of immediate war — its impracticability — and *not* the question of war itself. The Athenians, on the other hand, whatever one may think of their *apologia* or the validity of the Peloponnesian grievances, argue on one principle alone: it is not right for the

----

9. *Tolma* and *gnome*! ! !

10. Note too how it anticipates Archidamos. Both are concerned with the "complaints" (ἐγκλήμασι) of Sparta's allies and their persuasiveness. Cf. especially 73.1 and 78.1 with 83.3 and 85.1.

Spartans to begin war as long as arbitration is still possible. Technically this will make them the aggressors. Archidamos also recognizes this, for he states that "to proceed against one who offers arbitration as against a wrongdoer, law forbids" (85.2). So does Perikles (1.140.2). In 413 Thucydides attributes to the Spartans themselves an admission of guilt in beginning the first war. Their views at that time are identical with those held by Perikles in 432. Τὸ παρανόμημα was on their side because they refused "to listen to the Athenian offer of arbitration, in spite of the clause in the former treaty that where arbitration should be offered there should be no appeal to arms" (7.18.2). The Athenian envoys' speech is just such an offer. It is an argument from "justice" (δίκαιον) raising the question of moral responsibility. And the warnings it makes — like those of Archidamos — all prove true. Egged on by Sthenelaidas the Spartans reject εὐβουλία and do adopt a policy based on error (ἁμαρτία). Eventually the *paralogos* of war, the intervention of *tyche*, thwarts them. Made contrite by suffering, they are eager to come to terms.[11]

In other words, the Athenian envoys' speech anticipates the whole course of the war up to the Spartan embassy to Athens in 425.

The speech of the Spartan envoys at Athens in 425 (4.17-20) displays a number of formal similarities with that of the earlier envoys. Its main concern, for example, is to bring about careful counsel (17.3), advice which it also bolsters by a lengthy warning (17.4-18). They first offer an example of human behaviour to be avoided, i.e., a negative *paradeigma* concerning men "who meet with an extraordinary piece of good fortune, and are led on by hope to grasp continually at something further. . ." (17.4; cf. 1.78.3). In their second point, they cite the vast experience of both peoples, which should preclude their acting in this manner (17.5; cf. 1.78.4). They then use their own recent misfortune as a *paradeigma* upon which to base a warning about the nature of *tyche*, especially in war (18.1-4; cf. 1.78.1-2). Finally, to ignore this warning and not make peace, while their fortune lasts, is to invite disaster (18.5; cf. 1.78.3).

"Time and experience," it appears, have taught the Spartans the truth of the Athenian warnings made in 432 about the nature of *tyche*, and their present *logos* echoes these warnings. Sensible

11. They admit to "an error in judgment" (4.18.2: γνώμῃ σφαλέντες). See Chapter 4, pp. 77 ff.

men, they now concede, "think that war, so far from staying within the limit to which a combatant may wish to confine it, will run the course that its chances (*tychai*) prescribe. . ." (18.3). But just as much as the speech looks backward, it also looks forward. A major turning-point in the war has been reached; the end of one cycle of experience is drawing to a close. The Spartan role is to be reversed. It is now their turn to offer advice and be ignored. And it is correct advice, because its warnings and predictions will ultimately prove true. Chapter 4, p. 79, comments that "Thucydides later makes it clear that the envoys' warning was a forecast of how the Athenians actually would respond. . . ." This warning, as an anticipation of what follows, is correct in three major particulars: the mood (*pleonexia*) which unexpected good fortune brings; the ultimate betrayal of *tyche*, when, based on this mood, the Athenians overextend themselves in Sicily;[12] the disaster which results.

Finally, there is the following similarity between the two envoys' speeches. While Nikias' speech in 413 will concern the practicability of the expedition to Sicily, the Spartans raise the question of war itself. Theirs is an argument from "right" (δίκαιον) in two ways. In admitting to error and offering peace and alliance they absolve themselves of their original παρανόμημα in beginning hostilities in times of treaty and place the moral responsibility for continuing the war on the Athenians. Technically the latter now become the "wrongdoers."[13] But justice is also implied on another

12. See below, note 26.
13. See above p. 133 and p. 138 (13). Cf. Chapter 4, notes 25 and 26. Woodhead, *Thucydides on the Nature of Power*, p. 157, comments on the "extreme realism" of Thucydides, for whom "laws of power are involved which are completely neutral" and whose "attitude to power, like power itself in its nature, is neutral" (p. 9). (In general it seems to me that Woodhead does not distinguish sufficiently between power and its exercise, which can never be separated. The latter alone raises moral problems. Indeed, it was the changing nature of Athens' exercise of power and its disastrous results which primarily interested Thucydides.) He criticizes Cornford and Wassermann for building hypotheses on the plan of the *History*, implying "humane and moral factors" (p. 158) on Thucydides' part. Since Thucydides is nowhere explicit in his view of moral responsibility, it is certainly in order to study the structure of his work in an attempt to abstract what is implicit there. Very definite, in no wise morally neutral, concepts lie behind it, as Woodhead himself realizes. He points out, for example (p. 35), that a people "may or may not temper its rule with justice (δικαιοσύνη)" and later (p. 47) notes that *dynamis* had been misused, "exercised not with *sophrosyne* but with βία, force, and ὕβρις, arrogance." This is surely the crux of the matter. What the *History* records is a transformation on the part of the *demos* from *sophrosyne* to *pleonexia* (encouraged by Kleon at the time of Pylos-Sphakteria, but only reaching its full force with the Sicilian Expedition) and in the exercise of empire from *dikaiosyne* to *bia* (the

plane. There are "natural laws" too which men must respect.[14] Life is full of μεταβολαὶ ἐπ' ἀμφότερα (17.5). When one has had more than his share of "good luck," it is only "right" or indeed sensible to treat such "gains as precarious."

6) Γνώμης ἁμάρτημα.

Alkibiades' speech in reply to Nikias (6.16-18) does not answer the latter point by point. Rather it is a refutation of two of Nikias' claims. Challenged as to his youth and motives, Alkibiades proves his right to command by showing how his position and activities as an individual have been of benefit to Athens. And basing his statements on his own knowledge of the facts, he describes affairs in Sicily in such a way as to make the expedition seem most practicable.

characteristic of the *naukratores* in the Melian Dialogue). How this came about is clearly delineated in the *History* and no matter how inevitable Athens' ultimate ruin may appear, Thucydides never loses sight of man's role in the historical process, his choices and his responsibility. This is especially true where warnings to the contrary are issued: those who ignore such warnings must be held morally responsible for the ruin they bring on themselves and others. The problem arises, I believe, because Thucydides is attempting to answer questions raised by the Sophists which do not find a true resolution until Plato and Aristotle. These relate not so much to the abstraction, power, but to the nature of *dike* and the validity of *nomoi*, especially in their relationship to *physis*. It remains for Plato to evolve an ontology on which to base his ethics and politics. Thucydides can only grapple with the problem as essentially a human one, unrelated to a systematic ontology, against the background of earlier notions of a Herodotean kind — the morality cycle of *hybris*, *koros*, *ate*, *nemesis*, in which divine *phthonos* is instrumental in bringing about *metabole* and so restores equilibrium. In both Thucydides and Herodotus there is a kind of pattern or rhythm to catastrophe. The question Thucydides might have posed to himself is this: what happens to men or the *polis* which transgresses laws, both written and unwritten, and comes to depend on *physis*? Is there some resolution in *physis* itself, some natural order based on the principle of equilibrium? This is an ethical question concerning the validity of men's obligations both political and moral. Towards this question Thucydides is in no sense morally neutral, only less systematic than later philosophers. I would suggest very briefly these levels in the *History*. a) There is a change on Athens' part from *sophrosyne* and *dikaiosyne* to *pleonexia* and *bia*. b) In legal terms (what might be charged in an international court of law) Athens rejects *dike* by refusing offers of arbitration and invading the Peloponnese, thus committing the same *paranomema* as the Spartans in 431, when they invaded Attika. c) Having rejected *sophrosyne* and *dikaiosyne* and come to depend instead on mere *physis*, *pleonexia* and *bia*, i.e., disregarding the *nomoi*, both in individual and international relations, Athens transgresses natural law, thus courting disaster. Excess leads to *metabole*, since equilibrium must be restored. Where Athens transgressed, Thucydides makes obvious. She can thus be held to account. Her fault is no more neutral than that of Oidipous or Xerxes. Tragic as is the ruin of each, each must be held morally responsible for his own downfall.

14. Or so I interpret this almost "cosmic" principle.

Alkibiades' *apologia* will not concern us.[15] More germane at this point is the correctness of his evaluation of Sicily's power and the validity of his prognostications based on this evaluation.

As far as facts are concerned, Alkibiades' description of Sicily does not go unchallenged, for Nikias, who did not deal with this matter in his first speech, now hastens to correct his opponent. Based on his own knowledge of the facts, he presents a very different picture of affairs in Sicily. *Both* plead knowledge from ἀκοῇ, but clearly *both* cannot be correct. One *logos* must be κρείττων in its approximation of truth. In the *antilogiai* we have analyzed previously it was the *erga* which ultimately decided between two *logoi*. If our thesis is correct, this should also be the case here. P. 137, based on a study of these speeches in the light of the *erga* which follow, demonstrates very clearly that one and only one is correct. Nikias' *logos* is confirmed as truth. Alkibiades, it appears, is one of that majority of Athenians who are ἄπειροι about things Sicilian (6.1.1). Since he grossly underestimates his enemy, one is justified in suspecting that his prognosis will be quite unrealistic.

Alkibiades makes four predictions, all arguments from εἰκός: 1) It is improbable (οὐκ εἰκός) that such a "mob" will unite either in policy or in action. Rather they will "one by one come in as they get a fair offer, especially if they are torn by civil strife as we are told" (17.4). 2) The Athenians will have the help of many barbarians who will join them out of hatred for Syracuse (17.6). 3) The Peloponnesians at home will not offer any hindrance (17.6-8). 4) In the end they will either become masters of all Greece "through the accession of the Sicilian Hellenes, or in any case ruin the Syracusans . . ." (18.4).

In order to establish the validity of the above prognostications a detailed comparison with Nikias' *logos* is unnecessary. A simpler method is to refer directly to the *erga*. Naturally, the *erga* which follow, events in Sicily itself, will be of primary importance. But certain *erga* which precede must also be taken into consideration. For past *erga* exist as *paradeigmata* from which Alkibiades may or may not have learned, and in light of which, in any case, the

15. Nikias accused Alkibiades of being motivated by "private interests" (12.2). Thucydides' own judgment confirms this view, ". . . he hoped . . . personally (τὰ ἴδια) to gain in wealth and reputation by means of his success" (15.2). The word private then recurs throughout Alkibiades' *apologia* (16.2, ἰδιώτης; 16.3, τοῖς ἰδίοις τέλεσι; 16.6, τὰ ἴδια ἐπιβοώμενος).

Alkibiades – ἥττων λόγος	Nikias – κρείττων λόγος	erga as confirmation
17.6: ἐξ ὧν ἐγὼ ἀκοῇ αἰσθάνομαι.	20.2: ὡς ἐγὼ ἀκοῇ αἰσθάνομαι.	7.55.2: (Thucydides' own judgment)
Sicily not a great power (17.2: μεγάλην δύναμιν)	The cities of Sicily are both great (μεγάλας) and numerous	"These were the only cities that they had yet encountered, similar to their own in character (ὁμοιοτρόπους), under democracies like themselves, which had ships and horses, and were of considerable magnitude (μεγέθη). They had been unable to divide and bring them over by holding out the prospect of changes in their governments (μεταβολῆς), or to crush them by their great superiority in force (παρασκευῆς)...."
1) nature of cities (17.2) — "peopled by motley rabbles" — unstable (frequent μεταβολάς)	1) nature of cities (20.2) — not subject to one another — in no need of "change" (μεταβολῆς)	
2) resources (17.3) — "not provided with arms for their persons" — not regularly established on the land (τὰ ἐν τῇ χώρᾳ νομίμως κατασκευαῖς)	2) resources (20.3) — the very same as Athens' (παρεσκευασμέναι τοῖς πᾶσιν ὁμοιοτρόπως μάλιστα τῇ ἡμετέρᾳ δυνάμει) especially Selinous and Syracuse	e.g., importance of cavalry obvious from very beginning (6.63.3; 64.1; 70.3) 6.71.2: most of difficulties foreseen by Nikias appear at outset (first winter)
e.g., hoplites are not what they boast (17.5)	e.g., hoplites (20.4) archers darters ships manpower	
no mention of money cavalry food supply	money cavalry (cf. 21.1) food supply	lack of money cavalry food allies must delay until spring

reader can assess his predictions.

1) Alkibiades does not know − or, perhaps, ignores − history. Otherwise, he might remember that in 424 that "mob" did unite at the urging of Hermokrates, whose speech to the assembled Sicilians (4.59-64) rang with the words ἡ Σικελία πᾶσα and κοινῇ ("Sicilian unity").[16] The result was that the Athenians left Sicily for ten years. Thus, the example of the past would seem to indicate that Alkibiades is mistaken about Sicily's lack of patriotism and her inability to unite against a common enemy. And later events do prove him quite wrong. Right from the outset the reluctance of the Greek cities of Sicily to join Athens aggravated the constant problem she faced in acquiring sufficient cavalry and food (6.50 ff. and esp. 71.2). Kamarina is typical. For a time she was neutral (6.88.1-2). When she finally did throw her active support behind Syracuse, the end was near. For then not only Kamarina but "almost the whole of Sicily . . . actively joined Syracuse against the Athenians" (7.33.1-2). As Nikias predicted, only Naxos and Katana stood beside Athens to the end (6.20.3; cf. 7.57.11).

2) Alkibiades greatly overestimates the barbarians. While it is true that the Egestaians and most of the Sikels remain faithful to Athens, they never compensate for the loss of those cities they were merely to augment.

3) Alkibiades explains his casual attitude to the Peloponnesians as follows: "Our fathers with these very adversaries, which it is said we shall now leave behind us when we sail, and the Mede as their enemy as well, were able to win the empire, depending solely on their superiority at sea." This is a misuse of the past, for again the *erga* (the *Pentekontaetia*) refute him. It was the *united* Greeks who defeated the Persians. Only then did Athens assume leadership of what later became the Delian League, with Sparta's acquiescence. Pausanias had taught her a lesson (1.95.7). In actual fact, the apathy of the League members themselves was what permitted Athens to consolidate her *arche* (1.96-99). According to Thucydides the Spartans put up little opposition to this until "their own confederacy became the object of its encroachments" (1.118.2). The past then does not conform to Alkiabiades' view of it.[17] There is no reason to be oversanguine. Later it is just these

16. For ἡ Σικελία πᾶσα see 59.1, 60.1, and 61.2 and for κοινῇ 61.2, 61.3, 61.6 (κοινῶς). Cf. his general remarks at 64.3.

17. Cf. K. J. Dover in Gomme 4, pp. 252-253: "He ignores the fact that the Delian

forces from Greece which turn the tide of the war, e.g., the
Corinthian Gongylos, who arrives just in time to prevent the
Syracusans from capitulating (7.2.1-2) and the Spartan Gylippos,
who ends Athens' hopes of investing the city (7.6.4). In addition
to leadership, manpower, and ships the Syracusan war-effort is
also aided by the fortification of Dekeleia, which proved to be
"one of the principal causes of their (the Athenians') ruin"
(7.27.3). Where was Alkibiades' second navy then?

4) In the end neither aim is realized. The overconfident
ναυκράτορες are forced to flee on foot. (The use of the word
ναυκράτορες by Alkibiades evokes memories of the Melian
Dialogue where it appeared for the first time, symbolic, as it were,
of Athens' new arrogance, especially towards islanders. See 5.97
and 109.)[18]

Thus the logos of Alkibiades, "by far the warmest advocate of
the expedition" (15.2), is not only factually incorrect, a product
of "hearsay," but it ignores or misrepresents the lessons of the
past. Small wonder then that his inflated expectations are never
fulfilled: they are nothing more than "wishful thinking." Based on
the latter (ἐπιθυμία),[19] Athens' policy is from the outset one of
γνώμης ἁμάρτημα.[20]

League was created, at a time when Athens and Sparta were allies, on the initiative of the
Ionian states, and that essential steps towards the conversion of the League into an
empire (i.98.4 − 99) had been taken while the Spartan alliance was still in force."
Without going into the vexed problem of chronology but accepting Thucydides' general
order of events, I suggest that by the end of the Pentekontaetia it is becoming
increasingly clear that Athens cannot successfully cope with invasions at home while
engaged in expeditions abroad, whether of conquest or against allies in revolt. One thinks
of her defeat by the Lakedaimonians at Tanagra (1.108.1) while her forces are engaged
in Egypt. The latter expedition itself ends in disaster (109-110). Perhaps as a result of it,
she makes a five-year truce with the Peloponnesians (112). In any case, she is then free
to sail against Cyprus with stunning success. Similarly, after the Thirty Years' Peace
(made at some loss to herself in Greece proper) she is able to deal with the Samian revolt
without fear of the Peloponnesians' interfering as they did when Euboia and Megara
revolted (114 ff.).

18. On the other hand, Nikias' major prognostications are correct. E.g., Naxos and
Katana were the only cities which seriously joined Athens (20.3). The Egestaian money
was "readier . . . in talk than in any other way" (22.3). And Athens' major error was
failing "to become master of the country the first day" (23.2). The latter in anticipating
Lamachos' strategy of immediate attack, a strategy which Nikias himself will later
oppose, is but one of a series of contradictions in Thucydides' characterization of Nikias.

19. Alkibiades personifies this ἐπιθυμία. Note the prevalence of this word in
Thucydides' description of his motives in 6.15 (15.2, ἐπιθυμῶν; 15.3, ταῖς ἐπιθυμίαις;
15.4, ἐπιθυμοῦντι).

20. The words are from 2.65.11. I agree with Westlake's interpretation of οὐ
τοσοῦτον . . . ὅσον in "Thucydides 2.65.11," CQ 8, 1958, pp. 102-110. It must be clear

Earlier we stated that Alkibiades plays the same role vis-à-vis Nikias as Corinth does in opposing Archidamos. As we have shown, both warners are correct in their prognostications about the course of the war and the probable failure of the enterprise. How realistic then is the counter *logos* which Corinth makes at the Second Congress at Lakedaimon (1.120-124)? By this time a declaration of war has already been decided upon (1.88). Corinth's self-appointed task is to refute Archidamos' predictions about the difficulties they will probably face, by making war with Athens seem eminently practicable. From the first the Corinthians are full of optimism. "We have many reasons to expect success. . . ." Briefly they are, superior numbers, more military experience, a source of money (their own resources and loans from Olympia and Delphi) to fit out a navy and buy off Athens' foreign sailors (121.3), natural courage which will be more than a match for Athenian *episteme*, once reinforced by practice in naval matters (121.4), and tactics like fomenting revolt among their allies to deprive them of their revenues and establishing fortified positions in their country (122.1).

There is little need to dwell on the above strategy; we have already discussed it in a general way in earlier chapters. As far as the Archidamian war itself is concerned, Thucydides does not mention any attempt to carry out three of the more significant proposals, loans from Olympia and Delphi, the buying off of Athens' sailors, or ἐπιτειχισμός. But their main error is under-estimation of the enemy. This is surely the essence of Perikles' counter *logos* which refutes their arguments point by point (1.140-144). To take only one argument, Chapter 3, pp. 56 ff. showed how the two speeches express opposing viewpoints on the relationship between natural qualities and acquired "skill." It is only finally Phormion's exploits which settle this debate by demonstrating "the importance of practice and experience in the acquisition of 'science' or 'skill,'" which is, in turn, "one of the

from the above that it is quite wrong to state as Woodhead does in *Thucydides on the Nature of Power*, p. 97: "Alcibiades' γνώμη should have succeeded, and the people ought to have believed; but, as we have seen, they did not." Mistaken as he was from the outset, it is difficult to see how Alcibiades could be called κράτιστος γνώμων and ἄριστος εἰκαστής (Woodhead, p. 91) where the Sicilian expedition is concerned. (I leave aside Alcibiades' later role in Book 8.) If, as Woodhead states (*ibid.*), the "ability to predict the future responses of men and likely course of events is the hallmark of the great leader," surely Alcibiades is no great leader. Unfortunately neither is Nikias and so a policy distinguished by its γνώμης ἁμάρτημα is adopted right at the beginning.

major ingredients of *tolma*, daring and initiative" (p. 58). His victories also prove what kind of military power, based on what qualities of character, actually does lead to success in the war. In fine, the Corinthians not only underestimate Athenian resources, experience, and determination, but are totally unrealistic in expecting to surpass them overnight in advantages which have taken years to acquire.

In actual fact it is the Spartans, (or the Spartan kind of warfare), who dictate the main tactic, annual invasion. And this is an act of futility, as Perikles foresaw; the Athenians never capitulate because of their land. As to aiding Athens' allies in revolt, one need only consider the case of Mytilene (3.26-33). Under Alkidas, "aid" to Mytilene is a fiasco of delay, blunders, and finally flight from the Athenian navy. The Lakedaimonians could never hope to challenge Athens in the Aegean. Far from defeating her at sea, they give up all such aspirations in 425 by handing over their entire navy as a pledge for their men on Sphakteria. Kleon is quick to find a pretext for retaining their ships (4.23.1). In the end, having suffered one *paralogos* after another, their famous "courage" gives way to demoralization and *atolmia* (4.55.4).[21]

Such in its outline is the cycle of human experience in the *History*. Having detected and described the patterns beneath the manifold and somewhat confusing variety of men's *logoi* and *erga*, Thucydides expresses the modest hope that his work be of use to "those inquirers who desire an exact knowledge of the past as an aid to the interpretation of the future, which in the course of human things must resemble if it does not reflect it. . ." (1.22.4).

"In the course of human things" perhaps best captures the spirit of κατὰ τὸ ἀνθρώπινον. It is not merely synonymous with human nature but is the totality of human experience.[22] It is the

21. Interestingly enough, the Corinthians were correct as far as the *entire* war was concerned. But time was necessary, as Archidamos saw, and experience as a counterweight to that lack of initiative which plagued the Spartans — experience to teach them the kind of enemy they were confronting. Though without enthusiastic support from home, Brasidas later demonstrated the effectiveness of breaking important allies from Athens. And in the Sicilian war foreign seamen *did* desert Athens for higher pay (7.13.2) and ἐπιτειχισμός *was* most effective (7.27-28). In the end it *was* necessary to defeat Athens by sea and deprive her of imperial revenues. But the money which effected this was Persian (2.65.12 and 8.58.5-6).

22. Cf. Stahl, p. 33, n. 100, "Ich halte die traditionelle Gleichsetzung von τὸ 'ανθρώπινον (I 22, 4) mit ἡ 'ανθρωπεία φύσις . . . für voreilig." He defines it as "das, was den Menschen angeht" or "die Bedingungen menschlichen Existenz" (p. 33).

cycle which first the Spartans, then the Athenians lived through. For though they differ in form (e.g., the specific *aitiai*, the magnitude of the disaster, etc.), they share the following essential features. Human nature (ἀνθρωπεία φύσις) is such that the mass of mankind is at the mercy of passions like fear, desire, and hope. While these emotions can often be kept under control for years, sometimes a crisis occurs in which deep-rooted feelings do come to the surface. Appealed to by the advocates of a certain course (πειθώ) such feelings are so intensified as to overpower all capacity for rational calculation. If in addition the majority are ignorant or inexperienced (ἀπειρία), or perhaps just young, they readily give in to their emotions in spite of the warnings of men who belong to an older generation or who at least have had enough experience to foresee the consequences.[23] They embark on a course full of dangers – war, expansion, or even revolt. The latter once begun seem to have laws of their own, a kind of immanent necessity (ἀνάγκη) which defies human control. Having entered the realm of the "unknown," men are easily thwarted in their plans, since they are now at the mercy of chance. (I.e., φύσις by submitting to φόβος, ἐπιθυμία, or ἔλπις because of πειθώ and ἀπειρία loses human control to ἀνάγκη and τύχη.)

The above process need not lead to total disaster; it can also have lesser consequences. Consider, for instance, what Thucydides writes about Athens' subjects in Thrace after the fall of Amphipolis. The news of its capture and Brasidas' "gentleness" induced them to translate a long-standing desire for independence into action. They "felt most strongly encouraged to change their condition, and sent secret messages to him, begging him to come on to them; each wishing to be the first to revolt" (4.108.3). Other factors such as the defeat suffered by Athens in Boeotia and incorrect information about Brasidas' success at Nisaia also added to their confidence and belief that no force would be sent against them. But in this they were wrong, for they underestimated the power of Athens. Thucydides is critical: ". . . their judgment was based more upon blind wishing (βουλήσει) than upon any sound prevision (προνοία); for it is the habit of mankind to entrust to careless hope what they long for, and to use sovereign reason to thrust aside what they do not fancy" (108.4: ἐλπίδι ἀπερισκέπτῳ as opposed to λογισμῷ αὐτοκράτορι).

23. Stahl, p. 73, also notes this opposition of young and old, experienced and inexperienced.

Thucydides describes the same process a little differently elsewhere. Kleon says of the Mytileneans (3.39.3-4):

the fate of those of their neighbours who had already rebelled (αἰ τῶν πέλας ξυμφοραί) and had been subdued was no lesson to them (παράδειγμα); their own prosperity (εὐδαιμονία) could not dissuade them from affronting danger; but blindly confident in the future, and full of hopes beyond their power though not beyond their ambition (μακρότερα μὲν τῆς δυνάμεως, ἐλάσσω δὲ τῆς βουλήσεως), they declared war and made their decision to prefer might to right, their attack being determined not by provocation but by the moment which seemed propitious. The truth is that great good fortune coming suddenly and unexpectedly tends to make a people insolent; in most cases it is safer for mankind to have success in reason than out of reason; and it is easier for them, one may say, to stave off adversity than to preserve prosperity (εὐδαιμονίαν διασῴζονται).

Ironic in the mouth of Kleon, because this is precisely what Athens herself will do, led on by Kleon. In miniature it expresses the tragedy of life as it appeared to Thucydides. Why are men unable to draw the lesson of others' misfortunes? Why do they not preserve their prosperity rather than cast it aside for unknown dangers, especially war? This being his concern, his praise of the Chians is most appropriate: "Indeed, after the Lacedaemonians, the Chians are the only people that I have known who knew how to be wise in prosperity (ηὐδαιμόνησάν τε ἁμα καὶ ἐσωφρόνησαν), and who ordered their city the more securely the greater it grew" (8.24.4).[24] Perikles himself expresses a somewhat similar view (2.61.1): "For those of course who have a free choice in the matter and whose fortunes are not at stake, war is the greatest of follies." To him the Archidamian war was a defence of the status quo; the Spartans were the aggressors.

But in 415 the situation is reversed. Τὸ ἀνθρώπινον is briefly this. Like the Mytileneans the Athenians have a paradeigma, Sparta's misfortune. They also have prosperity, lately restored after pestilence and war (6.12.1). Yet neither serves as a deterrent.

---

24. Yet even these two sober peoples made the mistake of underestimating Athens' power. Far too much concern has been registered over this passage. It is not a political judgment. Thucydides admired any people or system — including Athenian democracy — in so far as it kept in check those human passions which could be ultimately destructive.

Emotion prevails over reason and they vote for war. In this decision Alkibiades plays a triple role. As the type of ἐπιθυμία he symbolizes their major passions, ἔρως and ἔλπις. Along with the Egestaians he also represents πειθώ. And finally, sharing as he does in the general ἀπειρία, he increases their ardour with misinformation.

In Chapter 4 we predicted that "if the Athenians will not learn from example, 'time and experience' will teach them *what the Spartans now know*" (p. 82). Because he saw the voice of experience twice ignored, does this mean that Thucydides was totally pessimistic? *Must* every generation learn through suffering? If so, what is the purpose of the *History*? As a sequence of *paradeigmata* with a unity and coherent theme, it seems to assume that men *can* learn from the example of others.

Chapter 9 will attempt to answer this question, while offering further evidence of Thucydides' cyclic view of history.

1) The Request for Aid

Kerkyra	Egesta
1.31.2 and 35.1: an independent power outside both confederacies	6.2.3: an independent Sicilian power descended from the Trojans
Ibid.: asks alliance and support against Corinth	6.6.2: allies of Athens since 427
	Ibid.: asks support against Selinous

πειθώ = fear and expediency

1.33.3 and 36.1: raise spectre of war with Lakedaimon	Ibid.: raise spectre of Dorian Syracuse aiding Peloponnesians against Athens
1.36.2-3: offer convenient base and navy	Ibid.: offer money for war

2) Aitiai Lead to Confrontation

1.55.2: "This was the first cause of the war (αἰτία δὲ αὕτη πρώτη) that Corinth had against the Athenians, viz. that they had fought against them with the Corcyraeans in time of treaty."	6.6.1: The Athenians had "the specious design (εὐπρεπῶς βουλόμενοι) of succouring their kindred and other allies in the island"
1.56-66: fear and suspicion, the outcome of the above hostility, lead to the revolt of Poteidaia, the second aitia	6.6.2: first aitia — Syracuse was aiding her ally Selinous against Egesta
1.67-88: appealed to by her allies, especially Corinth, Lakedaimon becomes involved and pledges to declare war on Athens	Ibid.: second aitia — Syracuse had driven out the Leontinoi
	6.8.2: Athens pledges aid in these matters, thus involving herself in a confrontation with Syracuse (cf. 6.18.4)

3) The Real Motives

φόβος	τῶν πλεόνων ἐπιθυμία
1.23.6: (Thucydides' own judgment) "The real cause (τὴν μὲν γὰρ ἀληθεστάτην πρόφασιν) I consider to be the one that was formerly most kept out of sight. The growth of the power of Athens, and the alarm (φόβον) that this inspired in Lacedaemon, made war inevitable."	6.6.1: (Thucydides' own judgment) The Athenians were "ambitious in real truth (τῇ ἀληθεστάτῃ προφάσει) of conquering the whole (island). . . ." (cf. 6.1.1)
as expressed in the logoi	as expressed in the logoi
1.33.3: (the Kerkyraians) τοὺς Λακεδαιμονίους φόβῳ τῷ ὑμετέρῳ πολεμησείοντας	6.8.4: (Nikias' thoughts) προφάσει βραχείᾳ καὶ εὐπρεπεῖ τῆς Σικελίας ἁπάσης, μεγάλου ἔργου, ἐφίεσθαι
1.86.5: (Sthenelaidas)	6.13.1: Nikias warns against those who are δυσέρωτας τῶν ἀπόντων and motivated by ἐπιθυμίᾳ
	and confirmed by Thucydides

and confirmed by Thucydides

1.88: φοβούμενοι τοὺς Ἀθηναίους μὴ ἐπὶ μεῖξου δυνηθῶσιν

6.24 passim: note especially ἔρως ἐνέπεσε and τὴν ἄγαν τῶν πλεόνων ἐπιθυμίαν as descriptive of Athenian feelings

4) Ἀπειρία

Sparta	Athens
1.72.1: Athenian envoys aim "to enlighten the ignorance of the young" (ἄπειροι) about the power of Athens	6.1.1: most of the Athenians are ignorant of the size of Sicily and the number of its inhabitants (ἄπειροι οἱ πολλοί)
1.80.1: Archidamos contrasts his own experience (ἔμπειρος) in war with the inexperience (ἀπειρία) of the majority, presumably the young (cf. 2.11.1)	6.16-18: Alkibiades' logos reveals this ignorance
2.8.1: both sides are full of young men (νεότης) whose inexperience (ὑπὸ ἀπειρίας) makes them eager to take up arms	

5) The Tragic Warners

a) τὸ δίκαιον

1.72-78: Athenian envoys

4.17-20: Spartan envoys (see discussion above)

b) τὸ ξύμφορον

1.79-85: Archidamos

6.8-14: Nikias (see p. 129)

6) Γνώμης Ἁμάρτημα

1.120-124: Corinth's logos

6.16-18: Alkibiades' logos (see discussion above)

7) The Warner Becomes Leader

Archidamos

Nikias

8) Ὁ Καιρός

Archidamos' delay (2.18-20)

Alkibiades' gnome — delay (6.48)

2.18.4: The Athenians have time to carry in their property

2.21.1-3: Being psychologically unprepared the Athenians respond with emotion — shock and indignation — at seeing the unexpected before their very eyes (ἐν τῷ ἐμφανεῖ)

6.11.5: their fear later turns to contempt (καταφρονήσαντες)

6.49: Lamachos' gnome — attack at once because first sight most terrifying (τῇ τε ὄψει) — otherwise men become indifferent — also they might surprise Syracusans in the field

gnome rejected but predictions confirmed in erga

6.63.2: fear turns to contempt (κατεφρόνησαν)

(for full discussion see Chapter 6, pp. 100 ff.)

9) Fatal Errors — Human Responsibility[25]

4.5.1: The Spartans make light of Demosthenes' occupation of Pylos, thinking it would be easy to take the place any time (cf. 4.8.4)

4.8.2: No one intercepts Demosthenes' two ships going to Zakynthos for aid

4.13.4: The Lakedaimonians omit to close the inlets as they had intended

Result: a major turning-point in war

6.104.3: Nikias takes no precautions against Gylippos, despising the scanty number of his ships

7.2.1-2: No one intercepts Gongylos or Gylippos (cf. 7.42.3)

Result: from then on the tide turns against the Athenians (7.2.4 and 7.6.4)

10) Tyche — That Which Happens beyond Human Calculation
(1.140.1: ὅσα ἂν παρὰ λόγον ξυμβῇ)

2.84.3: The wind aids Phormion by throwing the Peloponnesians into confusion (cf. 85.2: a paralogos)

2.91.3: A merchantman which happened to be lying at anchor gives the Athenians an opportunity to turn near defeat into victory (91.4: a paralogos)

(see Chapter 4 for numerous references to tyche both in the erga describing Demosthenes' adventures and in the speech of the envoys)

4.55.3: Lakedaimonians totally demoralized by "their late numerous reverses of fortune, coming close upon one another without any reason" (τὰ τῆς τύχης πολλὰ καὶ ἐν ὀλίγῳ ξυμβάντα παρὰ λόγον)

6.61: Public agitation over the mutilation of the Hermai and the affair of the Mysteries combined with the advance of a force of Lakedaimonians to the Isthmus (61.2: ἔτυχε κατὰ τὸν καιρὸν τοῦτον) and a suspected plot of Alkibiades' xenoi at Argos results in the latter's recall and flight

7.2.1: Gongylos arrives at the very moment Syracusans were about to consider ending the war

7.2.4: Gylippos arrives just as the Athenian wall is almost complete (ἔτυχε δὲ κατὰ τοῦτο τοῦ καιροῦ ἐλθών)

7.50.4: An eclipse of the moon (ἐτύγχανε γὰρ πασσέληνος οὖσα) keeps the Athenians from leaving Sicily[26]

11) The Paralogos

4.33-37: The Spartans, unable to use their skill (33.2: τῇ σφετέρᾳ ἐμπειρίᾳ), are defeated on their own element

4.55.3: (Thucydides' own judgment) Spartan defeats a paralogos

7.55.1-2: ὁ παράλογος αὐτοῖς μέγας ἦν — defeated on own element where least expected

6.62.1-4: Compelled by circumstance the Athenians can make no use of their special

---

25. Obviously, these are not all the errors committed, but they are very significant ones.

26. This is, of course, an oversimplification. It is not so much a question of strokes of luck acting against the Athenians as no happy coincidences such as Demosthenes had enjoyed at Pylos. Tempted by the latter to overextend themselves and finally with virtually nothing but tyche and elpis left to depend upon (Nikias' last two speeches, 7.61 and 7.77) they are truly betrayed by tyche as Gylippos foresaw (7.68.1: τύχην ἀνδρῶν ἑαυτὴν παραδεδωκυῖαν).

skill (τὸ τῆς ἐπιστήμης) and so are again
defeated on their own element

7.75.7: (Thucydides' own judgment)
Athenian defeat a complete reversal

12) The End — Retreat and Encirclement

7.71.7: "They now suffered very nearly what they had inflicted at
Pylos; as then the Lacedaemonians with the loss of their fleet lost
also the men who had crossed over to the island, so now the
Athenians had no hope of escaping by land, without the help of
some extraordinary accident."

4.34.2-3: ἔκπληξις afflicts Spartans —
their situation hopeless (οὐκ ἔχοντες
ἐλπίδα καθ' ὅτι χρὴ ἀμυνομένους
σωθῆναι)

7.71.7: ἔκπληξις afflicts Athenians —
their situation is hopeless (τότε τοῖς
Ἀθηναίοις ἀνέλπιστον ἦν τὲ κατὰ γῆν
σωθήσεσθαι)

4.35.1: Retire to end of island

7.73.1: Decide to retreat by land

4.36.3: Demosthenes' gnome — to
surround and attack on all sides with
missiles (32.3: πανταχόθεν κεκυκλωμένοις
. . . ἀμφίβολοι γίγνωνται τῷ πλήθει) again
defeats them. They are completely
encircled (βαλλόμενοί τε ἀμφοτέρωθεν
ἤδη)

7.79.5: Strategy of the enemy is to surround and attack on all sides with missiles
(προσέβαλλόν τε πανταχῇ αὐτοῖς κύκλῳ —
cf. 81.4)

7.83.3: Nikias suffers the same
(περιστάντες πανταχόθεν ἔβαλλον)

4.37: the κήρυγμα

7.82.1: the κήρυγμα

13) Moral Responsibility

7.18.3: "But when, besides the ravages from Pylos, which went on
without any intermission, the thirty Athenian ships came out from
Argos and wasted part of Epidaurus, Prasiae, and other places; when
upon every dispute that arose as to the interpretation of any
doubtful point in the treaty, their own offers of arbitration were
always rejected by the Athenians, the Lacedaemonians at length
decided that Athens had now committed the very same offence as
they had before done (τὸ παρανόμημα), and had become the guilty
party. . . ."

Sparta	Athens
(cf. logoi — 1.78.4: The Athenian envoys; 1.85.2: Archidamos; 1.140.2: Perikles and full discussion above)	(cf. erga 6.105.1-2: Athens breaks treaty by aiding Argos, thus furnishing εὐπροφάσιστον μᾶλλον τὴν αἰτίαν)

For the Sicilian expedition itself see 3)
above and real motive — conquest

cf. Thucydides' own judgment (7.75.7):
"They had come to enslave others, and
were departing in fear of being enslaved
themselves. . . ."

Chapter 9
Ἄριστος Εἰκαστής:
Hermokrates' Counsels (Thuc. 6.33-34 and 72)

Late in the fall of 415 the Athenians land at Syracuse, where they are victorious in their first encounter with the Syracusans. In spite of this success, however, they experience a number of hardships — lack of cavalry, money, and food supplies as well as uncertainty about support from the cities of Sicily. As a result they decide that it is not possible for the moment to prosecute the war, but instead retire to Naxos and Katana for the winter. The defeated Syracusans make use of this unexpected respite to take counsel in an assembly at which their leader Hermokrates comes forward to address them. Thucydides describes him as "a man who with a general ability of the first order (ἐς τἆλλα ξύνεσιν) had given proofs of military capacity and brilliant courage (ἐμπειρία and ἀνδρεία) in the war . . ." (6.72.2). In his speech he offers advice and encouragement. Since, however, Hermokrates' *logos* is dependent on the *erga* which precede, some consideration must first be given to the defeat itself.

Just why *were* the Syracusans defeated? Thucydides mentions that they were unprepared. For some reason they did not expect an immediate engagement (69.1). This is repeated a few lines later where Thucydides explains that "they had not supposed that the Athenians would begin the attack. . . ." They are thus compelled to fight at short notice. Though clearly at a disadvantage from the outset, having forfeited the initiative, they nevertheless take up arms and hasten to meet the enemy. The factual account of the battle itself is extremely brief (70.1):

The armies now came to close quarters, and for a long while

fought without either giving ground. Meanwhile there occurred some claps of thunder with lightning and heavy rain, which did not fail to add to the fears of the party fighting for the first time, and very little acquainted with war; while to their more experienced adversaries these phenomena appeared to be produced by the time of year, and much more alarm was felt at the continued resistance of the enemy.

In the end, however, the Syracusans flee to the protection of their numerous cavalry, who prevent the Athenians from pursuing any significant distance.

In brief then the situation is as follows. Though taken unawares the Syracusans do not hesitate to confront the Athenians but fight tenaciously until an unhappy accident — a thunderstorm — occurs. Lacking experience, they react with fear and in the end flee. I.e., they are defeated by their own inexperience, after evincing both courage and vigour in resisting the Athenians. Only the most obtuse reader could fail to grasp this as the essential point of the *erga*, since Thucydides has directed him to this conclusion by foreshadowing it not just once but twice in the preceding chapters. First Nikias' *logos*, a brief παρακέλευσις addressed to his troops, anticipates the *erga* by describing the enemy's basic weakness. He predicts that they "will not stand against us, their skill not being at all commensurate with their rashness" (68.2: διὰ τὸ τὴν ἐπιστήμην τῆς τόλμης ἥσσω ἔχειν). Yet even this prediction, the usual reasoning after the fact, does not suffice. Apparently Thucydides was so concerned that this point not be lost on the reader that he added his own judgment, an elaboration of Nikias' view (69.1):

> Want of zeal or daring (προθυμία, τόλμη) was certainly not the fault of the Syracusans, either in this or the other battles, but although not inferior in courage (ἀνδρεία), so far as their military science might carry them (ἐπιστήμη), when this failed them they were compelled to give up their resolution also (βούλησιν).

This of course is just what the *erga* confirm: though the Syracusans have natural courage in abundance, they lack skill. Something as ordinary as a thunderstorm, because they have never experienced it before, defeats them, showing that native courage is alone insufficient. Success depends on a combination of courage and the skill that comes from experience.

Of what is all this reminiscent? Once again those events to which we have referred so often, Phormion's exploits against the Peloponnesians in 429. So closely are the two situations modelled on each other as to convince even the most sceptical that Thucydides saw life in patterns and, in writing, imposed such patterns on events. For the experience of the Syracusans duplicates that of the Peloponnesians in the Gulf of Patrai to the smallest detail. Consider the following similarities.

a) The Peloponnesians did not expect to fight at sea and so were unprepared, with ships "more like transports for carrying soldiers" (2.83.3; cf. 6.69.1: ἀπροσδόκητοι).

b) They did not imagine the Athenians would dare to engage them (ibid.: οὐκ ἂν οἰόμενοι; cf. 6.69.1: οὐκ ἂν οἰόμενοι).

c) They were, however, compelled to fight in mid passage, (ibid.: ἀναγκάζονται and 83.1: ἠναγκάσθησαν; cf. 6.69.1: ἀναγκαζόμενοι) thus forfeiting the initiative to the enemy.

d) It was their first attempt at sea (2.85.2: πρῶτον ναυμαχίας πειρασαμένοις; cf. 6.70.1: τοῖς μὲν πρῶτον μαχομένοις).[1]

e) An unexpected difficulty − choppy waters, the result of a sudden wind − threw them into confusion (2.84.3; cf. the storm, 6.70.1).

f) This confusion led to total disorder and in the end flight (2.84.3; cf. 6.70.1-2: inexperience, fear, and flight).

g) The conclusion reached in Chapter 3, pp. 45 ff. was that a lack of skill, the result of inexperience, caused the defeat (cf. above).

Like their earlier counterparts, the Syracusans also have a respite, an opportunity to assess their defeat. Will they make a realistic appraisal of what happened and learn from their errors?

---

1. Once again Thucydides "overdoes it a little." (Cf. Chapter 3, n. 10.) It is no more possible to believe that the Syracusans were "fighting for the first time, and very little acquainted with war" than that Patrai was the Corinthians' first attempt at sea. (See E. A. Freeman, A History of Sicily, Vol. 2, Oxford, 1891, passim, for a record of the major confrontations between Syracuse and the Carthaginians and Etruscans − admittedly naval − and following that her uneasy peace with the Sikels. Even from Thucydides' own work, e.g., 4.25.12, one has the impression that the Greeks in Sicily were constantly at war with one another.) The exaggeration of ἀπειρία in both peoples is part of the pattern and neatly underscores one difference between them: the Syracusans succeeded where the Peloponnesians did not in eventually combining natural qualities with experience and leadership to defeat the Athenians.

Or will they make the same mistake as the Peloponnesians? Remember that the latter considered inexperience the least important reason for their defeat. Instead they attributed it to lack of preparation and bad luck (2.87.2: τὰ ἀπὸ τῆς τύχης). Their main concern was courage; as long as the men had not shown cowardice, they believed a second encounter held no dangers.

It is against this background that we will now consider Hermokrates' *logos*. It has two main parts. First, it looks back to the *erga* which precede and attempts to offer an explanation for their defeat and secondly, it makes definite proposals for improvement, predicting success if they are adopted.

To what does Hermokrates attribute their defeat? Lack of discipline (ἀταξίαν). But he is optimistic because "they had not been beaten by so much as might have been expected, especially as they were, one might say, novices in the art of war, an army of artisans opposed to the most practised (ἐμπειρίᾳ) soldiers in Hellas" (72.3). In other words, they were quite inexperienced, especially in contrast to the enemy. There were also too many generals, (15 in all), giving too many commands and too little order. (The latter, of course, are the natural results of inexperience.)

Hermokrates suggests the following improvements. First, they must provide better leadership by electing just a few skilful generals (ἔμπειροι) with full powers. In addition, they must begin a rigorous training program (μελέτη) aimed at discipline and skill. If they adopt his proposals, he predicts that they will in all probability (κατὰ τὸ εἰκός)

> have every chance of beating their adversaries, courage (ἀνδρείας) being already theirs and discipline (εὐταξίας) in the field having thus been added to it. Indeed, both these qualities would improve, since danger would exercise them in discipline, while their courage (τὴν εὐψυχίαν) would be led to surpass itself by the confidence which skill inspires (μετὰ τοῦ πιστοῦ τῆς ἐπιστήμης θαρσαλεωτέραν).[2]

Note that Hermokrates makes no mention of their lack of preparation or the fortuitous thunderstorm. He does not try to

---

2. Compare Hermokrates' belief that "danger would exercise them in discipline" (τὴν μὲν μετὰ κινδύνων μελετωμένην) with the way in which the Athenians and Lakedaimonians gained their military skills "in the school of danger" (1.18.3: ἐμπειρότεροι ἐγένοντο μετὰ κινδύνων τὰς μελέτας ποιούμενοι).

offer excuses but gets right to the heart of the matter as Thucydides himself saw it (69.1). Since they already possess courage, how are they to achieve the kind of "skill" which will not dissolve in the face of the unexpected and turn to ἀταξία? The answer is experience, specifically rigorous training. Thus Hermokrates expresses what was the central issue of the *antilogia* between Phormion and the Peloponnesians. The same words recur in both passages, προθυμία, τόλμη, εὐψυχία, ἀνδρεία on the one side, ἐπιστήμη, μελέτη, ἐμπειρία on the other. Nor is it surprising, for both passages are contributions to the contemporary debate about φύσις vs. ἐπιστήμη. And the conclusion arrived at by both is the same. Φύσις alone is inadequate; achievement depends on the interrelationship of φύσις and ἐπιστήμη. The latter is the result of μελέτη and ἐμπειρία.

But more important for the present chapter is a second similarity between Phormion and Hermokrates. Both men are capable of drawing lessons from life, of learning from experience. While the Peloponnesians misread past experience and so doomed themselves to a repetition of their own errors, both Phormion and Hermokrates see the truth in the *erga* and incorporate it in a *logos*. The *logos* is τὰ δέοντα, a link between past and future, and in relation to its listeners, διδαχή.

In this process of learning from experience the reader also shares. Chapter 3 proposed that Thucydides "so selected his details — *erga-logoi-erga* — that the reader is inexorably led to reason as Phormion reasoned and discover for himself the truth contained in the events themselves" (p. 58). This is also the case here, but the process is somewhat more complex. Not only is the reader led to the truth by the *logos-erga-logos* combination, but he also learns from the past, from Phormion's exploits, which exist as a *paradeigma* in the pages of the *History* itself. He can compare one situation to another (εἰκάζειν) and make up his own mind about τὰ δέοντα even before Hermokrates speaks. Thus, while Hermokrates learns from experience, the reader learns from the example of the past, from *paradeigma* or history.

Let us revert to late summer of the same year, shortly after news of the Athenian expedition reaches Syracuse. An assembly is held at which, among others, Hermokrates and Athenagoras debate the truth of the report. Their debate is an *antilogia*, *logos* and counter *logos* on the same question: how should the Syracusans respond to the alleged expedition? On the one side,

Hermokrates asserts unequivocally that the news is true (32.3: ὡς σαφῶς οἰόμενος εἰδέναι; 33.1: περὶ τοῦ ἐπίπλου τῆς ἀληθείας and again σαφέστερον . . . εἰδώς). They must take action immediately with any and all means available. Concretely his advice is twofold. They should send to their allies for aid and meantime surprise the Athenians by going out to meet them at Taras. In his view success lies in seizing the initiative. Athenagoras, on the other hand, gives no credence to the report. He believes it improbable (36.4) that men so shrewd and experienced as the Athenians would leave an unsettled Greece to attack Sicily. And even if they did, Sicily would be more than a match for them. Thus he advises against any decisive moves but would leave matters to the generals. His is a wait-and-see policy.

Both men argue from εἰκός in basing their respective strategies on assumptions about the enemy. And both predict success if their policies are adopted. What must be underscored here however is that at the heart of one *logos* lies truth (ἀλήθεια), at the heart of the other, probability (εἰκός). Thucydides nowhere suggests that Hermokrates is operating on mere hearsay. On the contrary, twice he uses the term σαφής, a word which he normally reserves for what is clearly and accurately known.[3] In other words, Hermokrates is not being rhetorical in referring to his greater authority on the matter; he has apparently assured himself that the report is

---

3. Liddell and Scott (LSJ9) define the word σαφής as "clear, plain, distinct" and thus "sure" or "accurate." Sometimes Thucydides uses the word as a synonym for "truth." For example, in 3.29.2 the Peloponnesians put into Embaton wishing to know τὸ σαφές about the fall of Mytilene. Πυθόμενοι δὲ τὸ σαφές, they "began to consider what they were to do. . . ." In the affair of the Mysteries since no one then or after could say τὸ σαφές about who did the deed, speculations continued to be rife on either side (6.60.2: ἐπ᾽ ἀμφότερα γὰρ εἰκάζεται). Here then εἰκός substitutes for "accurate information." And so it does for "the events of remote antiquity." Thucydides admits that they "could not from lapse of time be clearly ascertained" (1.1.3: σαφῶς μὲν εὑρεῖν). Thus his conclusions about the period are a combination of τεκμήρια and εἰκάζειν. (See below.) With respect to Agamemnon he also mentions "the account given by those Peloponnesians who have been the recipients of the most credible tradition" (1.9.2: τὰ σαφέστατα . . . μνήμῃ). It may not be absolute truth, but it is as close as one can get. See too 1.22.4, where Thucydides expresses the hope that his own work will prove useful to "those enquirers who desire an exact knowledge of the past" (τὸ σαφές). Here τὸ σαφές is the product of that painstaking method described in 1.21-22. Elsewhere the word is often used to describe a proof for which convincing, if not irrefutable evidence exists (e.g., 1.32.1; 1.34.2; 1.95.5 and 1.140.5). In discussing Antiphon, Nestle, *Vom Mythos zum Logos*, p. 397, states: "Endlich erscheint das Lieblingswort des Thukydides für klare geschichliche Erkenntnis (τὸ σαφές) auch bei Antiphon als Ausdruck für die gerichtliche Klarstellung eines Hergangs." He cites the example of *On the Murder of Herodes* 67 and 84.

true. Moreover, *the reader knows he is correct*. The whole of Book 6 up to this point has been devoted to describing Athens' plans and preparations for this very expedition. In fact, so accurate is Hermokrates' evaluation that he echoes Nikias and Thucydides himself in suggesting Athens' aims, "professedly to help the Egestaeans and to restore Leontini, but really to conquer Sicily, and above all our city, which once gained, the rest, they think, will easily follow" (33.2: πρόφασιν μέν vs. τὸ δὲ ἀληθὲς Σικελίας ἐπιθυμίᾳ; cf. 6.6.1 and 6.8.4). Thus past *erga* lie behind Hermokrates' *logos*, for the assumptions and predictions — mainly arguments from εἰκός — which give rise to his strategy, whatever their worth, have at least the merit of being based on truth, ἀληθεία. This means, of course, that Athenagoras cannot be correct. When he gives advice about the "calculation of probabilities" (36.3: τὰ εἰκότα), he bases himself *not* on the report, which he apparently does not even consider worthy of investigation, but on the nature of the Athenians and their *probable* behaviour. Since they are shrewd men of experience, it is improbable (οὐ γὰρ εἰκός) "that they would leave the Peloponnesians behind them, and before they have well ended the war in Hellas wantonly come in quest of a new war quite as arduous, in Sicily. . ." (36.4).[4]

The reader is witness to a genuine dilemma. How are the Syracusans to distinguish truth from error? Unless they are as convinced of the facts as Hermokrates, i.e., have some absolutely trustworthy source of information about Athens' aims, what intrinsic superiority has one *logos* over the other? Any choice between the two must be subjective, in this case based perhaps on Athenagoras' personal attack on Hermokrates and his party. Thus are revealed the limitations of *logoi*. Both speakers cancel each other out. Rebuking them for διαβολάς the generals finally settle the matter. They neither discount the report nor launch a vigorous offensive. Instead they make preparations to repel the Athenians because there is no particular harm in it. It is a decidedly half-hearted policy.

Let us reconsider Hermokrates' *logos*. We have shown that in its major assertion it has a basis in fact. But is it κρείττων? There is only one objective way to determine this — to analyze the speech in terms of the *erga* which follow. Hermokrates attempts to

4. Incidentally, his disbelief underscores Athens' folly and Nikias' concern about enemies at home (6.10). Cf. Gomme 4, p. 301: "His statements of fact and estimates of probability are uniformly wrong. . . ."

do two things, a) to convince his listeners they are in real danger and b) to suggest action they might take to defend themselves.

a) 33.1-2. In asserting that the Athenians have set out with the aim of conquering Sicily, Hermokrates fails to convince his listeners. This is clear from chapter 35, where their reaction is described.

> Meanwhile the people of Syracuse were at great strife among themselves; some contending that the Athenians had no idea of coming and that there was no truth in what he said; some asking if they did come what harm they could do that would not be repaid them tenfold in return; while others made light of the whole affair and turned it into ridicule.

Having embarked on a rather unenthusiastic policy of defence, they later change their attitude. In chapter 45 Thucydides repeats the words of 32.3 (πολλαχόθεν . . . ἠγγέλλετο) with the following addition, καὶ ἀπὸ τῶν κατασκόπων σαφῆ. Eyewitnesses now convince them of what Hermokrates knew all along, that the report is σαφῆ, thus confirming the truth of his original assertion. Only now the enemy fleet is at Rhegion. At this point "they laid aside their incredulity and threw themselves heart and soul ito the work of preparation." They take immediate and vigorous measures of defence, even sending round to the Sikels.

b) 33.3 and 34. Above all Hermokrates urges them not to be taken off guard. In addition to preparations in Syracuse, they should send around to the Sikels and others in Sicily, to Italy and Carthage, and to Corinth and Lakedaimon. The latter he would ask to send help at once as well as renew hostilities in Greece itself. Since the above requires time, he proposes a *dianoia* which he believes the present emergency dictates. (It is ἐπίκαιρον, i.e., they will seize the *kairos* thereby.) They must take the offensive by going on board ship and meeting the Athenians at Taras and the Iapygian promontory. Such a move would strike dismay in the enemy because they would face the prospect of fighting for their passage across the Ionian Sea against men with a sure defensive base in Italy. In a display of *pronoia* Hermokrates anticipates probable expedients they might employ in such straits. Among other causes of discouragement would be uncertainty whether the cities of Sicily and Italy would receive them. In fact, this consideration alone might be enough to keep them from leaving Kerkyra. The result would be one of two things. What with deliberating and reconnoîtring they would find winter upon them or be so confounded by unexpected opposition as to give up the expedition altogether (34.6: καταπλαγέντας τῷ ἀδοκήτῳ). The fact that their most experienced general had taken the command against his will would also militate against them; he would surely be glad of an excuse to give up the whole project.[5] Hermokrates ends his *dianoia* with a *gnome* about human behaviour: ". . . the first to attack, or to show that they mean to defend themselves against an attack, inspire greater fear because men see that they are ready for the emergency." This he believes is what the Athenians would probably experience. "They are now attacking us in the belief that we shall not resist . . . but if they were to see us showing a courage for which they are not prepared, they would be more dismayed by the surprise than they could ever be by our actual power" (34.8). What the *kairos* demands then is *tolma*. And this is what he enjoins (34.9: τολμήσαντες again).

At first glance it would seem pointless to consider Hermokrates' *dianoia* any further. After all, since it was non-effective, there are no *erga* to confirm its correctness. Yet it cannot be dismissed so lightly. It raises the question why Thucydides has seen fit to supply minute details of a strategy which was not adopted, and furthermore make it the major part of a *logos* which, as we shall see, is in every other respect κρείττων. Did he himself believe that an aggressive strategy was "the better course" under the circumstances? We suspect he did, for two reasons: a) The psychological generalizations upon which the strategy is based have already been demonstrated as empirically true a number of times in previous *erga*. b) In a most general way, Hermokrates' *logos* foreshadows the way in which the Athenians were ultimately defeated.

a) Hermokrates' strategy is based on a simple rule of human behaviour. Men are confused and dismayed by the unexpected. In war this can work to the advantage of the weaker side, for the stronger may well be caught off guard just *because* he does not expect resistance. Sometimes then the best defence is offence, to recognize the enemy's vulnerability and take advantage of it. This requires perfect timing, a recognition of the moment of attack (*kairos*) and *tolma*. Of this truth the *History* itself provides several examples. Consider the two following *paradeigmata*: Twice Phor-

---

5. Again Hermokrates is amazingly accurate about Athenian affairs.

mion and his men recognize the *kairos* (2.84.3 and 2.92.1), the point at which to attack an enemy numerically their superior. In both cases the moment arrives when the unexpected throws the latter into confusion (84.3, the wind; 91.3-4, the incident around the merchantman). Then it is possible to take advantage of their weakness, lack of skill. But neither exploit would have been possible without *tolma*, which, as the *logos* revealed (2.89), was the result not only of greater skill and experience, but of Phormion's leadership, his *pronoia* or correct anticipations embodied in διδαχή.[6] It is just such a combination of *tolma* and the unexpected that Hermokrates now urges. In a second *paradeigma*, the same elements are present in the confrontation of Brasidas and Kleon at Amphipolis. In the first place Brasidas is wise enough to recognize that the Athenians are off guard because they do not expect resistance. He therefore encourages a small, picked force to take advantage of this weakness by seizing "the opportunity of the moment" (5.9.4). He also gives an accurate forecast of the probable outcome of a surprise attack. Thus when the right moment is at hand (10.5: τὸν καιρόν), they set to. The Athenians are "panic-stricken by their own disorder and astounded at his audacity" (10.6: τὴν τόλμαν). When Klearidas also enters the fray, the result is that "the Athenians, suddenly and unexpectedly attacked on both sides," fall into confusion (10.7: ξυνέβη τε τῷ ἀδοκήτῳ καὶ ἐξαπίνης).[7]

In other words the example of past history allows the reader

---

6. At least it seems to me that all these factors must be taken into consideration if one is not to do an injustice to the historian's subtlety. I would agree with the following statement of Gommel, p. 35: "Eine deutliche Anlehnung des Thukydides an die Rhetorik seiner Zeit zeigen die Stellen in den Reden, an denen die Eikos-Argumente auf der Syzygie Stark-Schwach und ihren Untersyzygien beruhen. Thukydides scheint sich hier bewusst der von der Rhetorik aufgestellten Technik bedient zu haben." A recognition of typology as one basis of the argument from εἰκός is, however, only the beginning. Gommel himself points out that both Phormion and the Peloponnesians use such arguments based on the "Schema Stark-Schwach" (p. 32). But he never really manages to show how and why Phormion's "Argumentation geht jedoch tiefer" (p. 34). In other words he has not seen that, as Thucydides presents them, Phormion's generalizations, whether they came from a hand-book of rhetorical *topoi* or not, derive directly from experience, from the *erga*. For this reason they do indeed seem more probable or, as we have expressed it, κρείττων. Missing this point, Gommel presents a rather formal study of Thucydides' *logoi* purely in terms of the rhetorical techniques of his day and, as such, a view of the historian as one-sided as that of Stahl, who greatly overemphasizes the irrational. (For a criticism of Stahl see Chapter 3, n. 9.) In the present chapter I will attempt to give my own explanation of what lies behind εἰκός and εἰκάζειν.

7. See Chapter 2, pp. 30 ff.

to judge of Hermokrates' strategy. Inductive reasoning would indicate that his predictions are eminently plausible.

b) Chapter 7 traced the decline in Athenian morale which culminated in the final defeat in the Great Harbour of Syracuse. What they suffered over an extended period is exactly what Hermokrates predicted would be their response to a daring and unexpected resistance at the outset. Even in the first meeting of the two peoples before Syracuse they are dismayed by the "continued resistance" of the Syracusans (6.70.1). The *logos-erga-logos* combination makes it clear that the main quality the latter possess is inherent if unschooled *tolma*. (See above, pp. 149 ff.) As their respective positions change, there is also a reversal of morale until the Athenians are completely demoralized by what seems to them a *paralogos*, defeat at sea (7.55.1 and see p. 118). This demoralization, the result of unexpectedly encountering a people similar to themselves in character (55.2), the Syracusans are quick to take advantage of. Once again they confront them boldly, their innate *tolma* now reinforced by experience and informed by the διδαχή of Gylippos. Reminiscent of Hermokrates' original prediction is Gylippos' belief that "the unexpected shock to their pride" has caused the Athenians "to give way more than their real strength warrants. . . (7.66.3: παρὰ ἰσχὺν τῆς δυνάμεως).

In other words Hermokrates' *logos* foreshadows the psychological decline of the Athenians in the face of unexpected setbacks, the result of unexpected *tolma*. Or to put it another way, knowing what *did* happen, Thucydides put in Hermokrates' mouth a strategy which makes use of the same psychology which proved so successful for Phormion and Brasidas and which later actually did defeat the Athenians. I would suggest that like Lamachos' *gnome*, it was very much the strategy he considered "the better course" under the circumstances.

Sensible as it may seem, however, the Syracusans do not follow Hermokrates' advice about immediate action. Nor do they make any haste to carry out his long-term proposal, that they send for aid to Corinth and Lakedaimon. In resolving the debate the generals do not mention the need for outside help, nor is there any reference to such a move even after the report of the Athenian expedition is confirmed (6.45). *Later*, however, they are once again forced to realize the correctness of Hermokrates' original *logos*. For after the first encounter at Syracuse this is just what they vote to do (6.73.2):

They also sent envoys to Corinth and Lacedaemon to procure
a force of allies to join them, and to induce the Lacedaemonians for their sakes openly to address themselves in real
earnest to the war against the Athenians, that they might
either have to leave Sicily or be less able to send reinforcements to their army there.

Thus is Hermokrates' first *logos* confirmed as κρείττων and all
that can be salvaged of it readily adopted by the Syracusans.

Two points are important here. First the situation has been
restored to what it was in 6.32. If the Syracusans erred by missing
the *kairos*, so did the Athenians. The delay that resulted from
adopting Alkibiades' *gnome* combined with their inability to
follow up their victory because of the onset of winter has brought
about just the kind of situation Hermokrates had envisioned.
Remember he predicted two possibilities; either the enemy would
delay until winter or give up the expedition altogether. Though
they do not abandon the expedition, as a result of their own errors
they do delay until winter, and so the Syracusans manage to get
the respite which Hermokrates had hoped to win by a display of
tolma. Thus Hermokrates has the opportunity to present a new
logos which transcends his earlier speech by incorporating the
truth embodied in the recent *erga*, i.e., that the Syracusans must
bolster their innate *tolma* with *episteme*, the result of *melete* and
empeiria.

Hermokrates, as we pointed out above, has learned from
experience. But just as important, *so have his listeners*. Previously
they had no means of determining which *logos* was intrinsically
superior. Until the news of the expedition was confirmed by
eye-witnesses as σαφῆ, the assumptions and predictions of both
logoi were mere εἰκότα. The Syracusans were a prey to πειθώ in its
worst aspects, slander (διαβολή) and encouragement to disdain of
the enemy based on overconfidence, and their fears were not
sufficiently aroused to overcome this complacency and wishful
thinking. *Empeiria* has changed all that. They now know from
experience not only that the Athenian expedition is a reality but
that the Athenians themselves are a formidable enemy.

Thus the *erga* are not only a source of truth for the man
capable of learning from experience, formulating a *logos* based on
them, but they can also be an important ingredient of πειθώ, the
effect of the *logos* on his listeners. Brasidas, for example, knew

this very well. In attempting to sustain the courage of his men against the Lynkestians, he reminded them of "the trial of strength which you had with the Macedonians among them" (4.126.3). I.e., they have personal experience of the enemy upon which to draw, experience which should convince them to accept τὰ δέοντα and evince *tolma* against the same enemy. Compare the *logoi* of Phormion and Gylippos. Both make use of their listeners' previous successes against their immediate enemies to inspire them to the same effort in the battles to follow (2.89.11 and 7.66.2).

In the present instance, mere probability has been converted to truth, truth from which Hermokrates himself learns and which serves to convince his listeners. Compare Antiphon, who also expresses this opposition between τὰ εἰκότα and *erga*. "I myself, using not arguments from probability but the facts of the matter, will prove . . ." (*First Tetralogy* 4.8: ἐγὼ δ' οὐκ ἐκ τῶν εἰκότων ἀλλ' ἔργῳ δηλώσω).[8] For both men then, the rhetor and the historian, truth resides in the *erga* alone, part of which derive from personal experience. (See p. 162.)

But there are other kinds of *erga*. In discussing Hermokrates' *logos*, we passed over 6.33.4-6 without comment. Let us return to this passage, even a cursory reading of which cannot fail to reveal the prevalence of the connective γάρ. In this respect it is somewhat similar to the Syracusan "thoughts" (7.36.3-6) analyzed in Chapter 5. Here too is "a series of statements . . . linked together by the connective γάρ and each explaining the one that preceded until every possibility is spelled out . . ." (p. 86). Again it is "reasoning from εἰκός in which every γάρ implies a question." For example, Hermokrates exhorts those who believe him not to be dismayed at the force or daring of the enemy. Why? His reason (γάρ) he formulates as a prediction. "They will not be able to do us more hurt than we shall do them. . . ." In fact, the very magnitude of the expedition is not without advantages: the bigger the better as far as the rest of the Sikeliots are concerned. Why? Their very terror (γάρ) will make them ready to join Syracuse. He continues his predictions, ". . . and if we defeat or drive them away, disappointed of the objects of their ambition . . . it will be a most glorious exploit for us, and in my judgment by no means an unlikely one." Hermokrates is sure enough of the latter

8. My translation. Cf. *First Tetralogy* 2.10, where there is a similar opposition between εἰκότως and ὄντως, "probabilities" and "facts."

logos	erga	logos	erga
Hermokrates (6.33-34)	Athenians at Rhegion (6.44-45)	Hermokrates (6.72)	Measures adopted (6.73)
a) the news of the expedition is true b) the Syracusans must take action at once, especially send for allies	eyewitnesses confirm the truth of the original report	advises that *andreia* be reinforced by *episteme* (through *melete* and *empeiria*) as well as improved leadership	the Syracusans not only vote everything as Hermokrates advises but carry out the suggestions of his first *logos* by sending to Corinth and Lakedaimon
Nikias (6.68) the *tolma* of the Syracusans will surpass their *episteme*	First Battle at Syracuse (6.69-70) Syracusans do not lack *tolma* but are defeated by lack of *episteme*		
διδαχή = τὰ εἰκότα	confirmation through experience *empeiria* = ἀλήθεια	διδαχή = *pronoia* based on ἀλήθεια = πειθώ based on *empeiria*	future *erga* will confirm all his predictions

to include his personal belief in a kind of parenthesis, "for (γάρ) I do not fear for a moment that they will get what they want." All this is, of course, mere assumption, since there can be no absolute certainty about the future. Thus in order to convince his listeners that what he predicts will very probably come to pass he adds a generalization, which serves to meet possible doubts by explaining (γάρ) the basis of his predictions. "Few indeed have been the large armaments, either Hellenic or barbarian, that have gone far from home and been successful." Again an explanation (γάρ). They cannot be more numerous than the inhabitants and their neighbours. Why? The latter (γάρ) all league together out of fear. Moreover, if they suffer disaster in a foreign land from lack of supplies, those who were the object of their attack win renown, even though the aggressors may well have brought about their own downfall. In itself, however, such a generalization may not be convincing unless his listeners know concrete examples from history to support it. Hermokrates assists them by supplying an example from the past which both illustrates his generalization and draws an analogy between the Syracusans and the Athenians of old. "Thus these very Athenians rose by the defeat of the Mede, in a great measure due to accidental causes (παρὰ λόγον), from the mere fact that Athens had been the object of his attack; and this may very well be the case with us also." (Here I might amend Crawley's translation. Παρὰ λόγον has the connotation "contrary to reason" rather than "due to accidental causes," although the latter were certainly present. I.e., their *logos* — deliberations, calculations, plans — did not take everything into account. Thus their defeat came as a complete surprise.)

The accuracy of these predictions will not concern us especially, although they do in fact later prove true and are part of the usual *erga-logoi-erga* combination.[9] What will interest us are the *erga* which lie behind Hermokrates' predictions. On what does he base his assumptions about the future (εἰκότα)? As we have pointed out above, they are based primarily on his generalization about the usual fate of large expeditions far from home. In itself this is not out of the ordinary, for in almost every speech studied

---

9. The concept of the *paralogos* stands out at once, since it is what primarily characterizes Athens' defeat. (See 7.55.1-2 and 75.7 as well as pp. 147 f.) Note too how he correctly anticipates "a most glorious exploit." The Syracusans in general come to recognize this possibility in 7.56.2 (καλόν ... τὸ ἀγώνισμα). It is also Thucydides' final judgment in 7.87.5 (τοῖς τε κρατήσασι λαμπρότατον).

up to this point the reasoning has followed a similar pattern, statement followed by explanation, usually a *gnome* or generalization, and then its application to the problem at hand. Here, however, we begin to discover what lies behind these generalizations. They are more than mere "commonplaces" in that they have a basis in "fact." Earlier (p. 120) we defined εἰκάζειν as the ability to learn enough "from past experiences (*erga*) to see similarities in the present (*logoi*) and so predict the future (*erga*)," meaning usually one's own experiences (*empeiria*). We now see that there is a form of εἰκάζειν which transcends mere personal experience, although it too depends on past *erga* as a source of truth. In this case the *erga* are the experiences of others which exist as examples (*paradeigmata*) and which as a totality constitute history.

Hermokrates has provided one *paradeigma* of a στόλος μεγάλος (cf. 1.18.2: τῷ μεγάλῳ στόλῳ). And surely no one would quibble with his evaluation. While he chose to stress the *paralogos* which resulted from depending primarily on superior *dynamis*, implicit in his exhoration is a recognition of the *tolma* and *gnome* of the defender, which was as much responsible for the *paralogos* as Persian overconfidence. Thucydides evidently studied Herodotus with great care and, while eliminating the religious overtones of the morality cycle, captured the essence of Xerxes' downfall. He thus makes good use of the Persian disaster to exemplify his generalization about "large armaments." But one example implies another. *Paradeigmata* of this kind usually conform to a pattern. And one has not far to seek to find the expedition pattern in earlier pages of the *History*. Two examples come to mind at once. Granted the details are sparse, since it is part of the synoptic *Pentekontaetia*, yet surely the Egyptian expedition conforms to this pattern. It too was a μεγάλη στρατεία (1.110.4) far from home which failed miserably. Though modern historians have reconstructed events in a manner which reduces the magnitude of the disaster,[10] Thucydides himself — whether consciously or not — leaves the impression that 200 ships sailed against and were lost in Egypt (1.104.2). "Of all that large host,"

10. See Gomme 1, pp. 321 f., for a discussion of the problem and W. P. Wallace, "The Egyptian Expedition and the Chronology of the Decade 460-450 B.C.," *TAPA* 67, 1936, p. 252, who argues "that most of the 200 ships returned via Phoenicia, enabling Athens to fight Tanagra with adequate forces; that only 40 (Ktesias' figure) were left to be destroyed in Egypt. . . ."

he tells us, failing to specify the number, "a few travelling through Libya reached Cyrene in safety, but most of them perished" (1.110.1). It was a major catastrophe.[11]

But the *paradeigma* which throws most light on the probable experience of the Athenians is the Trojan expedition which Thucydides describes as τὴν στρατείαν ἐκείνην μεγίστην ... τῶν πρὸ αὐτῆς (1.10.3). Its very success, (one of the ὀλίγοι of 6.33.5) allows Thucydides to ponder out loud, as it were, on the major prerequisite of expeditions abroad − supplies and money (1.11). Agamemnon's victory was a narrow and troublesome one requiring 10 years. Thucydides states his belief (1.11.2):

> If they had brought plenty of supplies with them, and had perservered in the war without scattering for piracy and agriculture, they would have easily defeated the Trojans in the field; since they could hold their own against them with the division on service. In short, if they had stuck to the siege, the capture of Troy would have cost them less time and less trouble.[12]

Hermokrates does not of course, refer to these earlier expeditions. But the reader knows of them, for they exist as *erga* in the pages of the *History* and thus as *paradeigmata* which increase the probability of Hermokrates' predictions. One might

11. At least this is so in Thucydides' account. I find rather interesting the remarks of Walker quoted by both Gomme and Wallace (p. 322 and p. 256): "Thucydides has devoted two whole books to the great Sicilian Expedition, while he disposes of the Egyptian in a couple of pages.... For all that, ... beyond all doubt, the Egyptian disaster is the greatest in Athenian history until we come to the battle in the Great Harbour of Syracuse and the surrender on the banks of the Assinarus." See Chapter 8, n. 17, where it was suggested that many events of the *Pentekontaetia* could have been paradigmatic for Alkibiades but were not. They can be for the reader.

12. Apart from the light it sheds on Thucydides' use of the ἄτεχνοι πίστεις and his critical attitude towards his sources (Gommel, pp. 6 ff.), the account of the Trojan expedition is valuable in that it demonstrates how Thucydides himself made use of εἰκός and εἰκάζειν in reconstructing the past. I would agree with the following statement of Gommel, p. 66: "Betrachten wir nun die Archäologie unter dem Gesichtspunkt, welche Faktoren die Entwicklung des frühen Griechenlands nach Ansicht des Thukydides bestimmt haben. Ein σαφῶς εὑρεῖν (I 1,3) war ihm nicht möglich, da die Begebenheiten so weit zurücklagen, dass er auf alte Berichte angewiesen war. Diese Berichte wertet Thukydides mit Hilfe des Eikos aus (I 9,4: εἰκάζειν δὲ χρὴ καὶ ταύτῃ τῇ στρατείᾳ οἷα ἦν τὰ πρὸ αὐτῆς). Er hat sie also auf ihre Wahrscheinlichkeit hin untersucht." He also agrees with Finley, pp. 48-49: "Dass die Methode des εἰκάζειν seiner Archäologie zugrunde liegt, sagt er selbst (I 9,4). Dieses εἰκάζειν nun beruht auf dem Abwägen der Kräfteverhältnisse" (p. 68). As I indicated above, mere typology − again the weak-strong relationship − is inadequate as the basis of εἰκάζειν.

go so far as to say that they foreshadow in truly Herodotean fashion the problems and ultimate destruction of the greatest expedition of all. Thucydides ends Book 7 with words which echo Hermokrates: "This was the greatest Hellenic achievement of any in this war, or, in my opinion, in Hellenic history . . ." (87.5: ξυνέβη τε ἔργον τοῦτο . . . μέγιστον; cf. 6.33.4: κάλλιστον δὴ ἔργον). Ἀκοῇ Ἑλληνικῶν includes all those former στόλοι. Like the Persian expedition the defeat was a *paralogos*, the result of an underestimation of the enemy and overconfidence based mainly on superior *dynamis*. And like Agamemnon's force the first major problem was lack of supplies and money – a harbinger of the increased difficulties they would experience once Sicily united and found allies in Greece. Finally, as in the case of the Egyptian expedition destruction was total: "few out of many returned home" (ὀλίγοι ἀπὸ πολλῶν in both accounts, 7.87.6 and 1.110.1). In other words, in its magnitude the defeat of the Athenian expedition against Sicily incorporates features of all previous "large armaments," thus attaining the level of the ultimate *paradeigma*.

To return to our main discussion, we will conclude with two points. First, past *erga* in the sense of *paradeigmata* have the same dual function as personal experience. They are a source of truth, and as such a guide to the future, for the man who is capable of abstracting this truth from a number of examples and formulating a *logos* based on it. In other words, the intellectual process of εἰκάζειν, and so *pronoia*, presupposes the ability to learn not only from *empeiria* but from *paradeigma*. Moreover, since the *paradeigma* is also a rhetorical device, it too, like *empeiria*, is a major ingredient of πειθώ, the effect of the *logos* on the listener. A speaker may make just as effective use of others' example as he does of the personal experience of his listeners in order to convince them. In fact, if the latter lack such experience, the experiences of others naturally take on added significance. For instance, we have seen above that before the Syracusans actually met the Athenians in battle, one of Hermokrates' major arguments was the example of earlier expeditions. On it he based his predictions of success and renown for the defenders.[13]

13. He does not of course convince them. The mass of mankind, as we indicated in earlier chapters (especially Chapter 8, p. 144), is little prone to learn from the example of others. Thus the *paradeigma* is severely limited as a form of πειθώ. The ability to persuade is extremely important to the statesman, for it is of little use to be adept at

Secondly, in discussing Hermokrates' later *logos* (6.72), we saw how the reader is himself led to use his powers of εἰκάζειν and so learn from the example of the past (p. 153). This is also the case here. In fact the reader is in a much better position to compare past and present than Hermokrates' listeners, since he has knowledge of not one large armament only but three. He is thus capable of evaluating Hermokrates' use of *paradeigma*. Is he factually accurate? Inductively speaking, is his generalization a reasonable one? In light of past *erga* are his predictions plausible? Hermokrates' reasoning, he will find, is unassailable on all these points. Thus it should come as no surprise when the *erga*, the final defeat of the Athenians, do conform to his *logos*. Having been foreshadowed in this as in so many other ways, they should in fact seem all but inevitable — a mere confirmation of a truth he has long known. Being yet another *paradeigma*, they should in turn render the generalization about "large armaments" all the more secure for future generations.

It is possible to confirm the above conclusions by consulting a third *logos* of Hermokrates (7.21). Though no attempt will be made to analyze this speech in detail, it is certainly worthwhile to indicate the more striking similarities. The passage begins with an appeal by Gylippos to the Syracusans to try their hand at a sea-fight, an appeal in which Hermokrates joins by "trying to encourage his countrymen to attack the Athenians at sea." Essentially he gives them the same advice as he did in his original *logos* (6.33-34): they must meet *tolma* with *tolma* and cause the enemy dismay by unexpected daring (τῷ τολμῆσαι ἀπ-ροσδοκήτως), "the advantages of which would far outweigh any loss that Athenian science might inflict upon their inexperience" (21.4: *episteme* vs. *apeiria*). In other words, he encourages them to do by sea what they have already accepted as possible on land — gain experience in the school of danger (6.72.4). Since, however, they do not yet have personal experience of the sea upon which to draw, he uses a *paradeigma* to reinforce Gylippos' hope of "some deed worthy of the risk" (my translation). Note that it is basically the same analogy as he used in his first speech, for he again compares the plight of the Syracusans with that of the Athenians

prognosis, if one cannot convince the masses to accept one's advice. Perikles expresses this point thus: "A man possessing that knowlege (i.e., of the proper policy, γνῶναι τὰ δέοντα) without that faculty of exposition (σαφῶς διδάξας) might as well have no idea at all on the matter. . . (2.60.6).

defending themselves against the Persians (21.3):

> the latter had not inherited their naval prowess (*empeiria*)
> nor would they retain it for ever; they had been landsmen
> even to a greater degree than the Syracusans, and had only
> become a maritime power when obliged by the Mede.

Thus once again the *paradeigma* in the sense of others' experiences
or past history proves to be a source of truth and so a guide to the
future (εἰκάζειν) as well as a means of convincing one's listeners.
And once again the *erga* will confirm this truth.

To complete the discussion of *paradeigma*, let us examine one
more *logos* of Hermokrates, this time his appeal to the Kamarinaians (6.75-80). We will deal only with the introduction
(6.76-77.1), the arguments of which serve as a basis for the rest of
the speech. For if the Kamarinaians accept its reasoning, they
must see the necessity for unity.

Hermokrates begins by expressing the fear that the Kamarinaians
may not be impervious to Athenian arguments, for the latter have
been careful to provide themselves with a pretext (προφάσει) for
being in Sicily. (Presumably Kamarina may make the mistake of
accepting it at face value.) Yet everyone suspects their real
purpose (διανοίᾳ). They have come not to restore the Leontinoi
but to drive out the Sicilians. As far as his listeners are concerned,
this alleged aim is, of course, only an assumption. To prove that it
is highly probable, however, Hermokrates refers to Athens' past
history, examples (77.1: παραδείγματα) from which he brings to
bear on the present situation in order to convince his listeners that
his assumptions (εἰκότα) are reasonable. His first assumption
(above) is that the Athenians' real aim cannot be aid to their
Ionian kinsmen. Why? The example of the Chalkidians in Euboia
proves it. It is contrary to reason that they "should cherish the
Leontine Chalcidians because of their Ionian blood, and keep in
servitude the Euboian Chalcidians, of whom the Leontines are a
colony" (76.2). His second assumption is that they are following
the same policy that proved successful in Greece. Again he
explains, this time with the example of the Athenian *arche*.
Chosen as leaders of the Ionian Greeks in order to take vengeance
on the Mede, they eventually found reasons (failure in military
service or disputes among themselves) to subdue their allies. In
effect then the Athenians fought *not* for the freedom of the
Greeks but in order to enslave them, while the latter fought to

change one master for another.[14]

Such are the *paradeigmata*: "the Hellenes in those parts" were enslaved "through not supporting each other." This being so, the present arguments of the Athenians should be exposed for what they are, σοφίσματα. The conclusion is inexorable. Having suggested the motives and probable outcome of the Athenians' present policy, Hermokrates can make a stirring appeal for unity based on their common heritage of race and freedom. Let them unite as free Dorians and avoid being taken individually as were the earlier Greeks.

Interesting as they are, we will not analyze all Hermokrates' arguments,[15] but judge the strength of his *logos* by one criterion alone, the probability of his predictions in terms of past *erga*. For the reader can verify the *paradeigmata* which form the basis of his arguments by consulting the *erga* which precede.

It would seem perfectly reasonable for Hermokrates to challenge the Athenians' claim that they come with concern for Ionian kin in Sicily, when they have long held in subjection most of the Ionian Greeks, in particular the Euboians, who colonized Leontinoi. The Euboians, be it remembered, were not allowed to leave the Athenian *arche* in 446. Their revolt was immediately subdued by Perikles (1.114.3). And if anyone is shocked by the harshness of the word δουλωσαμένους (6.76.2), he need only refer to 1.98.4, where Thucydides describes the secession of Naxos: "After this Naxos left the confederacy, and a war ensued, and she had to return after a siege; this was the first instance of the engagement being broken by the subjugation (ἐδουλώθη) of an allied city. . . ." This was evidently the status Thucydides thought most of the "subjects" enjoyed. There follows (1.99) an analysis

---

14. Naturally no one would suggest that these were the Athenian motives in fighting the Persian Wars. Objectively speaking, however, it is an accurate description of their effects.

15. In a direct appeal to Kamarina (6.78-80.2) he argues both from "expedience" and from "justice." He also uses two further *paradeigmata*, the immediate example of others rather than past history. As proof of the real nature of Athens' expedition, he uses the example of the Rhegians. Though Chalkidians, even they refused to help restore the Chalkidian Leontinoi. *A fortiori* then it is wrong for the Kamarinaians to assist their natural enemies to destroy their natural kinsmen. As for fear of Athens' armament, if they unite they need have no fear. The proof of this? The example of Syracuse herself in the recent encounter: ". . . even after attacking us by ourselves and being victorious in battle, they had to go off without effecting their purpose" (79.3). If none of the above arguments convinces them, he meets fear with fear, by adding a threat. The Syracusans will hold them responsible whatever the outcome. In the end this is what does convince them: ". . . they feared the Syracusans most of the two. . ." (88.1).

of the transformation of the Delian League to empire. Hermokrates is not far wrong in his view of how the Athenians gained complete control. One of the chief causes of defection (and so of the subjugation which was its consequence) was failure of military service (6.76.3: λιποστρατίαν; 1.99.1: λιποστράτιον).[16] "Fighting against each other" also had disastrous results. It was a war between the Samians and Milesians over Priene which precipitated Perikles' expedition against the hitherto independent Samos in 440. In the end both she and Byzantion were reduced to subject status (1.115-117).

In light of the past then as well as the more recent example of Melos, it is highly probable that Athens' concern for the Leontinoi is merely a pretext behind which lurks a policy of divide and conquer — highly probable for Hermokrates' Sicilian listeners, that is, for the reader *already knows the truth* about Athens' aims and can recognize at once the validity of his main assumptions. In 6.6.1 Thucydides himself stated unequivocally that the Athenians were "ambitious in real truth of conquering the whole (of Sicily), although they had also the specious design of succouring their kindred and other allies in the island." What is more, the historian motivated Alkibiades, the main advocate of the expedition, with even more grandiose schemes — conquest of Carthage as well as Sicily (6.15.2). Just how closely his desires approximated public policy it is difficult to say with certainty.[17] In any case, Thucydides himself believed that the masses entertained a variety of similar far-fetched ambitions. He states, for example, that "the idea of the common people and the soldiery was to earn wages at the moment, and make conquests that would supply a never-ending fund of pay for the future" (6.24.3). In other words, previous *erga* incorporating Thucydides' own judgment indicate that Hermokrates is perfectly correct in distinguishing Athens' real aims from her stated purpose.

Thus using the *paradeigma* as a method of reasoning Hermokrates approximates what the reader knows to be ἀλήθεια and

16. Cf. the *logos* of the Mytilenean envoys at Olympia (3.9-14).

17. We need not accept Alkibiades' *logos* to the Lakedaimonians (6.90.2) as an accurate statement of Athenian policy. On the other hand, the references in Aristophanes' *Knights* (174 and 1303) certainly indicate that the idea was in the air. See too Plutarch, *Perikles* 20.3, *Nikias* 12.2, and *Alkibiades* 17.2. For modern opinions see H. D. Westlake, "Athenian Aims in Sicily, 427-424 B.C. A Study in Thucydidean Motivation," *Historia* 9, 1960, pp. 385-402 and W. Liebeschuetz, "Thucydides and the Sicilian Expedition," *Historia* 17, 1968, pp. 289-306.

what later *erga* will confirm to be so.

In his recent work, *Rhetorisches Argumentieren bei Thukydides*, Jürgen Gommel spends a number of pages discussing the use of εἰκός in Book 8.[18] In so doing he hints at a problem we have already raised a number of times. Anyone can make use of arguments from εἰκός. In the lawcourts, in fact, both sides used this method of reasoning. And so, as we have seen, do the speakers in Thucydides' *History*. For instance, both Phormion and the Peloponnesians use arguments from εἰκός to predict the outcome of their confrontation at Naupaktos. But obviously both are not correct. Thus εἰκός in itself, as Gommel states, affords "keine absolut gültigen Ergebnisse."[19] But I would question his distinction between "einem vorurteilslosen Eikos-Schluss und einer vagen Vermutung. . . . Als einer solchen stellt er (Thucydides) dem εἰκός des Theramenes und der Athener sein eigenes εἰκός entgegen."[20] This is impossibly subjective. Moreover, one example after another drawn from the *History* has revealed that as *some* men use εἰκός it brings results that are truly startling, for their predictions prove true to the smallest detail. Thucydides, it seems, believed in the *human* – as opposed to the oracular or religious – possibilities of confronting the future.[21] In this he would undoubtedly have agreed with the statement of Antiphon quoted by Gommel: τίς ἐστι μαντική: ἀνθρώπου φρονίμου εἰκασμός.[22]

A recapitulation shows clearly what lies behind correct εἰκασμός and hence *prognosis*. Chapter 7 gave a partial answer, describing the successful leader as a man who "can read the message of the past, one who can combine his own and others' experiences with the intellectual tools of εἰκός and εἰκάζειν to predict and so conquer the future" (p. 120). Up to that point,

18. Pp. 41 ff.
19. P. 44. Cf. Chapter 3, p. 57: "*In itself* then εἰκός is not infallible or even dependable as a guide to the future."
20. Gommel and myself are each approaching the problem with a different purpose. Gommel's main aim is to show how Thucydides himself used contemporary rhetorical techniques to make his history more credible (p. 80). My primary concern has been with εἰκός and εἰκάζειν as intellectual tools for correct *prognosis*, hence tools useful to others besides the historian. In other words I am working in the spirit of the passage of Antiphon quoted below. To study this aspect of εἰκός involves one in the broader question of "truth" and its establishment.
21. See n. 29 below.
22. DK 87A 9.

however, we meant mainly personal experience (*empeiria*), such as Phormion had in the Gulf of Patrai. Having learned from life, from the first naval battle with the Peloponnesians, what earlier he merely assumed, he was able to formulate a *logos* based on this knowledge. Lamachos and Gylippos, as Thucydides presents them, were also such men. The predictions they made, in both instances correct, were the very ones one might assume of men who had lived through similar experiences and had learned enough from them to cope with the present. The past then, in the sense of personal experience, was their guide.

But men also learn from the example of others (*paradeigma*). Chapter 5 showed how the Syracusans did just this: following the Corinthian example they made significant innovations in their naval tactics. This too was a "lesson in εἰκάζειν" in which the ability to learn from example "almost surpasses personal experience" (pp. 91-92). Thus the past in the sense of *paradeigma* is also a guide to the future.

In the same way, Brasidas had evinced the capacity "to go beyond mere personal experience and see the similarities of numerous experiences, even those of others" (p. 92). This, as the present chapter has shown, is the very capacity Hermokrates evinces, the capacity to learn not just from his own personal experiences but the experiences of others, *paradeigmata* in the sense of history. Thus if εἰκάζειν in its widest sense implies the ability to predict on the basis of both *empeiria* and *paradeigmata*, Hermokrates is truly the most fully developed statesman in the *History*, in Thucydidean terms, ἄριστος εἰκαστής.[23]

The test of an εἰκαστής lies in his *logos*. What relationship does it have to past *erga*, the source of truth? Does he incorporate this truth in his *logos*? If so, future *erga* should confirm his assumptions (εἰκότα) as ἀλήθεια. Indeed, all our analyses have revealed that a man who evinces *pronoia* by making correct predictions usually understands the past, i.e., mediates past and future by formulating a *logos* which is the central portion in an *erga-logos-erga* combination. Those who fail to do this, fail, that is, to consult or perhaps do not understand past *erga*, though they use arguments from εἰκός, do not predict correctly.[24]

23. Taken from 1.138.3, where it is used to describe Themistokles. Compare Finley, p. 203, who points out that "only the Syracusan Hermocrates combined" all four characteristics which Perikles claimed (2.60.5). This is also the view of G. F. Bender, *Der Begriff des Staatsmannes bei Thukydides*, Würzburg, 1938, pp. 106-107.

24. See, for example, the analysis of Alkibiades' *logos* (6.16-18) in chapter 8,

Finally, a corollary, Hermokrates' example answers the question raised at the end of Chapter 8. Some men, if only a very few, learn as much from others' example as they do from personal experience and thus are capable of using history as a source of truth for their *logos* or future plans. This is a ray of optimism implying as it does that not all men are doomed to learn through "time and experience," through suffering.

But if past *erga* lie behind a correct use of εἰκός and εἰκάζειν, one must be certain he has accurate information. If, for example, past *erga* are his own experiences he must not ignore some facts and exaggerate others so that he ends by distorting reality as the Peloponnesians did after the Battle of Patrai. On the other hand, if the "facts" on which he bases his *logos* are information in the form of messages or reports, he must be equally scrupulous about their soundness. This was the point of our earlier discussion of Hermokrates' first *logos*. The latter referred to himself as σαφέστερον ... εἰδώς (6.33.1; cf. 32.3: ὡς σαφῶς οἰόμενος εἰδέναι). To the best of his ability, we suggested, he had ensured himself that his information was correct and so was able to formulate a policy which later *erga* indicate was the best strategy under the circumstance.[25]

Where the uses of history are concerned, the above is also true. One must be scrupulously accurate about the past. Thucydides is severely critical of mankind in general for the ready acceptance of "the first story that comes to hand." He states: "The way that most men deal with traditions (1.20.1: τὰς ἀκοὰς τῶν προγεγενημένων), even traditions of their own country, is to receive them all alike as they are delivered, without applying any critical test whatever" (ἀβασανίστως). After giving three examples, one from Athenian, and two from Spartan history, he concludes, "So little pains do the vulgar take in the investigation of truth. . ." (20.3: οὕτως ἀταλαίπωρος τοῖς πολλοῖς ἡ ζήτησις τῆς ἀληθείας). But this does not close the question. In Book 6.54-60 he returns to the uncritical attitude of the Athenians towards their own history and again the example of the alleged

---

especially pp. 138 ff. It is possible to analyze Euphemos' *logos* in answer to Hermokrates (6.82-87) in the same way. The latter has the additional feature of much truthful irony. Again the example of Athens in the Persian Wars lies behind many of Euphemos' predictions except that now Athens herself is forcing Syracuse to assume the same role she herself assumed in the face of Xerxes' invasion.

25. This contrasts with the ἀπειρία of the Athenians in making their decision to attack Sicily. See p. 146.

tyrannicides, Harmodios and Aristogeiton, his aim being to demonstrate just how dangerous it may be for people to be inaccurate or misinformed about the past. He relates the story at length "to show that the Athenians are not more accurate than the rest of the world in their accounts of their own tyrants and of the facts of their own history" (6.54.1: περὶ τοῦ γενομένου ἀκριβὲς οὐδὲν λέγοντας). In so doing he demolishes three points: that Hipparchos was tyrant, that the purpose of the attack was to free Athens from tyranny, and that the tyranny was "violent, impious, illegal, and burdensome."[26] He then reconstructs history. On at least one point, that "Hippias was the eldest son and succeeded to the government" he states that he has had "more exact accounts than others" (55.1: εἰδὼς μὲν καὶ ἀκοῇ ἀκριβέστερον ἄλλων). Second, he makes use of extant evidence such as inscriptions and monuments. Finally, he welds the facts into a new form with arguments from εἰκός. On the basis of his reconstruction he is then able to "undermine every point of the popular 'knowledge,' on which the fear and suspicion of 415 B.C. was based, and so deny the validity both of the analogy and of the fearful suspicions."[27] Accuracy about past erga is proven essential to analogy or εἰκάζειν. Without it "his fellow-citizens both misunderstood the past and by so doing mishandled the present situation."[28]

Thus is explained Thucydides' unparalleled concern for accuracy. He was a "critical" historian because of the significance he attached to ἔργον, πρᾶγμα or παράδειγμα. The latter did not concern him merely as isolated "facts" however, but as part of a continuum of experience, erga-logoi-erga. They are a source of truth for εἰκασμός, man's τέχνη μαντική, for correct prediction (pronoia) depends on correct analogy (εἰκάζειν), which is in turn dependent on accurate erga.[29]

26. I am following the analysis of Mabel Lang, "The Murder of Hipparchus," Historia 3, 1955, p. 398.

27. Ibid.

28. Ibid. Commentators, it seems to me, have underestimated the significance of the Harmodios and Aristogeiton episode. See, for example, Gomme 4, p. 329: "The most plausible explanation is that he succumbed here to the temptation before which all historians and commentators are by their very nature weak, the temptation to correct historical error wherever they find it, regardless of its relevance to their immediate purpose." For Thucydides it was most relevant.

29. Since the τέχνη μαντική is specifically human, based on intellectual abilities such as gnome, logismos, pronoia, etc., it is evident why Thucydides was so distrustful of other non-human or religious means of predicting the future (oracles, divination, etc.). To quote Finley, p. 312: "All this is not to say that he may not have believed in the

gods. He mentions disbelief as a symptom of social disintegration and goes out of his way to praise the high character of the pious Nicias. He simply did not believe that the gods intervened in the working out of the political forces which he thought operative in history." Thus oracles or seers are never a dependable guide to the future. (See especially Thucydides' rather cryptic remarks on Nikias' reaction to the eclipse in 7.50.4.) Thus too his especial contempt for *elpis*, a groundless projection usually based on mere emotion or wishful thinking (e.g., 4.108.4).

Chapter 10
General Conclusions:
The Least Objective Historian

Factual accuracy and objectivity have long been considered the major qualities of Thucydides' *History*. This is a one-sided, if not totally distorted view of the historian and his method of composition. For if, as Thucydides states, his aim was "the truth," and his search for this truth led him to be critical of his sources, to apply "the most severe and detailed tests possible" to the reports of his informants in order to ensure accuracy,[1] it need not follow that a random accumulation of data or facts, however "exact," would be of any worth to posterity. Thucydides' "facts" cannot be considered in isolation from the schema or pattern which informs them. "Truth" then is not just the *erga* but the *erga* (and the *logoi* too) as they conform to a coherent and meaningful pattern. In other words more important than the facts themselves are the preconceptions about history, the historical process, and the purpose of the historian with which Thucydides approached his task of recording "the war between the Peloponnesians and the Athenians" (1.1.1). Chapter 8 demonstrated the pattern of history, a recurring sequence of events which in its totality constitutes the cycle of human experience — the human tragedy. Having detected this pattern beneath the confusing variety of men's *erga* and *logoi*, Thucydides' purpose was twofold: first, to select and dispose his facts in such a way that events themselves would conform to and so demonstrate this pattern of history and second, to show how far and by what means man is capable of intervening in this process.

The present chapter summarizes the historiographic methods

---

1. 1.22.2.

Thucydides used to achieve this purpose. From the analysis of isolated passages will emerge the architecture of the work as a whole and with it the concepts which lie at the base of this formal structure.

A. Motivation and Anticipation

The basic unit in the structure of the *History* is the *logoi-erga*[2] combination. In most *successful* action the *logoi*, whether direct or indirect (e.g., Archidamos, 2.11 and 20, Phormion, 2.84.2 and 89, and Brasidas, 5.8-9), anticipate the *erga* which follow. In turn the *erga* provide confirmation that the plan or strategy, and so the reasoning on which it was based, was correct. Such *logoi-erga* combinations, however, do not exist in isolation. For instance in the case of Phormion, there is a complex pattern of *logoi-erga-logoi-erga*. Phormion's second *logos* takes account of the *erga* which preceded. In effect, he learns from experience and so anticipates a second victory in the final *erga*. This technique of juxtaposing *logoi* and *erga* becomes almost infinitely extensible as it is used to anticipate the final naval encounter in the great harbour at Syracuse. P. 117 illustrated a complex series of *erga* and *logoi* representing cumulative knowledge gained through both personal experience and the example of others. Moreover, certain *logoi*, usually major debates (e.g., that between Archidamos and the Corinthians or Nikias and Alkibiades) anticipate whole periods. Just as in the case of the isolated *antilogia*, the *erga* which follow decide immediately between the two *logoi*, (e.g., between Phormion and the Peloponnesians or Nikias and Gylippos), so in major debates later *erga* eventually demonstrate the superiority of one *logos*. This *logos* we call the "stronger" ($\kappa\rho\epsilon\acute{\iota}\tau\tau\omega\nu$) on the principle that life itself, the *erga*, confirmed it as true. On the same principle the other *logos* is the "weaker" ($\mathring{\eta}\tau\tau\omega\nu$).

First conclusion:

The juxtaposition of *logoi* and *erga* permeates the work from beginning to end. By means of this technique men are represented as learning or incapable of learning from their own and others' experiences, from *empeiria* and *paradeigma*.

---

2. Isolated *logoi-erga* combinations have been thoroughly analyzed by de Romilly, *passim*.

B. Pattern and Inevitability

A puzzling characteristic of the second half of the *History*, the events leading up to and including the Sicilian expedition (5.84-7.87), is its aura of *déjà vu*. Time and again characters, events, and even sequences of events are reminiscent of counterparts and parallels in the "first war." For example, the predictions and advice of Lamachos in the first council of war are very similar to those of Archidamos before the invasion of Attika. They assume, moreover, that the Syracusans will respond to attack just as the Athenians did in 431. Similarly Gylippos' predictions about Athenian demoralization and defeat are the very ones one might expect of a man who had witnessed Spartan demoralization at and after Sphakteria. When events unfold as predicted, having been foreshadowed by the *logoi*, they all the more clearly establish a link between the first and second half of the work. Other types of situations also recur. Archidamos and Nikias are not just tragic warners — plausible enough — but their *logoi* approximate one another in structure and substance. (See p. 129.) In the same way the first confrontation of the Syracusans and Athenians, though a land-battle, duplicates to the smallest detail the first naval encounter of the Peloponnesians and Athenians in the Gulf of Patrai.

Cumulative evidence leads to inescapable conclusions. The *History* is a veritable complexity of repetitive patterns — patterns not merely of human behaviour but type-characters, events, and even sequences of events. In this respect Thucydides' method is thoroughly Herodotean. Earlier writers have already pointed out patterns of human behaviour:[3] it is in fact such patterns which lie behind the above-mentioned predictions of Archidamos at the Isthmus, Lamachos, and Gylippos. But just as significant are recurrent type-characters who appear as if modelled after some idealized paradigm. There are, for example, those who play the role of tragic warner, older men of experience like Archidamos and Nikias;[4] there are the statesmen, Themistokles, Perikles, and Hermokrates, all of whom evince formidable powers of prediction (*pronoia*); there are men who reject *gnome* or *logismos*, reason and intellect, even discussion, and represent emotions and passions

---

3. E.g., Finley, pp. 57 ff., 98, and 110 and Gommel, pp. 21 ff. and 49 ff.

4. The recurrence of such type-characters is, of course, far more complex, since, as Chapter 8 demonstrated, not only the characters but the very circumstances in which they appear to give their unheeded warnings seem to recur.

(θυμός), Kleon, the type of *pleonexia*, Alkibiades, ἐπιθυμία, and Demosthenes, *tolma alogistos*. Events too conform to patterns. Verbal echoes going far beyond the mere accidental indicate that the retreat and encirclement of the Spartans at Sphakteria and that of the Athenians in Sicily were written in light of one another. So startling are the similarities as to tax credulity. We have already referred to the battle of Patrai and the first land encounter of the Athenians and Syracusans. The central point of both battles would seem to be ταραχή, its cause and effects and the possibility of overcoming it by experience and training. Ταραχή seems in fact to have haunted the historian. It recurs in the battle of Naupaktos as well as in the first, second, and final naval confrontations of the Athenians and Syracusans in the great harbour. Thus all the earlier sea-battles serve as models against which to set the final battle.[5]

Second Conclusion:

As the *logoi* foreshadow, so do the *erga*. Foreshadowing of this kind is based on repetitive patterns to which events and characters usually conform. Each instance of a pattern we call a *paradeigma*. For the reader earlier events exist as *paradeigmata*, model situations, the outcome and possibilities of which he knows. By bringing this knowledge of the past with him into the present, he is equipped to compare and judge, even to predict.[6] This technique − repetitive patterns and *paradeigmata* − together with the juxtaposition of *logoi* and *erga*, gives the *History* its aura of inevitability.

If the characters in the *History* are represented as learning from their own and others' experiences, the reader himself learns from the example of others, *paradeigmata* in the sense of history.

C. Cycle

So far does analysis lead. But to end here would be to leave the *History* in fragments, a series of isolated events, with

---

5. I would go so far as to include the Battle of Leukimme, the central point of which, a πεζομαχία on board ship resulting in ταραχή, also foreshadows the final encounter in the Great Harbour. The latter, once Athenian skill and experience become useless, represents a kind of regress to that "old imperfect armament" (1.49.1, but note the circumstances and vocabulary throughout 1.49).

6. As W. P. Wallace, p. 252, put it, "he feels that he knows, where those who took part in the events could only guess."

discernible pattern and structure, yes, but without unifying principle. This is not the case: synthesis is possible. The fact that events recur in a definite sequence indicates that there is a pattern to history itself. In the *History* Thucydides delineated two parallel cycles of experience — that of the Spartans and that of the Athenians — and hinted at a third, the downfall of Xerxes. The central point of each is reversal, μεταβολή. It is the same process Herodotus described in terms of the individual ruler or tyrant. The lives of Kroisos, Polykrates, and Xerxes, for example, all follow a similar pattern, a morality cycle of ὕβρις, κόρος, ἄτη, νέμεσις, in which the φθόνος of the gods is instrumental in bringing about μεταβολή and so restores equilibrium.[7] In Thucydides' *History* the individual ruler is replaced by the *polis* and the gods do not interfere. But there is μεταβολή nonetheless and a similar restoration of equilibrium. Τὸ ἀνθρώπινον, as described in Chapter 8, is the interaction of ἀνάγκη, τύχη, and φύσις, the last comprising human nature and so human responsibility. What causes this cycle Thucydides does not indicate. He merely describes how and when it begins and what are its various stages. Like the plague, the symptoms and stages of which he also describes without attempting a causal explanation, it is, once begun, an inexorable process which seems to defy human control. Perhaps the cycle is in the nature of things. Certainly this is implied in Perikles' last speech (2.64.3), ". . . even if now, in obedience to the general law of decay (πάντα γὰρ πέφυκε καὶ ἐλασσοῦσθαι), we should ever be forced to yield. . . ." Interpreted in its strictest sense "the general law of decay" implies a kind of immanent necessity (ἀνάγκη).[8] On

---

7. For an excellent analysis of Herodotus in these terms together with relevant bibliography see Henry Immerwahr, *Form and Thought in Herodotus*, Cleveland, Ohio, 1966, pp. 306 ff. For too long too much has been made of the differences between Herodotus and Thucydides and not enough of the similarities, or, one might even say, the debt of Thucydides to his predecessor. I would suggest the following as a point of departure for a fresh comparison of the two historians. If great tyrants or rulers bring about their own downfall, how is this same process manifested in the *polis*, and especially in one ruled by the *demos* where responsibility cannot be attributed to a single man? If one follows the major tragedy of the *History*, the downfall of Athens, it is not difficult to see that Athens, the *polis* itself, is Xerxes, Nikias, Artabanos, Alkibiades, Mardonios and Hermokrates, Themistokles. It would be necessary to leave aside the φθόνος of the gods and instead disentangle human errors and responsibility for them from ἀνάγκη and τύχη. I am confident that the gulf between Herodotus and Thucydides would be substantially narrowed and that in the latter one would discover an outlook less religious but no less metaphysical.

8. Cf. 3.82.2, where φύσις ἀνθρώπων is abstracted as a major factor in this process.

the other hand, there are suggestions that if a people do not overstep certain bounds but live with respect for law and exercise σωφροσύνη they may be able to avoid this cycle. Or such is my interpretation of Thucydides' remarks about the Chians (8.24.4). Men then are themselves responsible for upsetting a kind of cosmic equilibrium, and reversal becomes inevitable. Indeed, the very existence of the *History* as useful to posterity implies one of two things: If men understand the past, the human tragedy as it recurs, they may be able to avoid reaching that point of overextension which must result in μεταβολή. But even if such a process is in the nature of things, men would still be more effective if they understood history in its full sense. In the declining *polis* a man who had read the *History* would have the same possibility of intervening in the process of history as a physician who had read his account of the plague. He would recognize the stage reached and so what was to come. As for the rising *polis*, such knowledge would be invaluable.

Third Conclusion:

For Thucydides events happen with a definite regularity and order, and there is a pattern to history. Thus informed by pattern and cycle the facts of history are made meaningful. Moreover, the first cycle, shedding light as it does on the second, is paradigmatic. And even if the characters in the *History* are not explicitly represented as learning from the Spartan experience, the reader himself does carry the past with him into the present, does sense how events will turn out, and when events actually do conform to his predictions, he is all the more convinced of the truth which the cycle in its totality conveys.

In the *History* men are represented as learning from their own and others' experiences, *empeiria* and *paradeigma*, the latter in its broadest sense meaning both the immediate example of others and the historical example. By taking into account, evaluating, or interpreting past *erga* in one or all these senses men are capable of mediating past and future. For the reader, whatever his personal experience, the *History* represents the accumulated experiences of others. As a set of *paradeigmata*, patterned and so meaningful and completely accurate by the historian's standards, it is the basis of a *logos* if and when such events should recur.

But *erga*, even informed, are of no worth to men if they do not know how to use them. *Erga* must always be related to *logoi*, the intellectual processes whereby man intervenes in the historical process. Thus, though the *erga* embody truth, being what actually happened, it is the *logoi* which are the historian's major preoccupation.

Throughout the *History* certain intellectual qualities (*pronoia*, *logismos*, *gnome*, etc.) are depicted as valuable. Men who evince them are usually successful. Thus the man who does understand the past and so can foresee the future, does formulate a *logos* based on *pronoia*, must also be adept at διδαχή. The form in which he presents his *gnome* must be persuasive or be of no use. Among other things he must understand and so dominate men's emotions.

All this the *History* illustrates — and something more. Through the technique of foreshadowing the reader shares in the experiences of the protagonists. Not only does he see time and again which *logos* is correct and why, but as events recur he can criticize and predict himself. Having learned from the first cycle, he should find events of the second cycle all but inevitable. When they occur they should in turn reinforce his original knowledge. Thus he is not only prepared if such should occur again in his lifetime, but having shared so often in correct intellectual activity, he should be himself a kind of εἰκαστής.

The term Thucydidean has become synonymous with epithets such as "critical," "scientific," and "objective." Appropriate as these adjectives may or may not be, they are certainly meaningless if they fail to take account of the historian's overriding purpose. This purpose, we suggested earlier, was twofold, to select and dispose his facts in such a way that events themselves would conform to and so demonstrate the pattern of history and to show how far and by what means man is capable of intervening in this process. What emerges most clearly from our analysis of the historiographic methods Thucydides used to achieve this purpose is the intensity and artistic skill of the man, and the almost architectonic quality of his mind, which grasped in a single vision not just the war which he claimed to record but all of human history, as it were. His standard of relevance was strict in the extreme. Hence the omissions. No one can deny, furthermore, that he was critical, though always *according to his own criterion*,[9] i.e., his twofold purpose, which was to make history meaningful. His

9. See the remarks of Collingwood, pp. 137 ff., in reference to a work of F. H. Bradley entitled *The Presuppositions of Critical History*.

preoccupation with forces and processes which go beyond the mere human is part of an outlook which, if not religious, surely approaches the metaphysical. He was thus no scientist in the 19th century sense, but rather a scientific enquirer, even as Herodotus was before him.[10] And if objective means *not* to allow one's own outlook, philosophical or otherwise to obtrude, then Thucydides was surely the least objective of historians.

10. Again I am following Collingwood, pp. 17 ff., in his definition of history in general and especially that vexed term "scientific."

Appendix to Chapter 6 (Thuc. 6.47-49)

ꙩꙩꙩ

There are several problems in the council of war as presented by Thucydides. One might expect a disagreement over strategy, but it is surely odd that there is no general consensus about the *aims* of the expedition. Only Lamachos gets right to the point by making Syracuse the object of attack. Both Nikias and Alkibiades would apparently turn around and go home *if* Selinous and Egesta came to terms and, in Alkibiades' case, *if* the Leontinoi were restored.

Yet this contradicts much that preceded. First, Thucydides himself made it clear that aid to Egesta and the restoration of the Leontinoi was nothing but a pretext, the Athenians "being ambitious in real truth of conquering the whole" (of Sicily, 6.6.1). Could anything be more straightforward? Moreover, the desires attributed to every level of the population (24.3), combined with the cost and magnitude of the armament (31) indicated that this was no mere display in aid of distant allies. This must have been clear to all three. In fact, this is just what impelled Nikias to speak out in the first place, even though the assembly had already voted to send 60 ships to Sicily. The rather vague object "to order all other matters in Sicily as they should deem best for the interests of Athens" (8.2), he interpreted as aspirations "to the conquest of the whole of Sicily" (8.4). And in his second speech he was wise enough to predict that the sums promised by Egesta would probably not be forthcoming and that they "should be prepared to become master of the country the first day" or find everything hostile (23.2). In short, *at this point* he was most realistic and had an insight not unlike that later attributed to Lamachos. Yet in 6.47 he never goes beyond the "ostensible" object, to reconcile

Selinous and Egesta, as if he recognized no other.

Alkibiades' viewpoint is even more contradictory. Right from the start his aims were clear. According to Thucydides, he was "exceedingly ambitious of a command by which he hoped to reduce Sicily and Carthage, and personally to gain in wealth and reputation by means of his successes" (15.2). There follows an account of his personal tastes and expenditures. In his speech Alkibiades was no more equivocal about the course Athens should follow. Speaking of empire he stated categorically (18.3): "And we cannot fix the exact point at which our empire shall stop; we have reached a position in which we must not be content with retaining but must scheme to extend it, for, if we cease to rule others, we are in danger of being ruled ourselves." He predicted that "we shall either become masters, as we very easily may, of the whole of Hellas through the accession of the Sicilian Hellenes, or in any case ruin the Syracusans, to the no small advantage of ourselves and our allies" (18.4). In light of this it is patently absurd for Alkibiades even to suggest he would be content with the reconciliation of Egesta and Selinous and the restoration of the Leontinoi (6.48). Yet this is what Thucydides tells us, making Alkibiades no less than Nikias accept the "ostensible" object of the expedition. Lamachos alone is single-minded in wanting a confrontation with Syracuse.

Clearly there is something wrong here. And if the passages cannot be reconciled, perhaps they can be explained in terms of what we believe were Thucydides' methods in writing the *History*.

Let us assume first that Thucydides did not just fabricate the opinions but had their general purport from some informant, perhaps even Alkibiades himself. He knew then that Lamachos was for immediate attack, Alkibiades for negotiations first, and Nikias for a return to Athens as soon as possible. He also knew the kind of men they were, Nikias, a conservative, Alkibiades, a back-room machinator, and Lamachos, an energetic military man. The particular arguments of each he could readily assume, keeping two things in mind, what actually did occur later and the purpose this debate was to have in the *History*.

First Lamachos. I think we have made it clear that his opinion is based on after-the-fact reasoning. It is what happened and so what might have been. It is the κρείττων λόγος, here the rejected alternative. The fact that Thucydides later saw fit to point out, through Demosthenes, that Lamachos' view should have been followed, indicates it was the strategy he himself would have followed under the circumstances. It was decisive and alone took advantage of the *kairos*. And what better person to express it than the shadowy Lamachos, who did not even live long enough to see Demosthenes arrive.

But if the historian wanted this "truth" implanted in his readers' minds, he must also respect the fact that the Athenians adopted a different strategy. This too could be easily explained after the fact. One need only spell out in Alkibiades' opinion the actual moves made and the allies approached. Here too everything would be true as far as later *erga* were concerned except the prediction of success. In this it would prove very much the ἥττων λόγος because none of its major predictions would come true.

Nikias' opinion was the most difficult. Nothing was to confirm or refute it later. Indeed, it was a dead-end, quite irrelevant to the main purpose of attacking Syracuse now or later. Everyone knew Nikias opposed the expedition or at least wanted to keep it as limited as possible. It would be easy enough to represent Nikias as still stubbornly holding to this position even after the expedition sailed, just as he spoke against the expedition after it was decided upon. Really the problem lies not so much in Nikias' intransigence at this point as the shift that takes place in his character as Thucydides represents him. Earlier he played the role of the tragic warner whose *logos* was κρείττων in the debate with Alkibiades and who was gifted by the historian with an amazing long-term clairvoyance. In effect, he predicted just what would happen. (See Chapter 8.) Having issued his warning, Nikias then becomes the source of missed opportunities and fatal errors in the actual expedition. There is just no way to get around the contradictions inherent in this change of role. (A thorough study of Nikias *per se* would probably yield some answers.) Here it seems that Thucydides made his opinions accord with his overall characterization of Nikias as a conservative man who wanted to end the expedition as soon as possible. Whether intended or not, it creates a neat irony: not only is he leader of an expedition he opposed but once he is in the field and the opportunity Lamachos saw is lost, he is forced to carry out the strategy of his opponent Alkibiades.

Bibliography

Ancient Authors and Texts Cited

Antiphon. *Minor Attic Orators*. Translated by K. J. Maidment. Vol. 1. Loeb Classical Library. London and Cambridge, Mass., 1960.

Aristophanes. *Comoediae*. Edited by F. W. Hall and W. M. Geldart. Second edition. Vols. 1 and 2. Oxford, 1906-1907.

Aristotle. *Ars Rhetorica*. Edited by W. D. Ross. Oxford, 1959.

Diodoros. *Diodorus of Sicily*. Translated by C. H. Oldfather. Vol. 5. Loeb Classical Library. London and Cambridge, Mass., 1962.

Herodotus. *Historiae*. Edited by C. Hude. Third edition. 2 vols. Oxford, 1927.

[Plato.] *Opera*. Edited by J. Burnet. Vol. 5. Oxford, 1907.

Plutarch. *Vitae Parallelae*. Edited by C. Lindskog and K. Ziegler. Third edition. Vol. 1. Parts 1 and 2. Leipzig, 1960-1964.

Thucydides. *Historiae*. Edited by H. S. Jones. Revised and augmented by J. E. Powell. Second edition. 2 vols. Oxford, 1942.

[Xenophon.] *The Constitution of the Athenians*. Edited by H. Frisch. Copenhagen, 1942.

Modern Authors

Abbott, G. F. *Thucydides. A Study in Historical Reality*. London, 1925.

Adcock, F. E. *Thucydides and his History.* Cambridge, 1963.
Andrewes, A. "Thucydides on the Causes of the War," *CQ* 9, 1959, pp. 223-39.
Awdry, H. "Pylos and Sphacteria," *JHS* 20, 1900, pp. 14-19.
Barker, E. *Greek Political Theory. Plato and his Predecessors.* London, 1960.
Bender, G. F. *Der Begriff des Staatsmannes bei Thukydides.* Würzburg, 1938.
Bétant, E. A. *Lexicon Thucydideum.* 2 vols. Hildesheim, 1961.
Blass, F. *Die attische Beredsamkeit.* Second edition. Vol. 1. Leipzig, 1887.
Brunt, P. A. "Spartan Policy and Strategy in the Archidamian War," *Phoenix* 19, 1965, pp. 255-80.
Burn, A. R. *Persia and the Greeks.* London, 1962.
Burrows, R. M. "Pylos and Sphacteria," *JHS* 18, 1898, pp. 147-59; 28, 1908, pp. 148-50.
Bury, J. B. *The Ancient Greek Historians.* New York, 1958.
Busolt, G. *Griechische Geschichte.* Vol. 3.2. Gotha, 1904.
Chambers, M. H. "Studies in the Veracity of Thucydides," *HSCP* 62, 1957, pp. 141-43.
Cochrane, C. N. *Thucydides and the Science of History.* Oxford, 1929.
Collingwood, R. G. *The Idea of History.* Oxford, 1961.
Cope, E. M. *The Rhetoric of Aristotle with a Commentary.* Revised and edited by J. E. Sandys. Vols. 1 and 2. Cambridge, 1877.
Copi, I. M. *Introduction to Logic.* Second edition. New York, 1961.
Cornford, F. M. *Thucydides Mythistoricus.* London, 1907.
Danninger, O. "Ueber das εἰκός in den Reden des Thukydides," *WS* 49-50, 1931-32, pp. 12-31.
Delebecque, E. *Thucydide et Alcibiade.* Aix-en-Provence, 1965.
Diels, H. and Kranz, W. *Die Fragmente der Vorsokratiker* (Greek and German). Sixth edition. Vol. 2. Berlin, 1952.
Eliade, M. *Cosmos and History.* New York, 1959.
Erbse, H. "Die politische Lehre des Thukydides," *Gymnasium* 76, 1969, pp. 393-416.
Finley, J. H., Jr. *Thucydides.* Ann Arbor, 1963.
―――― *Three Essays on Thucydides.* Cambridge, Mass., 1967.
Fliess, P. J. *Thucydides and the Politics of Bipolarity.* Louisiana, 1966.

Freeman, E. A. *A History of Sicily*. Vol. 2. Oxford, 1891.

Gardiner, T. "Terms for Thalassocracy in Thucydides," *RM* 112, 1969, pp. 16-22.

Gomme, A. W. *Essays in Greek History and Literature*. Oxford, 1937.

____ *A Historical Commentary on Thucydides*. 4 vols. Vol. 4 revised and edited by A. Andrewes and K. J. Dover. Oxford, 1945-70.

____ "Notes on Thucydides," *CR* 1, 1951, pp. 135-38.

____ *The Greek Attitude to Poetry and History*. Berkeley, 1954.

____ *More Essays in Greek History*. Oxford, 1962.

Gommel J. *Rhetorisches Argumentieren bei Thukydides. Spudasmata* 10, 1966.

Gomperz, T. *Greek Thinkers*. Vol. 1. London, 1901.

Greene, W. C. *Moira*. New York, 1963.

Grene, D. *Man in his Pride*. Chicago, 1950.

Grote, G. *A History of Greece*. Third edition. Vol. 7. London, 1855.

Grundy, G. B. *Thucydides and the History of his Age*. 2 vols. (Vol. 1, second edition.) Oxford, 1948.

Gundert, H. "Athener und Spartaner in den Reden des Thukydides," *Antike* 16, 1940, pp. 98-114.

Hammond, N. G. L. "The Arrangement of the Thought in the Proem and in other Parts of Thucydides I," *CQ* 2, 1952, pp. 127-41.

Henderson, B. W. *The Great War Between Athens and Sparta*. London, 1927.

Hignett, C. *Xerxes' Invasion of Greece*. Oxford, 1963.

Hinks, D. A. G. "Tisias and Corax and the Invention of Rhetoric," *CQ* 34, 1940, pp. 61-69.

Huart, P. *Le Vocabulaire de l'Analyse Psychologique dans l'Oeuvre de Thucydide*. Paris, 1968.

Immerwahr, H. R. "Ergon: History as a Monument in Herodotus and Thucydides," *AJP* 81, 1960, pp. 261-90.

____ *Form and Thought in Herodotus*. Cleveland, Ohio, 1966.

Jaeger, W. *Paideia*. Second English edition. Vol. 1. Oxford, 1947.

Jebb, R. "The Speeches of Thucydides," *Essays and Addresses*. Cambridge, 1907, pp. 359-445.

Kennedy, G. *The Art of Persuasion in Greece*. Princeton, New Jersey, 1963.

Kirkwood, G. M. "Thucydides' Words for 'Cause,'" *AJP* 73, 1952, pp. 37-61.

Kranz, W. *See* Diels.

Lang, M. "The Murder of Hipparchus," *Historia* 3, 1955, pp. 395-407.

___ "A Note on Ithome," *GRBS* 8, 1967, pp. 267-73.

Liebeschuetz, W. "The Structure and Function of the Melian Dialogue," *JHS* 88, 1968, pp. 73-77.

___ "Thucydides and the Sicilian Expedition," *Historia* 17, 1968, pp. 289-306.

Löwith, K. *Meaning in History.* Chicago, 1949.

Madden, E. H. "The Enthymeme: Crossroads of Logic, Rhetoric, and Metaphysics," *Phil. Rev.* 61, 1952, pp. 368-76.

McBurney, J. H. "The Place of the Enthymeme in Rhetorical Theory," *Speech Monographs* 3, 1936, pp. 49-74.

Meyerhoff, H. (ed.) *The Philosophy of History in our Time.* New York, 1959.

Momigliano, A. D. *Studies in Historiography.* New York, 1966.

Navarre, O. *Essai sur la Rhétorique Grecque avant Aristote.* Paris, 1900.

Nestle, W. *Vom Mythos zum Logos.* Stuttgart, 1940.

___ "Thukydides und die Sophistik," *Griechische Studien,* Stuttgart, 1948, pp. 321-73.

Pearson, L. "Thucydides as Reporter and Critic," *TAPA* 78, 1947, pp. 37-60.

___ "Prophasis and Aitia," *TAPA* 83, 1952, pp. 205-23.

Pritchett, W. K. *Studies in Ancient Greek Topography.* Part 1. Berkeley and Los Angeles, 1965.

Rittelmeyer, F. *Thukydides und die Sophistik.* Leipzig, 1915.

de Romilly, J. *Thucydides and Athenian Imperialism.* English translation. Oxford, 1963.

___ *Histoire et Raison chez Thucydide.* Paris, 1956.

___ "La Crainte dans l'oeuvre de Thucydide," *C&M* 17, 1956, pp. 119-27.

___ "L'Utilité de l'histoire selon Thucydide," *Entretiens* 4, 1958, pp. 41-66.

___ "Les Intentions d'Archidamos," *REA* 64, 1962, pp. 287-99.

Sealey, R. "Thucydides, Herodotus, and the Causes of War," *CQ* 7, 1957, pp. 1-12.

Seaton, R. C. "The Aristotelian Enthymeme," *CR* 28, 1914, pp. 113-19.

Shorey, P. "Implicit Ethics and Psychology of Thucydides," *TAPA* 24, 1893, pp. 66-88.

_____ "Φύσις, Μελέτη, Ἐπιστήμη," *TAPA* 40, 1909, pp. 185-201.

Smith, B. "Corax and Probability," *QJS* 7, 1921, pp. 13-42.

Stahl, H. *Thukydides: Die Stellung des Menschen im geschichlichen Prozess. Zetemata* 40, 1966.

Stern, F. (ed.) *The Varieties of History.* Cleveland, 1956.

Untersteiner, M. *The Sophists.* Oxford, 1954.

Walker, P. K. "The Purpose and Method of 'The Pentekontaetia' in Thucydides, Book I," *CQ* 7, 1957, pp. 27-38.

Wallace, W. P. "The Egyptian Expedition and the Chronology of the Decade 460-450 B.C.," *TAPA* 67, 1936, pp. 252-60.

_____ "Thucydides," *Phoenix* 18, 1964, pp. 251-61.

Walsh, W. H. *Philosophy of History.* New York, 1960.

Wassermann, F. "The Melian Dialogue," *TAPA* 78, 1947, pp. 18-36.

_____ "The Speeches of King Archidamos in Thucydides," *CJ* 48, 1953, pp. 193-200.

_____ "Thucydides and the Disintegration of the Polis," *TAPA* 85, 1954, pp. 46-54.

_____ "Thucydidean Scholarship 1942-1956," *CW* 50, 1956, pp. 65-70 and 1957, pp. 89-101.

_____ "The Voice of Sparta in Thucydides," *CJ* 59, 1964, pp. 289-97.

West, A. B. "Pericles' Political Heirs," *CP* 19, 1924, pp. 124-46 and 201-28.

Westlake, H. D. "Nicias in Thucydides," *CQ* 35, 1941, pp. 58-65.

_____ "Thucydides and the Pentecontaetia," *CQ* 5, 1955, pp. 53-67.

_____ "'Ὡς εἰκός in Thucydides," *Hermes* 86, 1958, pp. 447-52.

_____ "Thucydides 2.65.11," *CQ* 8, 1958, pp. 102-10.

_____ "Athenian Aims in Sicily, 427-424. A Study in Thucydidean Motivation," *Historia* 9, 1960, pp. 385-402.

_____ *Individuals in Thucydides.* Cambridge, 1968.

Wilcox, S. "Corax and the *Prolegomena*," *AJP* 64, 1943, pp. 1-23.

Woodhead, A. G. *Thucydides on the Nature of Power.* Cambridge, Mass. 1970.

_____ "Thucydides' Portrait of Cleon," *Mnem.* 13, 1960, pp. 289-317.

Index

1. INDEX OF GENERAL SUBJECTS

accident 7, 47, 71, 78. See also
παράλογος and τύχη.
accuracy 93, 173-74, 177, 182.
Achaia 90.
Acharnai, Acharnian 12, 14, 16-19,
101.
Agamemnon 154, 165-66
Aitolia, Aitolian 68, 71-73, 104-105.
Akarnania, Akarnanian 43-44, 48,
61, 69, 112.
Alkibiades 27, 82, 96-97, 123, 126-
28, 131, 135-40, 144, 146-47,
160, 165, 170, 172, 178, 180-81,
185-87.
Alkidas 141.
Ambrakia 125.
Amphipolis 30-34, 38-40, 68, 142,
158.
anticipation 8-9, 11, 13, 18-21, 25,
32, 37, 39-40, 45-46, 55, 58, 60-
61, 63, 67, 70, 78-79, 85-86, 91,
93, 96, 98-99, 103, 105, 112-13,
115, 119-21, 123, 125, 127-28,
132-34, 139, 150, 156, 158, 163,
178.
antilogia, see ἀντιλογία.
Antiphon (rhetor) 29-30, 41, 78,
154, 161.
Antiphon (sophist) 171.
Archidamos 11-21, 26, 30, 45, 74-

75, 77-78, 80, 93, 99-101, 127-33,
140-41, 146, 148, 178-79.
Argos 147-48.
Aristogeiton 68, 174.
Ariston 92
Aristophanes 16.
Aristotle 27-28, 135.
Arrhabaios 23.
Artabanos 181.
assumption 7, 13, 26-27, 35-36, 38-
39, 44-45, 49-52, 55, 57, 63-65,
70, 86, 88, 92, 96, 100-101, 103,
125, 154-55, 160, 163, 168, 170,
172.
Athenagoras 100, 153-55.
Athens, Athenian, passim.
Attika 11-12, 14-15, 18, 20, 30, 63-
64, 77, 100, 135, 179.

bias 31.
Boeotia 126, 142.
Brasidas 9, 23-40, 45, 47, 50, 55, 67-
68, 74-75, 81, 92, 104-105, 112-
13, 120, 141-42, 158-60, 172,
178.
Byzantion 170.

calculation 49, 66, 68, 70, 78, 104,
129, 142, 147. See also λογισμός.
Carthage, Carthaginian 151, 156,

2. INDEX OF GREEK TERMS

3. INDEX OF MODERN AUTHORS

4. INDEX OF REFERENCES TO THUCYDIDES

Book 3

5. OTHER ANCIENT REFERENCES CITED

DATE

8/12/17